SANTA BARBARA DAY HIKES

RAYMOND FORD, JR.

Santa Barbara
Day Hikes

SHORELINE PRESS

SANTA BARBARA • 2000

Published by Shoreline Press, Post Office 3562, Santa Barbara, CA 93130
Printed by Kimberly/Williams, Goleta, CA
Distributed by Pacific Books, Post Office Box 3562, Santa Barbara, CA
93130; (805) 687-8340

Design and typography by Jim Cook
Maps and photographs by Ray Ford, Jr.

First Edition
ISBN 1-885375-07-7

Contents

Mountain Crest Hikes

Santa Barbara
Day Hikes

Rattlesnake Canyon

Introduction

SENSE OF PLACE

The beauty begins immediately. Just a few yards from the road's edge there is a sharp delineation between the world being entered and the one left behind. Upstream are the first pools, and the breeze. Light and cool. Airy. Invigorating. The sound catches at you, grabs you, and pushes you on up into the mountain wall. Farther to the interior are waterfalls, sun-bathing spots, and hidden valleys.

The spot where I am presently sitting is a perfect kind of place, solid bedrock to lean back against, the deep V of the canyon leading my eye steeply down and across the edge of the city to the harbor. Santa Cruz and Santa Rosa islands shimmer in the distance. The sound of the water is incessant but satisfying; the waterfall above cascades down into a fifteen-foot-wide, five-foot-deep pool. The water churns and froths a bit, then slides by my feet and down the twin spouts of a thirty-foot waterfall.

Spacious, apple-green in color, and cold even in the summer heat, the pool is as inviting as my present perch on the rock. This is a niche that suits a personal need of mine, to be by myself for a while.

I slide into the pool, gasping a bit at the cold bite of the mountain water, submerge fully, then bounce up and back onto the rock, letting the deep warmth of the bedrock warm my back.

Nearby I spy I lizard, motionless except for the pushups it does every half-minute of so. I am told this helps with depth perception, the lizard being able to get a little bit better bead on its prey, perhaps a fly, by viewing it from the perspective of differing heights.

I lie still, watching it. It is deathly still for a handful of minutes more. Then it bursts forth, scurrying over the rock in a frenzy of action, and out of my sight. Lunchtime, I think.

Life in the Santa Barbara outdoors has many moments such as this to offer, and loads of secrets. Whether it is a quiet walk on the beach, a strenuous hike up into mountain depths such as I am at now, or a top-of-the-mountain ride over the sensual curves of East Camino Cielo Road, the secrets are there to be found. Perhaps, if like the lizard, you spend time enough, listen carefully, shift perspective now and then, the sense of this place will come to you.

This is an invitation to go beyond, to push yourself a bit further than you thought possible, to explore hidden places and seek what is just around the corner.

REVISIONS AND CHANGES

Those of you who have older versions of this book will notice a lot of changes. In the very first edition (*Day Hikes of the Santa Barbara Foothills*, 1975) the focus was on the frontcountry and getting to know the Santa Ynez Mountains. In subsequent editions the book expanded beyond the front range to cover hikes as far distant as Figueroa Mountain.

I've come back to the former approach in this edition, partly because I want to focus readers on getting to know each region of the county more intimately, and partly to make the book easier to pack with you and take on the trail. There is also more to the frontcountry than hiking in the mountains. Tucked away in the little corners of the coastal valley are a handful of hikes—more walks than hikes, actually—they, too, offer a wonderful opportunity to get away for a few minutes and enjoy nature.

There are the beaches, too, nearly 50 miles of them, most of them open for public access. These also offer great places for remote walks, and the sound of the ocean is never far away, a comforting companion that will almost always soothe you to the core. Best of all, kids love beaches, and beaches are the easiest places you can take kids to begin their acquaintance with nature.

HIKING WITH KIDS

In looking back, I think I was a very fortunate kid. We lived in Cincinnati, a large city, but in the Midwest even the big cities had lots of open space within them. I grew up not two blocks away from a good-sized creek. In chaparral country it would be called a river.

For a second-grader this was wild country, and I felt every bit the adventurer. But that wasn't the best of it. My grandparents owned a farm near Blanchester, about an hour's drive outside Cincinnati. It wasn't a huge farm (160 acres) but to a young boy it was paradise. Third grade was very special for me because Grandpa decided I was old enough to drive the tractor and to lead the cows out to pasture and do a bunch of other things like collect the eggs. Best of all, I was finally allowed to go across the railroad tracks to the other side of the farm, where the ponds and forests were.

Frog hunting was what I really liked to do, and one day my dad took me a little farther into the forest than I'd ever been, to a place called Seven Swamps, where it was rumored that there were water moccasins and all sort of other wildlife. I never did see any snakes, but what I spied were lots of giant bullfrogs, huge ones, a foot or so in length. What a treat!

Looking back in later years I realized it was these experiences that had shaped me, imprinted on me the need for being out in the country, close to the sounds and smells you find out back, and the sense of adventure to keep me whole and alive. These were good years, but more important, they provided me with the basic appreciation for and love of the wilderness and all things wild that still guide me today.

We are fortunate in Santa Barbara to be blessed with an abundance of country in which our children can grow up closely in touch with nature, just as I did. If you are thinking about what you can do to make sure your children have plenty of opportunities to explore nature or what exactly you should teach them when you are out there, here are a few things you might consider.

When I was on the farm no one ever taught me the name of anything or droned on about this and that. What my parents and grandparents did for me was a far better thing: they shared these places with me and more importantly, encouraged me to go out and explore for myself. We had fun together running through the cornfields, jumping fences, fishing in the pond.

Along the way they shared their love of the places we went, the excitement of seeing a rainbow, the joy of just being out there. One of the rewards for them, I am sure, was the squeals of happiness that came out of me. Shared experiences—these are what was important to me—and I think for kids today they still are.

Going to the hills or beaches to discover what's out there, sharing adventures, reveling in the pleasure of being out in nature—these are far more important than knowing the names of things. What kids need to learn is a sense of the beautiful, to be excited by new discoveries, to yearn for a view of what is just around the corner. Once they have experienced these things, and the imagination has been inflamed, the quest for knowledge will come.

When I think of nature I think of this: There is what is overhead, the sky, the sense of immensity and distances reaching back to the beginning of time. Then there is what is beneath us, the world of little things to be found at ground level, things that from an adult level seem small and inconspicuous, but from the child's view, with the aid of a magnifying glass, seem very important and mysterious. Then finally there is what is inbetween: the tall mountains and the rolling hills and creeks and canyons. It is important to acknowledge all three.

This is what I would suggest:

- take kids to the beaches as often as you can
- walk out to the end of the breakwater every so often
- watch the pelicans from the end of the wharf
- have plenty of picnics at the parks
- camp overnight at Skofield Park
- fly kites together at Shoreline Park
- let kids scramble over the rocks and splash in the creeks
- go walking with your kids whenever you can (but let them tell you when you should stop)
- get a magnifying glass and check out all the little things
- sit under the stars and enjoy their beauty
- take a moonlit walk on the beach or on East Camino Cielo Road
- drive to the high country, where the kids can run around in the rocks
- share a sunset together from Knapp's Castle
- go fishing together at Lake Cachuma
- get a tide table and go tidepooling on the minus tides
- and, of course, look for rainbows wherever you can find them.

If there is just one place in the canyons I would take my child to sit and talk or to play in the pools, it would be the bench at the intersection of the east and west forks of Cold Springs Creek. It is a beautiful walk through the oaks, not too difficult, and the waterfall and pools at the edge of the bench are a perfect place to begin exploring nature with your children.

Other favorite places of mine are the sycamore logs at the edge of the bluff in the Douglas Family Preserve, where you can sit and look out at the islands; the end of the breakwater, the perfect place to get a sense of the mountain wall; and the beach walk from Arroyo Burro to Shoreline Park. These are all great places to take a child, and to re-awaken the child within you.

Rachel Carson understood what a child needs as well as anyone. In *The Sense of Wonder* she wrote:

If I had influence with the good fairy who is supposed to preside over the christening of all children I should ask that her gift to each child in the world be a sense of wonder so indestructible that it would last throughout life, as an unfailing antidote against the boredom and disenchantment of later years, the sterile preoccupation with things that are artificial, the alienation from the sources of our strength.

To share this sense of wonder, visit the Santa Barbara Outdoors website (see below) where you will find lots of information you can use to help you in the process. I have created a number of journals there that are designed to help you introduce your children to the out-of-doors. Whether you want to share an expedition to Cachuma Lake, a tidepool visit, or the wonders you will find in the pools up in Cold Springs Canyon, check out these journals.

BEACH TIME

If you are a surfer you will know what I mean when I say it is easy to fall in love with the ocean, to give it unconditional love and to want to protect it like you would a newborn baby.

I have lived almost my whole life with the smell of sea salt in my nostrils, the island views before my eyes, and the sound of waves ringing in my ears. It is difficult to think of living without these things. Since fourth grade, when my family moved from Cincinnati to Hermosa Beach, I have never lived much more than a mile from the ocean, the top of San Marcos Pass the farthest.

My earliest memories of the beach are of the long stretches of sand that seemed to disappear into the distance in either direction and the mostly gentle waves we played in. In fifth grade we moved a few miles away, to El Segundo, where I lived until graduation. By then we were old enough to ride our bikes to the beach, and we did so quite often, heading for the sand dunes on the western edge of town or toward Bollona Creek, where we would fish for sand dabs.

By the time high school was ending I had been surfing for more than a year. I knew I would only go to college where I could con-tinue to do so. That eliminated almost every college except UC Santa Barbara. I surfed whenever the waves were up, and most days we'd walk out to the the cliffs overlooking Campus Point and check the waves, only then deciding if we would head for the beach or to classes.

Waves were everything. To race toward the huge one, paddling furiously out to it, the one I'd been waiting for all day, this was an exciting moment. To cut down the face, gaining speed for the turn off the bottom, using the momentum I gained to rise high up over the lip, gliding along the edge of the breaking foam, riding the high of infinite time, this was what it was all about—at least then.

As I have grown older I have felt less the need for the excitement that comes with being out there on the edge of a wave, and more a need just to be near the ocean, to walk along the beaches every so often and enjoy the moments that come with this.

We are truly lucky in Santa Barbara to have so may beaches from which to choose, so many places where we can take our children to play, to discover for themselves the excitement and mysteries the beaches and ocean offer. Beaches are good beginning places for kids to learn about nature, to feel nature's power and beauty, and to begin a long-term relationship with it. Take them often.

SANTA BARBARA OUTDOORS

For those of you who have access to the Internet, I have created a website on which you will find up-to-date trail information, image galleries, and lots of other stuff that is impossible to fit into a book of finite size.

The name of the site is *Santa Barbara Outdoors* and the web address is http://www.sb-outdoors.org. The site is fully searchable, which means you can type in the name of any trail hike, beach walk, or town stroll and almost instantly be presented with links to updated trail info reports, galleries, and other information. To help guide you I have given the web address and keywords to use for each of the routes listed in this book. You will find these in the trail descriptions.

Most important about the site, however, is that it is more than a repository of information I have added. Thanks to the programming efforts of my good friend Dan Rabinowitz, the site has been constructed so that it is truly a community site. If you become a member (registering is easy and free) you will be able to add beach or trail reports, contribute information you have about flora and fauna, Santa Barbara history, or even add bird sightings or surf reports!

The idea is to harness the power of the web—which is its strength—to allow us to become an on-line community working together to build a library of knowledge and experiences about our local area.

A main feature of the site is the creation of a "personal portfolio" for each registered user, in which you can begin building your own library of environmental and outdoor information.

Whether you want to check out the thousands of images con-

tained on the site, see what others have contributed about a specific trail, or become a member yourself, do stop by.

THE ADVENTURE PASS

Unfortunately, one of the new truths about hiking in the Los Padres National Forest is that you will need an Adventure Pass if you want to park your car and head out on a trail or even have a picnic.

The Adventure Pass is very controversial, and there are many pros and cons regarding the need for it. From the point of view of the forest personnel, whom I know well, the money is badly needed to support recreational facilities in the forest. From the point of view of those who oppose the pass, use of the public forest for such things as day hikes or walks in the hills is a basic right.

Regardless, the bottom line is that you will need an Adventure Pass if you want to spend time in the forest. Fortunately, most of the trailheads on the front side of the mountains are outside the forest. But if you plan on hiking on either East or West Camino Cielo you will need a pass.

Seasonal passes cost $30. If you would like to find out where you can obtain one, or to register your opinion pro or con, call the Forest Service Headquarters at (805) 683-6711.

TAKING PERSONAL RESPONSIBILITY

Throughout this guide you will find ample encouragement to get out and experience all of what Santa Barbara's natural environment has to offer. The rewards are evident; but perhaps the dangers aren't quite so.

Each time you venture out into the mountains or along one of the beaches there are potential dangers. Beach walkers have been stranded by high tides, and occasionally the cliffs come tumbling down. The weather can change quickly, and poor planning can leave you stuck in a predicament. There are snakes out there, too, and poison oak and ticks.

If you take care, plan well, walk within your ability, watch where you put your feet and hands, and look before you leap you will most likely be safe. Thousands of hikers go out each year and rarely have problems.

But please remember this: what you read here is just a guide, a suggestion of what you might find if you head out there. But there are no guarantees. You are responsible for your actions, and you should act accordingly. This is especially true if you venture off-trail, where conditions can change drastically with the weather, the season, and the amount of available light.

WHEN THINGS DON'T GO RIGHT

There may come a time when you need the help of trained personnel to help you out of a predicament or to give medical treatment. If this should occur, most likely the response will come from the Los Padres Search and Rescue Team.

LPSAR is a non-profit, all-volunteer organization that mobilizes when an emergency occurs in areas that normal rescue personnel cannot reach. Should you get into trouble, don't hesitate to seek their help.

You cannot contact the team directly; it operates under the auspices of the Santa Barbara County Sheriff's office. Call 911 and explain the nature of your situation. If warranted, they will transfer you to the watch officer at the Sheriff's office.

If help is not immediately available, rather than trying to do something immediately, take a few moments to asses the situation and develop a plan of action. Evaluate each of the alternatives you have available to you. If time permits, talk out the pros and cons of each. Talk over the choices with each member of your group and try to reach a consensus with which everyone feels comfortable. Continue to evaluate the situation as conditions change.

As a precaution, you might think about bringing a cellular phone with you, especially if hiking alone. You will be able to phone out from most locations on the front side of the mountains. A GPS device can help pinpoint your location; consider taking one with you on all of your hikes.

Setting the Scene

The mountain wall rises steeply behind Santa Barbara, an enduring quality that defines those of us who live here. Natural forces spanning many millions of years have carved five canyons into the mountain wall directly behind Santa Barbara—Mission, Rattlesnake, Cold Springs, San Ysidro, and Romero—each with its own unique charm. There are also countless other beautiful canyons hidden deep in the flank of the Santa Ynez Mountains, the upper reaches of the Santa Ynez Valley, and the San Rafael Mountains whose enchanting nature will lure you back time and again.

THE CHAPARRAL

From the perspective of the city, however, the abruptness of the mountain wall as it rises nearly 4,000 feet to its crest at La Cumbre Peak, the spiny layerings of sandstone, and the insipid color of the chaparral combine to convey a sense of inhospitality and dullness.

Upon first glance, the Santa Ynez Mountains do not appear inviting. For fifty miles they run unbroken, and because of the peculiar way they have been juxtaposed on the countryside in an east-west direction, the sun pours down on their southerly slope at nearly right angles. This scorches all but the hardiest chaparral plants, and the vegetation that is visible from Santa Barbara survives mainly by adapting to the lack of summer rain and the searing Santa Ana winds with a uniform, colorless appearance.

In addition, the dense chaparral cover gives sense of impenetrability. The thick, interlocking branches and the needle-sharp points of the tough, leathery leaves seem more to say *Keep Out, No Trespassing* than to invite closer inspection. "Meshed and tangled like concertina wire, and mined with rattlesnakes," one writer has said of the chaparral, "it is impossible to penetrate with anything less persuasive than a light tank."

The chaparral is an elfin forest dominated by shrubs seldom more than fifteen feet in height. What it lacks in stature, though, it makes up for in orneriness. It is primarily evergreen, which protects it from becoming desiccated during the long, rainless summer months, and the leaves are tough and leathery, with prickly edges.

It is also dry and resinous, which makes it extremely fire-prone, but this imparts its characteristic fragrance as well. This curious juxtaposition of opposites, of toughness and delicacy, marks chaparral country and makes it special to me.

DISTINCT ELEMENTS

Properly speaking, the chaparral has two distinct elements: coastal sage (also called soft chaparral), and hard chaparral. Coastal sage is the community of low herbaceous shrubs, rarely more than seven feet in height, that borders the canyons of the lower foothills. The small fuzzy leaves of yerba santa and the purple, black, and white sages are predominantly gray in color, but in the springtime the delicate purple buds of the sages and their overwhelming aromas make the soft chaparral community a treat to be sampled again and again.

This softer chaparral is found along the lower elevations of the Santa Ynez Mountains and on steep shale slopes that have insufficient soil to support grasses or species of the oak woodland community. Also found in the soft chaparral are California sagebrush, buckwheat, monkey flower, yarrow, and the wonderful bush that exudes a butterscotch aroma: pearly everlasting.

The hard chaparral is composed of duller green plants, which dominate higher elevations. These are dense woody shrubs that grow so thickly as to render travel through them nearly impossible, except for a few years after a wildfire. Despite the less-than-appealing aesthetics of this community, its species are well adapted to poor soil conditions, a short rainy season, and intense summer heat. These plants are like the tough kids on the block—on the surface neither delicate nor beautiful, but well structured for survival here—and in a Darwinian sort of way, there is a grace to these plant types.

This chaparral can be subdivided into two groups. The lower half grows to elevations of about 1,500 feet and is sometimes called "chamise chaparral" or *el camisal*. Though big pod and greenbark ceanothus, sugar bush, and black sage are also found here, chamise dominates, often in pure stands such as those around Inspiration Point. Chamise is a member of the rose family and has tiny needle-like leaves that grow in bundles. Its reddish-brown seed pods, which open during the flowering season, remain on the shrubs for much of the following year and give chamise chaparral its characteristic rusty color. Known as "greasewood" because of its high oil content, chamise is responsible for the intensity of many mountain wildfires.

Manzanita and scrub oak are the predominant species of the upper half of the hard chaparral. Other shrubs found near the crest are holly-leaf cherry, chaparral pea, toyon, yucca, bush poppy, prickly phlox, and mountain mahogany. Holly-leaf cherry was called *islay* by the Chumash, who harvested it in the fall and ground it into flour for use during winter months. Along with acorns, holly-leaf cherry formed a substantial part of the Chumash diet.

The name "chaparral" dates to the time when gaunt Spanish cattle roamed the valleys and foothills of the county, their wanderings unimpeded by either barbed wire or concrete. Rousting these half-wild steer from brush-choked canyons was the task of the rugged, hard-riding *vaqueros,* who protected their legs from sharp branches and thorns by wearing tough leggings, "chaps," that extended from belt to boots.

The plant that caused the *vaqueros* the most annoyance was the interior live oak, known scientifically as *Quercus wislizenii.* A similar oak that grows in Spain is called *el chaparro* ("short"), and this was the name given to the scrub oak that the Spaniards found in California. The "-al" suffix, added to the root word *chaparro,* means "the place of" and has led to the dense southland brush being called chaparral, even though today it includes far more than the pockets of scrub oak where Spanish cattle used to hide out.

MEDITERRANEAN CLIMATE

Santa Barbara, and the chaparral countryside that lies behind it, is a product of a Mediterranean climatic system. It is characterized by moderate, moist winters and long, hot, dry summers. Rainfall is generally sparse—about 17 inches per year—and often occurs during a few high-intensity winter storms. Summer temperatures often exceed 100° Farenheit. and relative humidity is low, often less than 5 percent.

Plant communities similar to chaparral grow in several other parts of the world, including the shores of the Mediterranean Sea, central Chile, South Africa, and southwestern Australia. These regions compose about 3 percent of the earth's land surface. All are located on the western borders of continental landmasses in a narrow strip between 30° and 45° latitude.

The weather patterns in these areas are dominated by a pressure zone known as the Pacific High. Locally, in the summer, as the Southwest begins to heat up, this mass of warm stable air moves slightly north and inland, deflecting storms originating in the northern latitudes eastward across Washington and Oregon. Only in the winter does the Pacific High retreat south and seaward and allow storm fronts access to the Southern California coastline.

CHAPARRAL SEASONS

Seasons in the chaparral differ from the norm. The primary season for plant growth and flowering is between March and May, and this season might be likened to summer elsewhere. June and July can be considered as autumn. The hot, dry months of August, September, and early October, during which no new growth occurs, is essentially winter. Spring really commences with the first rains in November or early December and continues until the rainy season ends in early April, when the weather warms and new plant life shoots forth.

MOUNTAIN CANYONS

On a warm spring or summer day there is no finer place to spend an afternoon than along one of Santa Barbara's many creeks. The rock is hot from the sun, perfect to lie back on and relax, and after a plunge in the chilling apple-green water, it feels good to lie back and absorb the sun's energy. The weariness of the hike will

Lizard's Mouth

begin to drain away, and the frantic pace which always seems to be the rule back in the city will start to evaporate.

It is a lazy, unpretentious way to enjoy the mountain wall and its hidden treasures. Resting on the coarse sandstone, so many years in the making, it is possible to assimilate the sense of deep time silently offered to you.

Light filters through the oak leaves in canyon country. Beneath, in their shade, are smaller shafts with bulbous, bright-red flower pods, known as hummingbird sage, and the intense nuclear yellows of the bush poppy. In the springtime these wildflowers create a Mondrian landscape of pastels that soften and give vibrance to the countryside. There are also the honeydew oranges of sticky monkey-flower, plumes of goldenrod, long vines of morning glory, and clusters of fragrant pearly everlasting.

Life in the Santa Ynez and San Rafael mountains begins in the canyons, the corridors into the mountain wall most often visited by Santa Barbarans, thin creases of abundance, a land where wealth is measured not in hard currency, but in liquid. Water is the life force here. I have spent many an afternoon hiking in the canyons of the front- and backcountry and what draws me back is this liquid gold and its cascading sound as gravity pulls it down to the sea. "If there be magic on this planet, it is contained in water," scientist Loren

Eisley wrote. "Water . . . its substance reaches everywhere; it touches the past and prepares the future."

The canyons are places that seem to allow an easier life. The vegetation literally has its feet in the water, and as a result the leaves are larger and greener than in other plant communities, for these plants can afford to transpire more freely than their chaparral neighbors, which live but a hundred or more feet above.

There are three distinct layers to the canyon plant community. At the top is the canopy, composed of the long branches of bay, willow, sycamore, alder, and, in the higher parts of the canyons, an occasional bigleaf maple. This overstory provides the shade, coolness, and humidity necessary to the lower layers. Next are the shrubs, including coffeeberry, elderberry, currant, the ubiquitous poison oak, and fuchsia-flowered gooseberry, which has brilliant red teardrop-shaped flowers with white inner petals.

Also in this middle layer are blackberry, wild rose, and the sunshine brightness of the canyon sunflower. Beneath is the herbacious layer, including a number of plants that can be classified as fire followers, plants that prosper in the years immediately after fire has swept through an area. Among the herbacious plants are miner's lettuce, hummingbird sage, cream cups, buttercup, lupine, brodiaea, shooting stars, blue-eyed grass, nightshade, watercress, and mint.

Here abundance is nowhere more evident than in the number of small creatures that inhabit the canyons. When one thinks of wild-

View from Inspiration Point

life in the mountains one usually thinks of the big creatures: the bear, the lion, the bobcat, or the coyote. But these are creatures of more open country—grasslands, wider canyon bottoms, higher country where the brush is sparser. In the deeper canyons, and especially in the chaparral, the thickets and the interlacing of ceanothus, manzanita, toyon, and scrub oak serve to keep the big life out. The chaparral and the canyons are worlds of small dimensions and the little creatures.

FIRE ADAPTATIONS

Just overhead is the chaparral, a sterile environment by comparison to the canyons. Because it is dry, dull, and difficult to make your way through, the chaparral is difficult to appreciate. The key element in the chaparral life cycle is fire, and nature has pre-adapted this scrubby brush to respond to the slightest spark. It is not uncommon for fuel moistures to drop to 8 to 13 percent during summer droughts or during Santa Ana conditions. In addition, the close spacing and continuity of the cover and the high surface-to-volume ratios in the chaparral community lead to a high percentage of available fuel.

Over time, the ratio of dead fuel to live plant material increases dramatically. For example, by age thirty often as much as 50 percent of the standing mass of chaparral is dead, and dry material litters the ground. Where such conditions exist over large mountainous expanses, fires, when ignited, tend to be quite large.

Though chaparral seems tough on the surface, it is actually a very delicately balanced community, well adapted to water stress. Over many millions of years, chaparral has evolved an equilibrium between water conservation and water use. One of the adaptive features is the solid continuity of brush cover and its nearly uniform height, which helps minimize evaporation and retain winter moisture through the long summer months of water deprivation. Holding fast to this soil moisture in the summertime is critical, and the even mantle acts like a blanket that protects the soil from wind and solar radiation.

While the cover tends to minimize soil moisture loss, the leaf structure of chaparral plants is sclerophylous, which means it is well adapted to resist water loss. Some plants, like scrub oak or hollyleaf cherry, have heavy wax cuticles on the leaves and stems, which help reduce water loss. On other plants, dense mats of hairs serve the same function. Another adaptation is vertical orientation of leaves, or, as in the case of sugar bush, leaves that are curled so that they do not receive sunlight directly. The grayish color of plants like white or purple sage or yerba santa also reduces the heating up of the plant tissues. Further, sunken stomata on the leaves of these plants help make water loss minimal.

Most of the leaves of chaparral plants are also desiccation-tolerant, which means that the leaf structure resists damage during long dry periods. Nevertheless, there are limits to the length of time these plants can survive water stress, and many are drought deciduous as well. Often, after 100 days or more of prolonged drought, many begin to lose their leaves, bringing evaporation loss almost to a halt. Plants that drop their leaves usually develop smaller leaves on side shoots of the main stems, and it is these tiny leaves that enable them to persist through extended drought.

Most chaparral plants produce chemicals that inhibit other plants from invading their territory. Through a process called allelopathy, the chemicals invade the soil from the leaf litter and prevent roots of other plants from competing for soil moisture. These toxins are so potent that in some cases, as with the bush poppy or certain species of ceanothus, the spaces that they occupy may remain incapable of being invaded by other species for as much as 20 to 40 years after the plants have been killed off by wildfire.

The main adaptation of chaparral to its arid conditions, however, is its response to fire, which initiates a new cycle of plant succession. In hard chaparral the buildup of dead plant material tends to ensure the continuity of fire, while in softer chaparral it is the volatile and highly flammable oils that do so.

After a fire, annuals and short-lived perennials, called fire followers, temporarily dominate the hillsides, producing spectacular displays of wildflowers. In about two to five years after a fire, though, almost all of these species stop growing, and their spaces are usually taken by the expanding canopies of resprouting or regrowing chaparral shrubs. The seeds of these herbaceous fire followers persist in the soil until released by heat from the next wildfire.

Once a shrub occupies the space held by fire followers, it physically dominates that site, primarily because of allelopathy. Not until the next fire will the cycle begin anew. Viewed on a linear scale, the chaparral life cycle can be seen as a series of "pulses," each initiated by fire. Removal of older brush by intense wildfires that occasionally sweep across the mountain wall is not just an adversity that these plants must overcome, but a necessary part of their life cycle. Unlike some other ecosystems, which require many years to redevelop a healthy diversity once fire has disturbed them, chaparral is actually healthiest and contains the widest variety of plant and animal species in the years immediately after fire. The concern is not so much if chaparral will recover after fire, or how long it will take, but rather how rapidly the ecosystem will decline if fire is withheld. Woven through the almost impenetrable tangle are the trails of small animals, though without fire, the wildlife does not fare well. As the fuel volume of chaparral increases, its food productivity decreases. Wildfire prunes out the dead wood, causes rapid regrowth, and permits the spread of annuals and herbs, which are retarded by a thick overstory. Generally, fire favors wildlife by setting the botanical clock back a notch to earlier periods of plant succession, thus forcing the vegetation to produce more food.

Almost anywhere off-trail you can see the effect of this fire ecology directly. The branches of the stiff-twigged shrubs make passage within this habitat difficult. Except for the recent Painted Cave Fire, these mountains have not burned in the past two decades, and except for the outer edges of the bushes, most of the limbs are dead. Chaparral plants grow only at their tips.

CHAPARRAL BIRDS

It wasn't until I began to spend time wandering off-trail, crawling through the chaparral, and sneaking up undiscovered canyons looking for new experiences that I began to see the wildlife.

The amount to be seen is often in direct proportion to the time spent away from trails, and most definitely to the value placed on smaller creatures, for this elfin forest harbors the little things. Mostly it requires patience and the ability to sit for long periods of time, immersed in the chaparral, to let life come to you.

My favorites are the chaparral birds, somewhat subtle in appearance. As California bird habitats go, chaparral harbors relatively few species. Though it produces great numbers of plants, there are few plant types, and as a wildlife habitat it is rather uniform and monotonous.

Because of the density of the brush, many of the birds that reside here are specially suited to life within and beneath the chaparral. Near ground level are surface dwellers such as the California thrasher, the Rufous-sided towhee, the brown towhee, and the mountain quail, whose running ability enables it to dash through narrow avenues in the vegetation. It is a pleasure to lie stretched beneath the chaparral and watch these birds scamper about as they forage through the leaf litter for seeds and insects and other invertebrates.

Living in the canopy itself are the Bewick's wren, the orange-crowned warbler, and the lazuli bunting. When the vegetation is

La Cumbre Peak

healthy, this layer of the chaparral produces vast quantities of food. Buds, berries, cherries, nuts, seeds, bulbs, corms, and flower leaves are all available. Insects add further to the rich diet afforded these birds, and it is not surprising that, despite the relatively few species, there are large numbers of birds here.

MOUNTAIN GEOLOGY

The Transverse Ranges, of which the Santa Ynez Mountains form the most westerly part, are among the few ranges in the United States that run in an east-west direction. Forming a continuous crest from Point Arguello to Ojai, a distance of 70 miles, the Santa Ynez Mountains are tilted steeply to the south at an angle of nearly 50 degrees.

From Point Arguello to Gaviota Pass, the range is generally less than 2,000 feet high. East of Gaviota, however, the mountains gain height rapidly, reaching 4,298 feet at Santa Ynez Peak, before dropping gradually to San Marcos Pass which has an elevation of 2,250 feet.

San Marcos Pass occupies a low saddle formed by a synclinal (V-shaped) fold that crosses the main axis of the range diagonally. East of San Marcos Pass, the mountains rise once again, averaging 3,500 feet behind Santa Barbara, with La Cumbre Peak measuring 3,985 feet in height. The range reaches its apex at 4,690-foot Divide Peak, near the Santa Barbara-Ventura county line.

The geologic history of the Santa Ynez Mountains is related to the slow movements of pieces of the earth's crust called tectonic plates. At present, Southern California marks the boundary between two of these plates, the North American Plate, which supports most of the continental United States, and the Pacific Plate, which supports a part of the California coast and Baja California. The point at which these two plates come into contact is called the San Andreas Fault.

The movement of tectonic plates is called continental drift. The action of this "drift" can cause several things to happen at the point of articulation between two plates. They might be pulled apart, which creates a trench between them. Or one plate can be pushed over the other, a process called subduction. Also, two plates can slide against one another, as presently occurs along the San Andreas Fault. Santa Barbara's geologic history involves all three of these processes.

THE SUBDUCTION BEGINS

One hundred and thirty-five million years ago, the North American and Pacific plates came into contact with one another for the first time, initiating a series of violent collisions that would shape the geology of all of Southern California. There was a much different topographic relief then, dissimilar vegetation (in the areas above water), and a climate much wetter than what we know at present.

There were no high mountains in California, perhaps only rolling hills, and a tropical sea lapped against a shore much farther east, near the base of what was to become the Sierra Nevada. What we now know as Santa Barbara was underwater and farther south, possibly as far south as northern Baja California.

Much of Northern California, however, and most of the Pacific Northwest was above water. Dense rain forests predominated in the Northwest, and the climate was temperate and humid. In the parts of Southern California that were above sea level, the climate was subtropical savanna, rolling grass-covered hills set in a warm, wet climate.

But gradually this began to change as two massive pieces of the earth's crust smashed together. While both the North American and Pacific plates drifted northward, the Pacific Plate moved north at a faster rate, causing it to collide with the North American landmass. Though the difference in rate of drift was minuscule, an average of only 2.25 inches per year (some 300 miles over the entire 135 million year period!), this difference was enough to produce Southern California's rugged topography.

Complicating this further, the Pacific Plate was composed not of a single sheet of the earth's crust, but of a series of connected pieces. In its middle portion was a break known as the Pacific Rise, out of which oozed molten materials from deep within the earth. Like escalators, the land on each side moved up and out and away from the rise.

Thus, as the Pacific Plate drifted north, there was also a part of it that moved to the east, causing the plate to be pushed, or subducted, under the North American Plate at some periods in its geologic history, and at others to slide north against it, as it does today along the San Andreas Fault.

As one of the pieces of the Pacific Plate subducted under the continental plate, the edge of the North American continent acted like a huge bulldozer blade, scraping portions of the crust off the ocean plate. This pile of rubble, called the Franciscan Formation by geologists, eventually became the basement rock beneath the Santa Ynez Mountains. Today it is exposed in Santa Barbara County mainly along the southern slopes of the San Rafael Mountains, especially near Figueroa Mountain.

Farther inland, subduction caused widespread volcanic activity in the Sierras, with friction between the two plates causing rock beneath the surface to melt and the land directly above the western edge of the North American Plate to sink. As the basin subsided, it formed a large depression shaped something like a bathtub.

This bathtub began to fill very slowly with the sediments that would one day make up the Santa Barbara front- and backcountry. Most of the geologic formations exposed in the Santa Ynez Mountains, including the Juncal, Matilija, Cozy Dell, and Coldwater formations, were deposited in this basin during the Eocene Epoch, 40 to 50 million years ago.

As the basin continued to sink, the shoreline crept inland to the base of an ancestral form of the Sierra Nevada, which was more rolling hills than mountains at that time. While the Sierra range was uplifted, torrential subtropical rains caused widespread erosion, covering the ocean floor with 20,000 to 30,000 feet of sediment that would eventually become the fertile Central Valley and the Santa Barbara coast.

The sinking of the basin and the subsequent sedimentation were not processes that occurred evenly, though. At some points as the basin sank rapidly the ocean was several thousand feet deep; at others, it subsided slowly or not at all, and the basin filled to become a shallow seashore environment.

When the sea was more shallow, a predominance of sands built up, like those in prominent peaks such as La Cumbre or Divide peaks, or in massive pieces of bedrock such as those at Lizard's Mouth or the Playground. Where the basin was deeper, shales prevailed, shales like the Cozy Dell, which lies in between the Matilija and Coldwater sandstones and forms the deep saddles that make Mission Crags so distinctive.

Finally, at the beginning of the Oligocene Epoch, approximately 35 million years ago, when the section of the Pacific Plate causing the basin to sink moved north of Southern California, Santa Barbara was about ready to surface for the first time. The basin, or bathtub, was almost full of sediment, and as the shoreline began to retreat westward, the land began to emerge.

At this point, Santa Barbara still lay beneath the ocean, but as more layers of sandstone and shale piled up in the channel, in the form of granitic sands and fine mud, the floor rose, and Santa Barbara timidly peaked its sand-and-shale-covered head above the ocean's surface.

Perhaps you've noticed the red-colored rocks exposed along the base of the Santa Ynez Mountains, especially visible on San Marcos Pass Road several miles above Cathedral Oaks Road. These are the Sespe "red beds," a series of rock layers composed of shale, sandstone, and a mixture of pebbles and larger cobbles called conglomerate. The reddish color is the result of iron oxides within the shales and sandstones, a vivid celebration of Santa Barbara's rise from its primeval depths. It also leads geologists to conclude that the Oligocene was a period of tropical or subtropical climate, since red soils similar to these are being formed in the tropics today.

With the subduction ended, California began to feel the first effects of the San Andreas Fault. When the subducting portion of the Pacific Plate moved north of Santa Barbara, it was replaced by a piece that began to slide against the North American Plate, a process that resulted in violent collisions.

The pressures built along the edges of these two plates were relieved suddenly in the form of earthquakes, releasing energy that began to lift thousands of feet of ocean sediments toward the heavens, making them into mountains. While earthquakes raised mountains from the sea, erosive forces labored to wear them back down. Streams carried sand and gravel toward the ocean, forming the broad alluvial plain we now call the Sespe red beds.

For 11 million years this gently sloping land had received deposits of sand, silt, and cobbles that would become the Sespe Formation. But rather than staying above water, almost as if in a last-ditch effort to return to its marine origins, the land sank one last time. For another 10 million years the red beds were gradually buried under ocean-bottom sediments laid down in Miocene seas.

The warm, shallow seas were more favorable to the development of marine life than those of any other time. Small single-celled organisms called diatoms flourished, as did many varieties of shellfish. Sea mammals, including whales, sea otters, seal, and sea lions evolved to maturity during the Miocene Epoch as well.

Sediments included the layers we know as Rincon Shale, Vaqueros Sandstone, and the Monterey Formation. The latter two layers, heavily saturated with organic material due to the abundance of marine life, now play a very important part in Santa Barbara's oil legacy.

Eventually mountain-building processes initiated by our restless earth shoved these rock layers out of the ocean, this time for good, to form the land we live upon today. No doubt though, someday we will once again be part of an ocean floor.

THE CHANGING CLIMATE

As Santa Barbara rose from the ocean depths, Southern California's subtropical climate was beginning to shift to a drier, cooler environment. Approximately 13 million years ago, at the beginning of the Pliocene Epoch, rainfall, a staple of evergreen forests and tropical plants such as ferns, lessened in its intensity and began to fall only in the colder months of the year. Colder ocean temperatures began to affect the positioning of the Pacific High and this blocked summer storms coming from the Gulf of Alaska, allowing them to occur only during winter and early spring months.

As the cooling, drying trend accelerated, mixed conifer and subalpine forests began to adapt to a narrowing range of environments, becoming stranded in small pockets and botanical islands, either in areas of high relief or abundant rainfall, where drought stress could be avoided.

By the beginning of the Pliocene open grasslands replaced the retreating forests, and as the Santa Ynez Mountains formed, they and other coastal ranges became important reservoirs for the survival and persistence of plants derived from the northern temperate rainforests. In addition, the uplifting of the Sierra Nevada began to protect coastal areas from even more intense periods of cooling and drying east of the Sierra, thus allowing the persistence of a number of relic plant species in Southern California.

Because of the climatic changes, another vegetative community much more suited to a developing Mediterranean environment spread toward California from the east. Fifty million years ago, as the layers now forming the basic rock units of the Santa Ynez Mountains were being laid down in the Santa Barbara Channel, live-oak woodland and associated trees such as madrone, bay, and pinyon pine appeared as far west as the Rocky Mountains. By the Miocene, some 20 to 30 million years later, they had assumed dominance over much of the interior of Southern California.

Another 10 million years later, during the Pliocene, grasslands and an oak-woodland setting covered most of Santa Barbara County, a land of soft rolling hills, luscious clumps of perennial grass, and thick clusters of oak trees—not unlike the Santa Ynez Valley on an April afternoon today. It was not the home of cattle, however, but of prehistoric land mammals such as camels, rhinos, three-toed horses, hedgehogs, and other species that thrived then on the wide expanses of grass.

As the Santa Barbara basin continued to fill with cobblestones, gravel, sand, silt, and other matter, these alluvia formed either rich, deep topsoils or, in areas where shale predominated, were compacted to form dense clayey soils. In the areas of good topsoil, grasses became the primary groundcover, with native bunch grasses covering most of the coastal plain. The clay soils, less hospitable, tended to support a combination of grasses and woodland.

The first oaks to migrate to the west coast were of the temperate forest, primarily deciduous oaks that originated in the cool, wet forests of the northern half of the continent before being driven from the plains, across the Rockies, and into the West. These migrating oaks were a mixture not only of deciduous, but also evergreen varieties such as the California coastal live oak, which evolved in a much drier environment, most likely similar to that of the warmer, drier parts of northern Mexico.

Today both the deciduous and evergreen varieties of oak are an integral part of what we call the Santa Barbara landscape. Valley oaks, the largest of the American oaks, still thrive in the deep, moist soils of the interior valleys, though where people inhabit the valley floors they are becoming an endangered species. Gnarled little blue oaks cover the grassy foothills surrounding the valleys, somehow getting enough moisture from the shallow soil to hold their leathery leaves through the dry summers. Living on stream flats or ravines where the topsoil is deeper and the moisture a bit more abundant are the equally gnarled interior live oaks, distinguished by having greener foliage than blue oaks. Higher on the slopes, where the grasslands give way to fir and pine, are California black oaks, a deciduous species with leaves similar in appearance to valley oak but having needle-like points at the ends of the lobes. Along the coast, forming huge oak forests in places such as Hope Ranch or Montecito, the California live oak is the prevalent species.

The drier climate also fostered the evolution of chaparral plant communities in Southern California. Able to survive in wetter climates, chaparral plants thrive in areas where dry, Mediterranean environments prevail.

Perhaps chaparral plants could be likened to hitchhikers, thumbs out, riding tectonic plates north into a more profitable environment as movement along the San Andreas Fault caused Southern California to drift northward, with forces exerted by this movement generating a power almost impossible to comprehend, ripping Baja California away from the mainland and creating a trench between it and the Mexican mainland that would become the Gulf of California.

Also breaking up the 30,000-foot thickness of sediments that had built up in the Santa Barbara Channel, tectonic movement pushed them more than a mile in the air, twisted the entire block from its original north-south direction to the east-west orientation it has today, and moved the Santa Barbara landmass with its newly evolving drought-resistant plant community toward an environment whose Mediterranean climate would allow them to thrive.

This mountain-building process began to occur about three million years ago, during the Pleistocene Epoch, uplifting the Santa Ynez Mountains to their greatest relief, perhaps as much as 7,000 feet in height, as the tectonic pressures being exerted by slippage along the San Andreas Fault caused layers of sedimentary rock in the Santa Barbara area to turn on their edges along the Santa Ynez Fault.

At this time a cooling trend also developed throughout the

Northern Hemisphere, causing the onset of a series of ice ages. Sheets of ice up to 10,000 feet thick covered much of the continent and the ocean level dropped about 350 feet. This caused the coastline to retreat between five and six miles and exposed the Channel Islands as one long landmass. For several million years the climate in Southern California was cool and wet.

Protected by the Sierra, the west coast endured not ice but torrential rain, which ate away at the rising mountains and provided the county with an environment much more like that of Monterey today. This was a period of rich and diverse plant life. Intermixed were conifers, redwoods, and deciduous woodlands. It was a period of pre-eminence in the Santa Barbara area for ferns such as the maidenhair.

The Pleistocene Epoch was not one long uniform period, but a series of recurring cool-moist, warm-dry cycles in which there was a constant reassortment of two primary elements: the temperate forests of the north, and the drought-resistant communities of the south. Some plants sought safety in the high country, others in the canyons or on the flanks of the developing mountain wall. Such plants, like the maidenhair fern, did not seem to mind sharing chaparral country as long as they could receive a share of the meager rainfall.

The overall trend, though, was one of drying, and after the Pleistocene ended, a warmer, less moist climate prevailed, allowing the spread of more drought-resistant plants like chaparral into Southern California and causing the elimination of the primeval forests and ferns from the low country.

This warming forced the development of narrower, more specialized local environments, causing plants to separate into distinct communities. Woodland forests segregated themselves into ecological islands where they could continue to exist. Alder, sycamore, and maple migrated to the canyons. While coniferous forests shifted to the mountaintops, evergreen oak species migrated onto the thin coastal strip. Other woodland species, which required either a colder climate or more rainfall, such as the cottonwood and valley oak, retreated to more equitable climates found in the interior valleys and the backcountry.

NATURAL HISTORY OF THE SANTA YNEZ MOUNTAINS

LATE JURASSIC TO EARLY CRETACEOUS
135 million years ago
Continental drift begins about 250 million years ago. 135 million years ago: North American Plate begins to override Pacific Plate. Subduction of Pacific Plate causes rise of Sierra Nevada. Along coast and to the base of Sierra, land subsides to create a large basin. Sea moves inland to the base of Sierra.

TERTIARY
PALEOCENE: 60 MILLION YEARS AGO
Santa Barbara is under a deep sea. Climate beyond Sierra to the interior becomes warmer. Sediments deposited on the ocean floor as mountains are weathered get subducted under the North American Plate. These do not appear in the strata of the Santa Ynez Range.

EOCENE: 50 MILLION YEARS AGO
Subduction slows. Pacific Plate is now being pushed north as well as being subducted. Sediments deposited on the ocean floor at this time become the basic geological units of the Santa Ynez Mountains: Juncal, Matilija, Cozy Dell Shale, and Coldwater Sandstone formations. Climate has become subtropical. Large mammals evolve in the lush jungle vegetation. Marine life begins to evolve.

OLIGOCENE: 35 MILLION YEARS AGO
Pacific Plate has almost passed north of Santa Barbara. Eocene and early Oligocene sediments begin to fill the large basin. The sea

becomes shallow. Santa Barbara area rises above sea level for the first time. The purplish-red Sespe Formation is the first non-marine sediment to be laid down. Climate becomes cooler and drier. Subtropical vegetation is replaced by savanna and oak woodland environments. Large mammals such as the wooly mammoth become extinct. Several grazing animals and their predators evolve.

MIOCENE: 30 MILLION YEARS AGO
Subduction ends when the Pacific Plate moves north of Santa Barbara and to its present position off the Washington coast. American and Pacific plates come into direct contact along the San Andreas Fault. Northward-moving Pacific Plate causes a shearing stress. Landmass moves north and into contact with the Sierra Neavada, creating a lateral compression giving rise to the Santa Ynez Range. Climate is cooler and drier and sea life more abundant than at any other time.

PLIOCENE: 13 MILLION YEARS AGO
Santa Barbara is above sea level for good, and present topography develops. Santa Ynez crest is forced upward by lateral compression, causing depression of the Santa Ynez Valley. Climate is warm and dry. Chaparral plant communities spread from the Southwest across Southern California. Many mammals reach their evolutionary peak of development.

QUARTERNARY
PLEISTOCENE: 3 MILLION YEARS AGO
Santa Ynez Mountains are uplifted from 1,000 to 2,000 feet higher than at present, and interior valleys subside further. Onset of a series of ice ages. Ocean level drops 350 feet, coastline retreats, and Channel Islands become one long island. Climate becomes cold and moist, and forest plant and animal communities flourish. Crest of mountains slowly erode to present relief.

HOLOCENE: 11,000 YEARS AGO TO PRESENT
Warming trend develops across continent and ice sheets melt. Sea level rises quickly. Canyons fill with creek sediments and valleys are covered with layers of alluvium. Evergreen plant communities retreat to canyons and mountain crests. Chaparral becomes the dominant plant community. Man migrates to the Santa Barbara area about 10,000 years ago and has become semi-sedentary by about 8,000 years ago.

GEOLOGIC FORMATIONS

There are eight main rock structures underlying the Santa Ynez Mountains. From the oldest to youngest they are: Juncal Formation, Matilija Sandstone, Cozy Dell Shale, Coldwater Sandstone, Sespe Formation, Vaqueros Sandstone, Rincon Shale, and Monterey Shale. All are composed of sandstone, shale, or interbeds of shale and sandstone. A small amount of conglomerate is also found in the area.

JUNCAL

The Juncal Formation is composed of alternating layers of sandstone and shale that are 4,000 to 5,000 feet thick. They are of the Eocene age (58 to 36 million years ago). Shale predominates and weathers easily, forming rounded clay hills. The more rapid erosion of the shale interbeds leaves the sandstone jutting out as prominent ledges or ridges. The layers accumulated in a cold, deep sea that supported little marine life. Because the soils formed by the Juncal shales are of poor quality, they support little but brushy growth on steeper slopes that have a southern exposure. Near the crest, such as behind Montecito, the shale has weathered to rolling, rounded hill-tops that have grassy cover, a sharp contrast to the jagged Matilija formation just to the west. The Juncal Formation is prominent in the upper Santa Ynez Valley and is the major rock structure in the Red Rock area.

MATILIJA SANDSTONE

Matilija Sandstone is the thick, resistant layer of sandstone that forms the 3,985-foot-high La Cumbre Peak. It is 2,000 feet thick at this point. This sandstone is grayish-white, weathers to a creamy buff color, and is extremely hard. This makes it highly resistant to erosion, and allows it to form the most rugged, craggy, and scenic strata found in the Santa Ynez Mountains. The sandstone was laid down in the later Eocene Epoch, and its origin is of granitic rock eroded from inland sources. After being washed into the ocean the granite was decomposed by underwater currents and spread out over the ocean floor as a uniform blanket of sand as the basin subsided. The Matilija Sandstone doesn't contain any fossils because the cold, inhospitable marine environment that emerged during the formation of the Juncal shales continued to prevail.

The upper part of Tunnel Trail passes through Matilija Sandstone, and the upper end of Rattlesnake Canyon ends at the base of this formation. Just above the large meadow you can see a large wall of sandstone. This is Gibraltar Rock, a popular climbing area. The narrow, upper part of San Ysidro Canyon is also formed of this sandstone.

COZY DELL SHALE

Formed in the upper Eocene, this formation is composed almost entirely of shale. Cozy Dell Shale is almost 1,700 feet thick and disintegrates readily into small fragments. This causes it to form markedly recessive topography, most graphically the deep saddles you can see in between the Matilija and Coldwater sandstones. It is dark gray and weathers to a brownish-gray or olive gray color. Cozy Dell Shale was deposited as a fine mud 35 to 40 million years ago, when the Eocene sea reached its maximum depth. While Coldwater and Matilija sandstones form spectacular peaks and cliffs, Cozy Dell saddles have their own gentle grace. This shale is exposed in several areas, most notably along the connector trail leading from Rattlesnake Canyon to the Tunnel Trail and on the saddle between Cathedral and La Cumbre peaks. The rolling, grass-covered knolls on the crest above San Antonio Creek are also composed of Cozy Dell Shale.

COLDWATER SANDSTONE

Coldwater Sandstone is the thickest of the marine sandstones found in the Santa Barbara area. Its resistant layers form the pyramid-shaped Mission Crags in the mountains directly above the

Botanic Gardens. Averaging 2,700 feet in thickness, it is composed mostly gray-white sands that weather on the outside surfaces to a buff color. Coldwater Sandstone is approximately 20 percent siltstone and shale, which can be seen in between the much thicker sandstone layers. The main part of the layer is composed of granitic sands washed down into an Eocene sea during a period when geologic activity was causing the sea to retreat. Most likely, the sandstone was deposited when the Santa Barbara basin was nearly full. This shallow marine environment was most likely much more favorable to the development of life. The shallow, brackish seas fostered the growth of large beds of oysters, a fossil found frequently in Coldwater Sandstone. Though not quite as resistant as Matilija Sandstone, it is extremely hard.

Coldwater Sandstone forms the picturesque ledges, cliffs, and boulder fields found at Lizard's Mouth and the Playground. Most of the rock exposed along the upper Jesusita Trail is Coldwater Sandstone, as are the formations in lower Cold Springs and San Ysidro canyons. Where it lies along the base of the Santa Ynez Mountains, Coldwater Sandstone forms beautiful narrow canyons that feature large pools and waterfalls. The best known of these narrows is at Seven Falls in the west fork of Mission Canyon.

SESPE FORMATION

The Sespe Formation is composed of interbedded shales, sandstones, and conglomerates that total 3,000 feet in thickness. The rock is primarily reddish-brown or maroon due to the high content of iron oxide found in it. The Sespe Formation contains the only non-marine layers of rock found in the Santa Barbara area. It accumulated on a nearly level plain as the sea became choked with sediment. Eventually the iron oxidized to become the rusty color it is today.

The Sespe Formation is found along the lower part of the foothills and makes up many of the rolling hills found in the Goleta area. Where there is a large percentage of clay in the strata, it weathers to a loamy soil that supports grassy slopes, many of which have avocado orchards on them. The red conglomerates are readily visible in the first few miles of Highway 154 above the San Antonio Creek bridge. The formation is also present along lower Jesusita Trail, and there are outcroppings of it throughout the Santa Barbara and Montecito foothills.

San Onofre Beach

Beach Walks

INTRODUCTION

I have always loved walking on the beaches. Perhaps it is because I grew up so close to the beach, never living much more than a mile from the ocean, that beachwalks have become a part of me.

There was a minus tide on the Sunday afternoon we headed up to El Capitan State Beach for a walk. There were just four of us—Gerry, Barry, Yvonne and I—a perfect number for what were about to do, which was to walk the coastline from the park down to Haskell's Beach.

This is one of Santa Barbara's very best beach walks. Though the highway is never more than a half-mile away, the tall cliffs swallow the sound of the traffic, and the feeling once you round the first corner is of being in a very faraway place. Along the way the are long stretches of hard-packed sand, boulder fields where you can stop and explore for all sorts of things, and tide pools filled with sea stars and huge, purple slugs feeding on the kelp. And lots of barnacles and sea urchins too.

It is a walk that can be done only at a lower tide, and minus tides are perfect since there is so much more to see. We started on the falling tide, having dropped off one car at Haskell's Beach and left a second car in the El Cap parking lot.

Turning around the point at El Cap reminded me of days long past, surfing the point. When it is up, the El Cap point break is the best Santa Barbara has to offer—at least in my opinion. The point turns in sharply, the bank's a solid wall of boulders stacked one on top of the other by the powerful waves, The surf isn't usually big here, perhaps four to six feet at its highest, but the shape of the point and the rocky bottom create a steep and fast-moving curl that is intense.

What a thrill!

There were a few surfers out as we carefully made our way over the boulders to the bottom of the cove where the sand begins. I saluted them silently. The first half-mile of the walk lead along a beautiful stretch of sandy beach, an easy walk at low tide. Fifteen minutes later we were around the first point, and the state park disappeared behind us. We saw a few fishermen and a couple who had

lugged a small cooler down the beach; otherwise it was deserted. What a treat.

There is a succession of small points, each of which is covered by water at higher tides, but that day the walking was easy. Then we came to the boulder fields, huge boulders, two to three feet in diameter, jumbled together at the end of one point. A great resting spot. Lunch time, I thought. Each of us snuggled down into a pocket of sand, resting our backs against the warm boulders. Perfect. As we leaned back, talking about something inconsequential, suddenly right there in front of us, barely twenty yards off shore, a whale sounded. Incredible! I assumed it was a gray whale but I didn't see enough of it to be sure.

We all scan the horizon, looking further up the coast to where we thought the whale would surface again. Sure enough, it did, blowing a snoutful of water high into the sky. In the next five minutes the whale surfaced twice more before it was far enough in the distance that we turned our attention elsewhere. We were all blown away; none of us had even seen a whale that close.

As we continued on down the coast there were more treasures to be found. The beaches are wide, a hundred yards of sand, rocky outcroppings, and scattered pools uncovered by the extremely low tide. We spied a few dolphins moving down the coast with us. The remaining few hours of the walk were just as pleasant. Plenty of time to let the psyche wind down, to readjust the soul to more pleasing rhythms, and to reawaken acquaintanceships with old friends. This is the essence of Santa Barbara's many beach walks: places where you can walk for long distances, often in complete solitude, where there is almost always a surprise awaiting you.

Enjoy these walks, as I have, and help take care of them. If you would like to know what you can do, please contact the Santa Barbara chapter of the Surfrider Foundation: Post Office Box 21703, Santa Barbara, CA 93101 (805) 967-9938.

1. Rincon Beach County Park

BEACH WALK INFORMATION
Distance—3 miles from Rincon to Carpinteria State Beach
Topo—Carpinteria
URL—http://www.sb-outdoors.org Keyword Search: Rincon Beach

DIRECTIONS
From downtown Santa Barbara, follow Highway 101 south for 13 miles to
the Bates Road turnoff (2.5 miles past Linden Avenue). There are two
parking areas. The parking lot directly across from the Bates turnoff leads
down to the main beach and surfing area. To the right, the upper parking
lot overlooks the bluffs just west of Rincon Point. A path leads down to the
beach.

A CAUTION
The Harbor Seal Preserve is closed to entry from December 1 through May
31. Please observe the closure. Dogs and seals make a bad mix. If you
bring your dog with you, make sure it is on a leash when you are anywhere
near the Seal Preserve. Please be respectful of private property rights.

THE WALK

There is excellent tide pooling at Rincon Point, with a long
stretch of sandy shoreline from the point west to the Chevron Oil
pier. When the surf is up this is a great beach to watch the riders
cruising across California's best waves. It is a few hundred yards to
the point. Along the way there is plenty of driftwood to sort
through and when the tide is low, plenty of rocks and pools to
check out along the way. You may have to take off your shoes to
make it across the creek, but once you are past this point the walking is free and easy.

West of the point the beach is wide and sandy. It is a bit more
than a mile of very pleasant walking all the way to the Chevron
pier. There is a very remote feeling despite being so close to
Carpinteria. From the bluff overlooking the pier you can watch
harbor seals frolic on the beach.

If you would like to avoid the creek crossing or the more
crowded point area, park in the upper parking lot and head directly
down to the west beach.

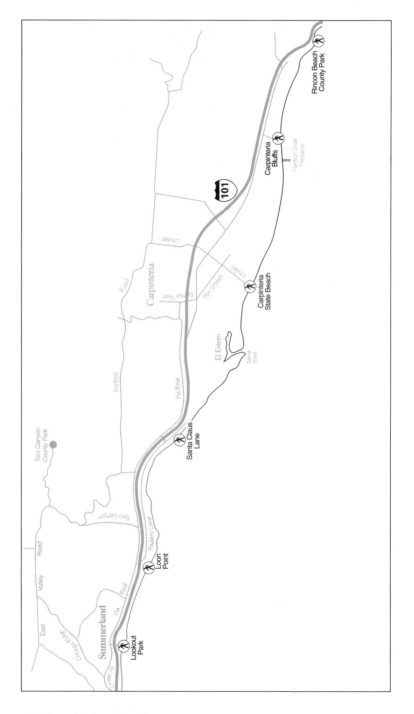

2. Carpinteria Bluffs

BEACH WALK INFORMATION
Distance—1 mile from the end of Bailard to the Chevron Oil Pier
Topo—Carpinteria
URL—http://www.sb-outdoors.org Keyword Search: Carpinteria Bluffs

DIRECTIONS
From downtown Santa Barbara, follow Highway 101 south for 12 miles to the Bailard Avenue turnoff. Turn right and park in the turnout just across Carpinteria Avenue where Bailard ends on the Carpinteria bluffs.

A CAUTION
The Harbor Seal Preserve is closed to entry from December 1 through May 31. Please observe the closure. Dogs and seals make a bad mix. If you bring yours with you make sure it is on a leash when you are anywhere near the Seal Preserve. Please be extremely careful when you are anywhere near the railroad tracks.

THE WALK

The Carpinteria Bluffs are now preserved as open space, thanks to the many local citizens who contributed to saving them. I always enjoy my walks there. Just off the freeway, there is almost always a catering truck nearby where I can get a snow cone or a drink before heading down to the beach.

The walk down to the bluffs leads through quiet, open meadows and a long row of stately eucalyptus trees. It is easy walking along the bluff edge to the Chevron Oil pier, where you can observe harbor seals on the beach.

There is access to the beach just east of the pier, leading down to a long sandy beach where you can enjoy a mile of secluded walking down to Rincon Point. To the west you will need to walk through the Chevron parking lot to reach more of the Carp bluffs. These will lead you along a very pleasant set of overlooks and eventually down to the ocean's edge. From there it is a bit more than a mile to the state park.

3. Carpinteria State Beach

BEACH WALK INFORMATION

Distance—.5 mile west from Linden Avenue to the rock jetty at Sandyland;
  1 mile from Linden Avenue east to the city park. 3 miles east to Rincon
  Park

Topo—Carpinteria

Telephone—684-2811

URL—http://www.sb-outdoors.org Keyword Search: Carpinteria State
  Beach

DIRECTIONS

From downtown Santa Barbara, follow Highway 101 south for 10.5 miles to
the Linden Avenue turnoff. To reach the beach, follow Lindena half-mile to
the ocean, where there is plenty of on-street parking. To reach the county
park, turn left on Carpinteria Avenue, then right two blocks east of Linden
onto Palm Street. Follow this toward the ocean to the park entrance.

A CAUTION

The Harbor Seal Preserve is closed to entry from December 1 through May
31. Please observe the closure. Dogs and seals make a bad mix. If you
bring your dog with you, make sure it is on a leash when you are anywhere
near the Seal Preserve. Please be respectful of private property rights.

THE WALK

Wide expanses of beach, gentle surf, and excellent clamming
during minus tides make this beach a walker's paradise. There is lots
of space in the park for day use or overnight stays, or you can walk
east through the park and blufftops to the city park with your picnic supplies for a more remote barbecue.

Carpinteria advertises its beaches as the world's safest, and they
surely seem that way; in either direction they are wide and flat, with
plenty of hard-packed sand for building sand castles or playing fris-
bee. I love hiking in either direction, though you can usually only
go a half-mile of so to the west unless the tide is extremely low or
you don't mind getting your legs wet. This is the more crowded
portion of the beach, but it is very nice walking along the beachfront houses to the rock jetties.

East of Linden Avenue the walking is very mellow as well, the
first half-mile of the beach leading you past the state park until you
eventually reach a series of bluffs. There are picnic tables situated in
very scenic locations along the bluffs, and your kids will love the

view down on the harbor seals from the point just east of the pier. To reach the viewing area you will need to walk through the Chevron parking area.

4. Santa Claus Lane

BEACH WALK INFORMATION
Distance—2.5 miles west to the Loon Point beach access; 1.5 miles east to Carpinteria State Beach (accessible only during minus tides)
Topo—Carpinteria
URL—http://www.sb-outdoors.org Keyword Search: Rincon Beach

DIRECTIONS
From downtown Santa Barbara, follow Highway 101 south for 8.5 miles to the Santa Claus turnoff. Continue east on the frontage road toward the village. There is plenty of beach parking for the next half-mile.

A CAUTION
Please be respectful of private property rights.

THE WALK
The beach near Santa Claus is wide and long, with plenty of space for sunbathing, picnicking, or long walks. It is a favorite spot for surf fishing and clamming as well. During minus tides you can walk to Carpinteria. If you can get around the first rock outcropping at lower tides, the walk to Loon Point leads past a mile of beautiful beachfront homes.

From the street long stretch of huge granite boulders hides the main part of the beaches from view, but once you clamber over the rocks you will discover the perfect place for an afternoon at the beach with the kids. Even at the highest tides there is always plenty of soft, white sand to pitch a tent or shade yourself with an umbrella.

You can walk in either direction, but, depending on the tides, you may not be able to get too far. Rock jetties will block your way in either direction at higher tides. I always come here at super low tides, when it is easy to get around these points. To the east a half-mile of beach leads past a very strange Middle Eastern sort of house, painted all white with tall fluted towers poking out above the jetty. If the tide is low enough you can get around the point. There is just one jetty you will need to get around, and after that it is easy walking all the way to the state beach.

To the west, once you are past the first obstacle, it is a very pleasant mile walk to Loon Point. The cove is crescent-shaped, and as you curve gradually around it you will spy some of the nicest homes to be found in the Summerland area. There are plenty of rocks to poke around at Loon Point, and if you can get this far you can make it all the way to Lookout Park if you want to.

SUMMERLAND

5. Loon Point

BEACH WALK INFORMATION
Distance—2.5 miles east to Santa Claus; 1 mile from Loon Point west to
    Lookout Park
Topo—Carpinteria
URL—http://www.sb-outdoors.org Keyword Search: Loon Point

DIRECTIONS
From downtown Santa Barbara, follow Highway 101 south for 6.5 miles to the Padaro Lane off ramp. Turn right on Padaro Lane. The Loon Point parking area is on the left side of Padaro Lane, .2 miles from the freeway.

A CAUTION
Please be respectful of private property rights.

THE WALK

The cliffs near the parking area for the Loon Point beach walk soar upward like a bird in flight. Below them is an isolated stretch of beach leading to Lookout Park, as well as a delightful stroll around Loon Point, if the tide permits, all the way to Santa Claus Lane.

The walk down from the parking area leads along the railroad tracks then under the freeway off ramp and down a short path to the beach. There is a more remote feeling on this route than most of the beach access areas. Once you are down on the beach you can head in either direction. A mile to the west is Lookout Park. In-between is a long, straight section of sand that can be walked at even the highest tides. There are plenty of spaces to stake out a picnic area and lots of sand for the kids to play in.

To the east, a quarter-mile of walking along the Loon bluffs leads to the point. It is rocky along the way and usually not passable at higher tides, but if you can get around the first point, this is a wonderful walk. There are plenty of huge boulders around the point to walk in and out of and several more small points that lead to a series of spectacular beach front homes.

6. Lookout Park

BEACH WALK INFORMATION

Distance—2 miles from Lookout Park to Eucalyptus Lane (near the Miramar); 3 miles from Lookout Park to the Biltmore and Butterfly Beach; 1 mile east to Loon Point

Topos—Carpinteria & Santa Barbara

URL—http://www.sb-outdoors.org Keyword Search: Lookout Park

DIRECTIONS

From downtown Santa Barbara, follow Highway 101 south for 5.5 miles to the Summerland off ramp. At the bottom of the turnoff, bear right across the railroad tracks and directly into the park.

A CAUTION

Be very careful crossing the railroad tracks when entering and exiting the park. Please be respectful of private property rights.

THE WALK

Lookout Park is tucked neatly along the Summerland cliffs, with picnic tables, barbecues, and playground equipment. An asphalt walkway leads directly down to the beach, with wide expanses of sand in either direction for walking, playing in the surf, or relaxing. At lower tides, the 3-mile walk to the Biltmore is delightful.

As you walk down to the beach, you will discover why this is such an attractive place to come: in front of you is a spectacular vista, a mile of wide beachfront, plenty long enough for a good walk to Loon Point and lots of space to set out towels and beach gear and still feel like you are by yourself.

My favorite walk here, though, is to the west. This part of the beach is at first hidden from view as you walk down the ramp. Turning right you will spot a few hundred yards of sandy beach that seem to disappear at a point where the seawall meets the ocean. Come at a lower tide, when you can get by the point and you will be well rewarded. The seawall stretches for a quarter-mile then eases back away from the edge of the water, and from there on the walking is easy. It is a mile from the park to a small cove where you will find a series of quaint beachfront houses, some of them very romantic looking.

Continuing around the point leads on to more houses and

Eucalyptus Lane and eventually Butterfly Beach and the Biltmore Hotel. We often leave a shuttle car there so we can make this a one-way excursion. This makes a fabulous afternoon walk.

MONTECITO

7. Eucalyptus Lane

BEACH WALK INFORMATION
Distance—2 miles east to Lookout Park; 1 mile west to the Biltmore & Butterfly Beach
Topos—Carpinteria & Santa Barbara
URL—http://www.sb-outdoors.org Keyword Search: Rincon Beach

DIRECTIONS
From downtown Santa Barbara, follow Highway 101 south for 3.5 miles to the San Ysidro off ramp in Montecito. Turn right (San Ysidro becomes Eucalyptus Lane on the ocean side of Highway 101) and drive a half-mile to the beach access point.

A CAUTION
Please be respectful of private property rights.

THE WALK
Hidden at the foot of San Ysidro Road, Eucalyptus Lane provides beach access to both Fernald and Hammond's points. There are excellent tide pools, long stretches of beach, and a host of beau-

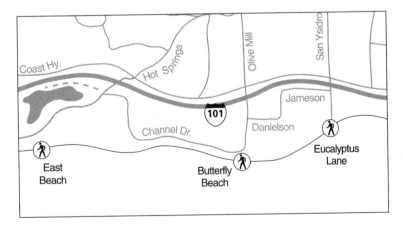

tiful homes to admire. This is an excellent spot to start for out-and-back walks to either Fernald Point or the Biltmore.

As you walk down the steps to the beach one of the first things you will spot is the Miramar Hotel, which can be seen from the freeway as well. Stepping onto the sand you will feel as if you have suddenly been dropped into a very private enclave. The cove is a solid wall of very unique homes, many of them with common side walls, and all of them very charming.

There is a long stretch of sandy beach leading east to a second cove, more homes, then more beach. At higher tides you won't be able to get around this point, but if you can, the walk will take you all the way to Lookout Park.

East of the steps is a long seawall and depending on the tide, it can be very exciting getting past it. The wall goes just a hundred yards, but even at medium tides the waves have a habit of sneaking right up to it. At lower tides the entire beach, almost all the way to Hammond's Point, becomes one long tide pool.

8. Butterfly Beach

BEACH WALK INFORMATION
Distance—1.25 miles west to East Beach; 1 mile east to Eucalyptus Lane; 3 miles east to Lookout Park
Topo—Santa Barbara
URL—http://www.sb-outdoors.org Keyword Search: Rincon Beach

DIRECTIONS
From downtown Santa Barbara, follow Highway 101 south for 3 miles to the Olive Mill off ramp. Turn right and drive a half-mile down to Channel Drive. There is ample parking along the beach. Note: Channel Drive no longer goes through to Cabrillo Boulevard.

A CAUTION
Please be respectful of private property rights.

THE WALK

A delightful quarter-mile-long beach sits right at the foot of the Biltmore Hotel and Coral Casino. There is plenty of room to relax and enjoy the sun and surf, or to take a walk in either direction at lower tides.

This may be Santa Barbara's most elegant beach. The long sea-

Butterfly Beach

wall is topped by an imposing stone railing, and tall palms blow back and forth in the breeze. There is enough of an edge to the wall that you can lie back against the railing and enjoy the full force of the sun or drop down to the sand and lean back against the seawall.

A half-mile of open beach leads toward East Beach. There is a series of cliffs along the way, rocky outcrops where you can find a more private place, and at lower tides you can make it all the way to the volleyball courts or the Cabrillo Bathhouse, which has a very nice outdoor café. A great loop can be made by crossing Cabrillo Boulevard and following the bike path along the estuary, turning on Channel Drive, and following it past the cemetery to Butterfly Beach.

Most people, however, head east toward Hammond's Point, as do the surfers. If you can make it past the Coral Casino seawall, you will be able to walk as far as your heart will take you. Passing several points will eventually get you to Eucalyptus Point and, if the tide is low, a series of great tide pools.

9. East Beach

BEACH WALK INFORMATION
Distance—1.25 miles from Stearns Wharf to East Beach; 1.25 miles west to
Shoreline Park
Topo—Santa Barbara
URL—http://www.sb-outdoors.org Keyword Search: East Beach

DIRECTIONS
Stearns Wharf is at the end of State Street. East Beach is a mile east of the
wharf on Cabrillo Boulevard. Both paid parking and street parking is
available along Cabrillo, though it may be hard to get on weekends

THE WALK

East Beach is quintessential Santa Barbara: wide stretches of soft
white sand, palm-lined boulevards, the red-tiled roofs of the East
Beach Pavilion, and one of California's most picturesque combina-
tions of wharf and harbor. There is even a carousel, as well as the
nearby Santa Barbara Zoological Gardens.

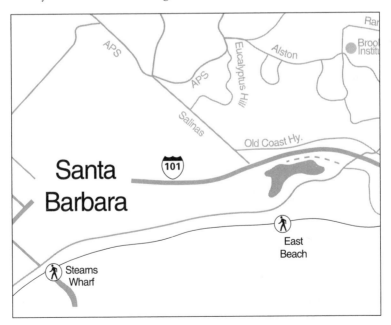

From the East Beach Pavilion, life seems idyllic: children swinging back and forth, family barbecues's next to spirited games of volleyball, scores of beachgoers lying back on their towels, the beachside tables filled with people relaxing to the island views while they sip cool drinks. For the moments spent along East Beach it is indeed idyllic.

To the west is perhaps the finest mile of beach you will find anywhere. With boats anchored just off shore, the wharf in the far distance, the islands on your left, and the long wall of mountains on your right, this is a perfect place to take off your shoes, wiggle your toes, and walk barefoot in the sand. What a delicious way to spend an afternoon, and what a perfect place to introduce your children to Santa Barbara.

To the east, a series of bluffs rise up, creating a different kind of walk. The beach is narrower, and within a quarter-mile you are restricted to a 50-yard-wide path. There are huge boulder fields piled along the cliffs, which do make for more isolated spots to sunbathe, and if the tide is low enough you can continue the walk all the way to Butterfly Beach. A nice loop is possible by returning via Channel Drive. Along the way you can stop for a side trip into the cemetery or spend a few minutes gazing at the ducks puttering about in the Andree Clark Bird Refuge.

10. Stearns Wharf/Breakwater

BEACH WALK INFORMATION
Distance—1.5 miles out and back to wharf and breakwater total
Topo—Santa Barbara
URL—http://www.sb-outdoors.org Keyword Search: Wharf or Breakwater

DIRECTIONS
Stearns Wharf is at the end of State Street. There is limited parking on or near it. You will find more parking near the breakwater, where there are several parking areas.

THE WALK
It may not seem so today, but there was a time when Santa Barbara was almost completely isolated from either the north or south. In the early 1870s John Stearns, with the aid of Colonel W. W. Hollister, helped remedy this by constructing a wharf almost a third-mile in length, in the process assuring the success of Santa Barbara's rising tourist trade and creating a landmark that defines the waterfront.

I absolutely love the Santa Barbara waterfront. Walking along the edge of the harbor, listening to the sound of the sailboat shrouds clinking in the breeze, watching the seals lazily making their way through the channels and the boats of such varying types and sizes slowing making their way in and out is wonderful.

One of my first memories of Santa Barbara is from the end of the breakwater, looking out over the harbor toward the city and the graceful palms and mountaintops. I couldn't think of a more beautiful place to live, and after nearly forty years of being here, I still can't.

This is an area you should take your children often. The walk to the end of the breakwater isn't difficult, though when the waves are breaking against the rocks it can be exciting. Near the end you can venture out onto the sandspit, a great place to sit a while and watch things.

Though you can drive over to the wharf and out to the end of it, you will find it much more satisfying to walk the quarter-mile, either along the bike path or on the edge of the water. It is a great walk out to the end of the pier, where you can watch the pelicans, check out what the fishermen are catching, or visit the Sea Center.

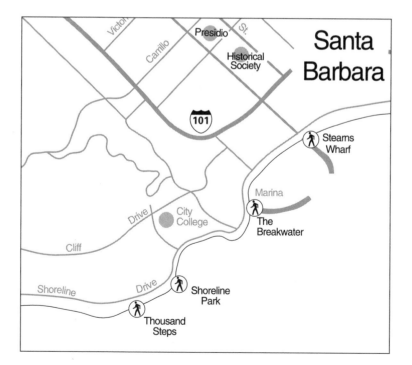

11. Shoreline Park

BEACH WALK INFORMATION
Distance—1.25 miles east to Stearns Wharf; 2 miles west to Mesa Lane;
   3 miles west to Arroyo Burro Beach
Topo—Santa Barbara
URL—http://www.sb-outdoors.org Keyword Search: Shoreline Park

DIRECTIONS
Shoreline Park is located a mile west of Stearns Wharf on the bluffs just past Leadbetter Beach. If you can't get around Santa Barbara Point due to high tide, there are steps leading down to the beach from the park's mid-point.

THE WALK
The park is long and thin, encompassing almost a mile of the bluff just west of Santa Barbara Point. There are plenty of places for picnics and barbecues, equipment for the kids to play on, and a stairway leading down to the beach, where you can enjoy a quiet walk along the cliffs all the way to Arroyo Burro Beach if you choose.

Surprisingly, given the proximity of downtown Santa Barbara, once you make the turn around Santa Barbara Point it is as if you had been transported to a remote beach. With the exception of a glimpse here and there of a clifftop house, you will see nothing of the city.

There are a series of points and small coves for the next three miles to Arroyo Burro Beach. Usually, if you can get around the point you will have clear walking for the next several miles, you should know whether you are on a rising or falling tide before you venture too far. At the lowest tides this is one of Santa Barbara's best walks. A long series of rocky shelves are exposed, and you can walk in and out of the tide pools almost all the way to Mesa Lane.

If you can't make it past the point, try walking up to the park. Follow the cement path along the edge of the cliff until you reach the stairs down to the beach on the harbor side of the point.

12. Thousand Steps

BEACH WALK INFORMATION
Distance—.5 mile to Shoreline Park; 1 mile to Mesa Lane; 2 miles to Arroyo
   Burro Beach
Topo—Santa Barbara
URL—http://www.sb-outdoors.org Keyword Search: Thousand Steps

DIRECTIONS
Follow Shoreline Drive west for a half-mile to Santa Cruz. Park along
Shoreline. It is just a half block to the steps.

THE WALK

As you walk out to the end of Santa Cruz you will marvel at the
houses on either side of the steps, which are perched almost right on
the cliff's edge. I love the patio of the one on the right. The chairs
look directly down onto the beach, with great views up the coast.

I often come here when higher tides block me from either
Arroyo Burro Beach or Shoreline Park. You won't able to make it
too far in either direction but I can almost guarantee you will have
the beach all to yourself.

The views once you reach the beach are equally as nice. There
aren't quite a thousand steps; in fact, nowhere near that many. If the
tide permits, the walk in either direction leads you in and out of
small coves. It is a quiet stretch, the tall cliffs sheltering you from
the houses above, and there are plenty of places to stop for a while
and enjoy the sound of the surf.

Heading toward the harbor it is a mile to Shoreline Park, and a
pleasant loop can be made by returning via the park and a few
blocks of walking along Shoreline Drive.

13. Mesa Lane

BEACH WALK INFORMATION
Distance—2 miles east to Shoreline Park and Leadbetter Beach; 1 mile
    west to Arroyo Burro Beach
Topo—Santa Barbara
URL—http://www.sb-outdoors.org Keyword Search: Mesa Lane

DIRECTIONS
From Santa Barbara, follow Highway 101 west for 2.8 miles to the Las Positas off
ramp. Turn left and drive slightly more than a mile to Cliff Drive. Turn left again
and go .7 miles up the Mesa to the first stop light, which is Mesa Lane. Turn right
and drive down to the end of it. There is no parking on the right (west) side of
the lane, but you can make a U-turn at the bottom and park on the east side.

A CAUTION
There are 241 steps down to the beach, as well as 241 on the way back up
to your car.

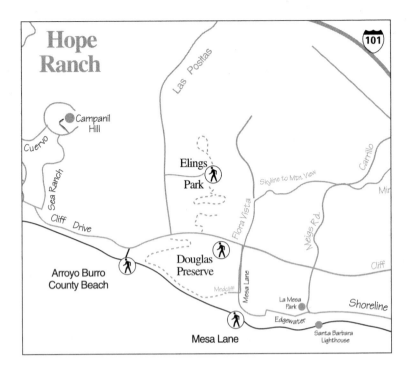

THE WALK

The coastline from Shoreline Park to Arroyo Burro Beach has a feeling of isolation despite its proximity to the city. While at higher tides you may not be able to get too far in either direction, at medium- or low-tide levels, you can walk to either the marina or Arroyo Burro.

Mesa Lane is a nice alternative access point to Arroyo Burro on really warm days, when there are huge crowds there. Ninety percent of the people who visit Arroyo Burro rarely venture more than a half-mile in either direction, which means if you drop down from Mesa Lane you won't see too many people.

The more secluded walk is to the east, in the direction of the harbor. There is a series of coves and stretches of sandy beach, along which you will rarely see more than a handful of people, and at lower tides, lots of rocks to explore. Toward Arroyo Burro the beach is more open, though there is one point near the end of the walk that you will need to make it around to get all the way to this area.

An alternative, and an excellent loop, can be made by returning via the Douglas Family Preserve. To do this, continue through the parking lot and veer right, following the parking area along the edge of the slough. At the Las Positas intersection you will find a path leading up onto the blufftop. There are plenty of small paths leading in and out of the preserve, all of them eventually reaching the edge of the cliff, where you will discover great views. Continue east along the cliffs to Mesa Lane.

14. Arroyo Burro Beach

BEACH WALK INFORMATION
Distance—1 mile east to Mesa Lane; 3 miles east to Shoreline park; 3 miles west to More Mesa; 6 miles west to Goleta Beach
Topos—Santa Barbara & Goleta
URL—http://www.sb-outdoors.org Keyword Search: Arroyo Burro Beach or Hendry's Beach

DIRECTIONS
From Santa Barbara, follow Highway 101 west for 2.8 miles to the Las Positas off ramp. Turn left and drive slightly more than a mile to Cliff Drive. Turn right and look for the park entrance on the left in several hundred yards.

THE WALK

Just having the Brown Pelican, a quaint beachside restaurant, here makes this beach a nice place to visit. The coastline in either direction provides access to long stretches of relatively deserted beach. At lower tides, the walk to either the marina or Goleta Beach is a pleasant way to spend a few hours on a weekend afternoon. This is considered by many to be Santa Barbara's best local beach walk.

Some call this Hendry's Beach. In the early 1900s the beachfront was owned by the Hendry family. Mistakenly, some have named it "Henry's Beach." But since 1947, when the land was purchased for $15,000, it has been known as Arroyo Burro Beach, after the creek that flows into the ocean here.

Regardless of whether you head east or west, you have the choice of two great walks. Heading east on medium or lower tides will allow you to make it all the way to Shoreline Park. A popular loop can be made by walking up the steps (all 241 of them) at Mesa Lane and returning through the Douglas Family Preserve. If you make the walk in the later afternoon, the walk along the edge of the cliffs through the preserve near sunset is absolutely spectacular.

Heading west leads you along a wide expanse of beach, with plenty of tidepooling at lower tides. There is a series of small points, but mostly what you will encounter for the next three miles to More Mesa are wide beaches, lots of sand, and great walking.

I recommend a shuttle for either of these walks. It is really nice to be able to make the trip all the way to either Shoreline Park or Goleta Beach without having to turn back because of the distance involved.

GOLETA

15. More Mesa Beach

BEACH WALK INFORMATION
Distance—3 miles east to Arroyo Burro County Beach; 3 miles west to Goleta Beach

Topo—Goleta

URL—http://www.sb-outdoors.org Keyword Search: More Mesa

DIRECTIONS
From Santa Barbara, follow Highway 101 west for 6.3 miles to the Turnpike off ramp. Go left over the freeway and down to Hollister Avenue. Turn left again and drive .4 miles to Puente (the first stop light). Go right and drive .75 miles to the intersection of Puente and Mockingbird Lane. There is no parking on Mockingbird, so you'll need to find a space on Puente. Walk east on Mockingbird several hundred yards to the end, then continue on the dirt path to the bluffs and a rough path down to the beach.

A CAUTION
More Mesa is known as a "clothing optional" beach, which means that you may encounter nudists there. If this offends you, there are many other beaches from which to choose.

THE WALK
More Mesa is the mid-point between Arroyo Burro and Goleta beaches, with long stretches of relatively deserted shoreline. There are many acres of blufftop that you can explore, with excellent views of both the Santa Ynez Mountains and the Channel Islands.

It is a quarter-mile walk from the road to the edge of the cliffs, and in the spring the fields are rich green and filled with the purples and yellows of wild mustard and radish. The main path leads directly down to the beach, but other trails seem to head off in every direction, making it possible to meander for several miles and never go on the same path twice.

The beach is isolated with a mile of wide, sandy beach to the east leading to the Hope Ranch area, and a very picturesque cove to the west. If you walk to the west, at higher tides the boulders scattered at the bottom of the cliffs may be difficult to get by, but once you do you will find yourself in a sheltered cove that is a very nice place for an afternoon of suntanning or picnicking. Just around the corner you will find huge blobs of tar in unusual shapes and, if you are lucky, a scattering of seals perched on the rock outcroppings just off shore. The three-mile walk to Goleta Beach is very nice.

16. East Goleta Beach

BEACH WALK INFORMATION

Distance—3 miles east to More Mesa; 6 miles east to Arroyo Burro; 1.25 miles west to Campus Point; 3 miles west to Coal Oil Point beach access

Topo—Goleta

URL—http://www.sb-outdoors.org Keyword Search: Goleta Beach

DIRECTIONS

From Santa Barbara, follow Highway 101 west for 7.5 miles to the Ward Memorial Drive turnoff (Highway 217—just past the Patterson off ramp). Follow this for 1.5 miles to the Goleta Beach turnoff. Go left under Ward Memorial, then right into the park.

A CAUTION

There is a fair amount of tar on the beach due to oil seeps in the channel. I recommend old tennies for walking and/or taking care where you put your feet.

THE WALK

Goleta Beach has excellent picnic and barbecue areas, with plenty of playground equipment for the kids and relatively calm (and safe) ocean water to play in. There are outdoor showers, restrooms, a great pier to walk out on, and both a snack shop and a restuarant for your enjoyment. Kayakers will find this a great place as well, whether for a trip out and around the pier, to Campus Point, or an inland adventure into the Goleta Slough.

The walk to More Mesa beach is one of my favorites. There is a small obstacle that is often present (a short "creek crossing" through the water exiting the slough) but after that you'll find

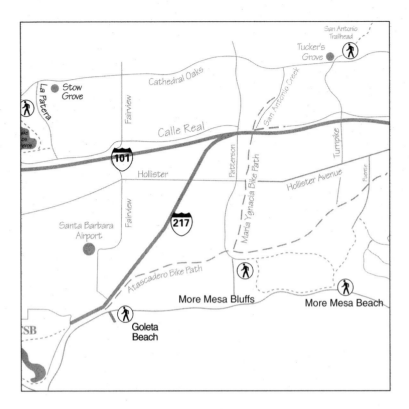

yourself mesmerized by the mile-long stretch ahead of you. You'll
have hundreds of seagulls, a few pelicans, and loads of sandpipers
and sanderlings for company. Along the way you may spot an
interesting scuplture made from driftwood, and when you near the
end of this stretch, huge gobs of tar thick enough to form large
boulder-like objects decorate the shoreline.

Several small points lead around to the More Mesa area. Just off
shore there are several outcroppings and usually a seal or two kick-
ing back on them, more so at lower tides when larger amounts of
the rock are exposed.

It is a six-mile walk to Arroyo Burro, a bit long for an out-and-
back walk, but with a shuttle car at the other end this is a perfect afternoon's walk. By walking east you'll have the sun at your back, and the
Brown Pelican restaurant is a great place to end the adventure. Have a
tidebook handy so you'll know when the next low tide is coming.

17. Campus Point

BEACH WALK INFORMATION
Distance— 1.25 miles west to Campus Point; 2 miles to lagoon access; 3.5 miles back to Goleta Beach
Topo—Goleta
URL—http://www.sb-outdoors.org Keyword Search: Campus Point, UCSB, or Goleta Beach

DIRECTIONS
From Santa Barbara, follow Highway 101 west for 7.5 miles to the Ward Memorial turnoff. Follow this for 1.5 miles to the Goleta Beach turnoff. Go left under Ward Memorial, then right into the park.

A CAUTION
There is a fair amount of tar on the beach due to oil seeps in the channel. I recommend old tennies for walking and/or taking care where you put your feet.

THE WALK
I am partial to the walk out to Campus Point since I spent so many hours surfing here when I was a student at UCSB. Depending on the tides you can walk along the beach to the point or follow the top of the cliffs. I often head out on the bluffs and return via the beach, but walking on the beach depends on the tide. At higher tides there are several places which are impossible to get by.

But if you are lucky and the tide low enough, the walk out and around the point is wonderful. Once you round the point you have nearly two miles of almost straight coastline and wide beaches which will take you all the way to Devereux Point if you want.

However, I often turn inland when I reach the edge of the UCSB lagoon, which is just a half-mile west of the point. A dirt road leads around the lagoon, the UCEN is right there, where you can stop for a snack or cup of java, and the route up to the top of the Campus Point bluffs is very nice. There are plenty of places to wander around on top of the bluffs before heading east back to Goleta Beach.

18. Isla Vista/Devereux Point

BEACH WALK INFORMATION
Distance—3 miles east from Coal Oil Point beach access to Goleta Beach;
   1.5 miles west to Ellwood bluffs; 3 miles west to Haskell's Beach
Topos—Goleta & Dos Pueblos Canyon
URL—http://www.sb-outdoors.org Keyword Search: Devereux Point or Isla
   Vista

DIRECTIONS
From Santa Barbara, follow Highway 101 west for 11.1 miles to the Glen
Annie turnoff which leads south to Isla Vista. Curve left onto El Colegio
Road, then turn right on Camino Corto and drive until it ends at Del Playa.
Go right a block to the access point. An alternate walk can be made by
parking near Isla Vista School and walking out along the West Campus
Road to the point.

A CAUTION
There is a fair amount of tar on the beach due to oil seeps. I recommend
old tennies for walking and/or taking care where you put your feet.

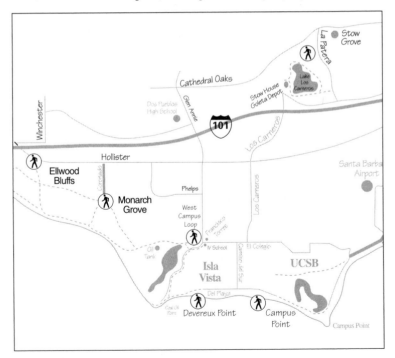

THE WALK

As you leave your car and head out to the edge of the bluffs, the view west to Devereux Point is outstanding. At sunset, the long peninsula-shaped point and the sihlouettes of coastal fir trees make for a perfect picture. You can reach the point either by following the top of the bluffs or dropping down the stairs and walking along the beach.

Once you are on the beach you can walk in either direction for long distances. There are several miles of almost straight beachfront to the east leading past Isla Vista to Campus Point. West is Devereux Point; three-quarters of a mile of wide, sandy beach leads to the rocky point. At lower tides the exposed rocks and pools make for great exploration. This is a kid's paradise.

As you round the point you will find miles of long beach ahead of you, long stretches where you will rarely see more than four or five people. A mile ahead are the bluffs below the monarch butterfly groves. A road leads up to the top of the bluffs, and from there you will find numerous paths leading to the eucalyptus forests where the monarch butterflies live in the wintertime.

On the way back you can follow the blufftops back to the east and drop back down to the beach not too far from Devereux Point. Or, if you still have the energy, paths lead north and then around the Devereux Slough. Follow West Campus Road back to the beach area and your car.

For a real treat, park a shuttle car at Haskell's Beach and make the hike from Isla Vista to Haskell's a one-way adventure.

19. Haskell's Beach

BEACH WALK INFORMATION
Distance—1.5 miles east to Ellwood bluffs; 3 miles east to Isla Vista; 6 miles west to El Capitan State Beach
Topo—Dos Pueblos Canyon
URL—http://www.sb-outdoors.org Keyword Search: Haskells Beach

DIRECTIONS
From Santa Barbara, follow Highway 101 west for 12.5 miles to the Winchester off ramp (4.8 miles from the Fairview Avenue overpass). As you get off the freeway, the off ramp leads directly onto Calle Real. Follow this west to the overpass. Go left across the overpass, then turn right onto the new frontage road directly in front of the Sandpiper Golf Course. Continue

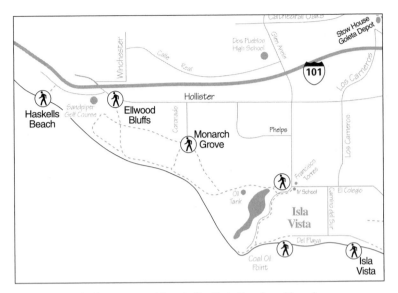

west on the frontage road for a half-mile to the signed beach-access parking area, which is just before the resort complex.

THE WALK

Most likely you will be bit intimidated by the huge resort complex that has just been completed on the far side of Tecolote Canyon. Surprisingly, what you will find once you reach the beach is one of the most remote and quiet sections of beaches along the coast, despite being only a few miles from downtown Goleta.

East of Haskell's the beach is fairly wide and excellent for sunning or a few hours' relaxation. The coastline leads along the edge of Sandpiper Golf Course, where you can spy a few of the holes, and passes an old wood-planked seawall. There are routes up to the Ellwood bluffs, the monarch groves, and, if you want a very pleasant two-mile stroll, all the way to Devereux Point.

To the west you will spot a long pier, which has been used for many years to service the oil industry. Symbolically, the pier acts as a threshold to another world. Once you walk under it the next several miles of beach provide what seems like a wilderness experience. The cliffs are steep, rocky ledges, fields of boulders provide great scenery, and there are plenty of small coves and long stretches of hard-packed sand to make you want to keep going on and on. It is six miles all the way to El Capitan State Beach, and when the tide is low, this is absolutely my favorite walk.

20. El Capitan State Beach

BEACH WALK INFORMATION

Distance—6 miles east to Haskell's Beach; 1.5 miles west to Corral Beach;
2.5 miles west to Refugio Beach
Topos—Dos Pueblos Canyon & Tajiguas
Telephone—(805) 968-1411
URL—http://www.sb-outdoors.org Keyword Search: El Capitan or Corral

DIRECTIONS

From downtown Santa Barbara, follow Highway 101 west for 20 mi es to the
El Capitan turnoff. A winding road leads under the freeway to the beach.
There are no parking areas outside the park; you'll have to pay for day use.

THE WALK

There is ample area at the beach for picnicking and frolicking on
the beach, as well as overnight camping. A bike path leads along the
blufftops from El Capitan to Refugio, providing a nice way to
enjoy the coastline from above, either by bike or on foot.

The walk on the beach to Refugio is one of the most enjoyable
of all, with lots of quiet beach and secluded coves. To the east you'll
find El Cap Point, a favorite of surfers when the swell is strong
enough for the waves to break there, and, beyond the point, a mile-
long stretch of beach that is wonderful to explore.

The beachfront at El Capitan is so pleasant it is difficult to think
of going anywhere else, but if you do you will find the beaches in
either direction a wonderful treat. To the west you'll notice a half-
mile-long stretch of very inviting sand. It is a mile to Corral Beach
and another to Refugio State Beach. Along the way there are several
points that can be very tricky to get around when the tide is up (and
fun too!). It is a four-mile round trip if you follow the beach one way
and return via the bike path, a very nice length for an extended walk.

Down the coast is one of Santa Barbara's best beach walks, a six-
mile trek that will take you along one of the most remote sections
of coast in Southern California. With a shuttle car left at Haskell's
beach beforehand, this is the perfect walk. For a taste of what the
walk is like, follow the path across El Capitan Creek and past the
surfing area. A hundred yards of rocks lead to the bottom of the
cove, and from there you'll have nearly a mile of great walking to
the next point.

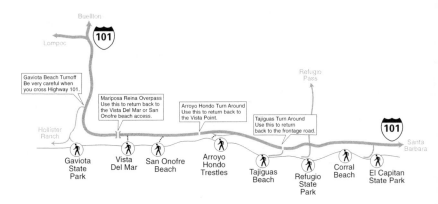

21. Corral Beach

BEACH WALK INFORMATION
Distance—1.5 miles east to El Capitan; 1 mile west to Refugio Beach
Topo—Tajiguas
URL—http://www.sb-outdoors.org Keyword Search: Corral Beach

DIRECTIONS
From downtown Santa Barbar, follow Highway 101 west for 22 miles to the Refugio turnoff. Go under the freeway and head back toward Goleta on Highway 101. The Corral parking area is slightly less than a mile east of Refugio Beach. Look for a rough but fairly large dirt parking area.

A CAUTION
Take care exiting the highway and returning onto it. There is no formally constructed path leading down to the beach. Take care when crossing the train tracks when walking down to and back up from the beach.

THE WALK
Corral Beach is a small cove tucked in the coastline between El Capitan and Refugio. It is a beautiful place for a secluded picnic, and the walks in both directions are lots of fun. The bike path provides an alternate way of enjoying the coastline, or you can walk on the beach to either of the state parks and come back on the bike path.

Many beachgoers end up at Corral Beach because it is much more secluded that the state beaches on either side of it and there is no cost to enjoy an afternoon on the beach. Because it is situated almost exactly between them, whether you walk along the beach or on the bike path, it is a short distance either to El Capitan or Refugio state beaches.

There are small points on either side of the small beach. At higher tides this creates the feeling of an isolated cove. As the tide drops you will be able to make your way in either direction.

22. Refugio State Beach

BEACH WALK INFORMATION

Distance—1 mile east to Corral Beach; 2.5 miles east to El Capitan; 2 miles west to Tajiguas Beach

Topo—Tajiguas

Telephone—(805) 968-0019

URL—http://www.sb-outdoors.org Keyword Search: Refugio or Refugio State Park

DIRECTIONS

From downtown Santa Barbara, follow Highway 101 west for 22.5 miles to the Refugio turnoff. There is free parking under the freeway, and a trail leads you directly into the park. For those who would like to drive into the park, there is a fee for day use.

A CAUTION

Refugio is crowded during the summer months but almost deserted from October through April.

THE WALK

Like El Capitan, Refugio State Beach has lots of space for picnicking and playing in the surf, and the water is usually calm, making this a relatively safe place for kids to play at the ocean's edge. This is a very nice place to hang out under the umbrella while the kids play in the water, share a barbeque, and take a short walk when the urge hits.

To the east it is a mile to Corral Beach, which is just long enough to make you feel like you've gotten somewhere and not too long for smaller kids. There is a long stretch of sand and then a series of small points that can be very tricky (or fun) to get by when the tide is higher. The return trip via the bike path provides views along the coast that are very nice.

The first half-mile of coastline west of Refugio Point is accessible only during lower tides, but there are loads of tide pools to explore at minus tides. There is a dirt path leading from the point for about a mile, providing an enjoyable way to explore this section of the coastline. Eventually you will be able to make your way back down to the beach and continue in the direction of Tajiguas if you want.

23. Tajiguas Beach

BEACH WALK INFORMATION
Distance—2 miles east to Refugio State Beach; 2.5 miles west to Arroyo Hondo vista point
Topo—Tajiguas
URL—http://www.sb-outdoors.org Keyword Search: Tajiguas

DIRECTIONS
Tajiguas Beach is 1.8 miles west of Refugio State Beach. Look for a turnaround on the freeway 2.1 miles past Refugio. Cross the freeway and turn right on the frontage road and go .6 miles west until the road ends near a railroad crossing. A steep trail leads down to the beach. You can find easier beach access by turning back toward Refugio State Beach, going .3 miles on the freeway to a large dirt parking area. The hike down to the beach is easy, but the point may block your access to the west at higher tides.

A CAUTION
You'll need to be in the fast lane to use the turnaround. Signal ahead to warn other drivers of your intentions.

THE WALK
Once upon a time there was beach access from the small enclave near the mouth of Tajiguas Canyon, but no longer. The frontage road serves nearly as well. It is a bit of a hike down to the beach on the rough trail, but once you are there you'll find a long stretch of wide open sand and plenty of places to set out your gear for the afternoon. You may see a fisherman here or there surf casting.

East of here the cliffs close in and the shore is rocky, so the walking is to the west of you. It is a mile of very pleasant walking to the Tajiguas homes, some of them very expensive wood-and-glass beach cottages perched on the cliffs above, others reflecting a more modest style. This would be a very nice place to live.

At lower tides there are plenty rocks to explore and lots of pebble-strewn sections where you can look for shells and pieces of well-tumbled glass. I always find a good amount of it here. In all, this is a section of beach on which it is easy to go slow and enjoy in a very unhurried fashion.

As you continue along you will notice a series of points and then seawalls closing in on you. This signals that you are approaching the Arroyo Hondo area and have come almost two and a half-miles! You will find the walk back just as pleasant. I love doing this in the late afternoon when the sun is drifting across the horizon and the yellow glow creates a very mellow feeling.

24. Arroyo Hondo Trestles

BEACH WALK INFORMATION
Distance—2.5 miles east to Tajiguas Beach; 3 miles west to San Onofre Beach
Topo—Gaviota
URL—http://www.sb-outdoors.org Keyword Search: Arroyo Hondo

DIRECTIONS
The Vista Point and old freeway trestles at Arroyo Hondo Canyon are 4.3 miles west of Refugio. Look for a turnaround .4 miles past the vista point (4.7 miles from Refugio). Turn around and go back .4 miles toward Refugio to the well-marked turnoff for the "Vista Point."

A CAUTION
You'll need to be in the fast lane to use the turnaround. Signal ahead to warn other drivers of your intention. The drop down to the beach is a bit tricky. Be careful and go slow.

THE WALK
The trestles at the mouth of Arroyo Hondo Canyon are very picturesque, as is the beach below. To the west you'll find a series of points leading eventually to San Onofre Beach, three miles away, a wonderful walk when the tide is low. This is a very remote and quiet place to enjoy the Santa Barbara coastline.

This is absolutely my favorite out-and-back walk on the Santa Barbara coast. It starts with a tricky bit of down climbing to reach the beach, which is a hundred feet below the parking area. Walk down to the old Highway 101 bridge, turn left, and drop by the side the railroad trestle. There is a series of steps cut into the concrete ramp, but they are pretty steep and the dirt path below them is slippery. With a bit of care you will make it just fine.

There is a huge pile of boulders at the mouth of the creek, and often scattered piles of driftwood to meander through to reach the sand. Turning to the left—or east—will lead you in the direction of Tajiguas, a beautiful hike in itself, but the real treat is the western coastline. Along this stretch the shales are turned almost vertical, and you will find yourself walking right on top of the edges, which are rounded enough that it isn't too difficult to do.

For the next three miles there is a series of rocky ledges similar to this, small coves, and geological formations that create a sort of ocean wonderland. There are plenty of points, too, often with a fisherman perched on top of the rocks, and loads of solitude.

There is one long beach walk I try to do every year, either from Arroyo Hondo to Gaviota or the other way around, depending on when the lowest tides are. If they are early in the morning I head west; if in the afternoon I start from Gaviota. It is always nice to have the sun at your back for as much of the time as possible. This walk requires a shuttle, but I think you will find this six miles of beach to be Santa Barbara's finest.

25. San Onofre Beach

BEACH WALK INFORMATION

Distance—3 miles east to the Arroyo Hondo trestles (vista point); .5 miles
to the Vista Del Mar beach access; 3 miles west to Gaviota Beach
Topo—Gaviota
URL—http://www.sb-outdoors.org Keyword Search: San Onofre

DIRECTIONS

San Onofre Beach is 7 miles west of Refugio Beach. Continue to the Mariposa Reina turnoff (8 miles from Refugio), cross the freeway, then head back toward Refugio on the freeway. The beach is 1.2 miles and is marked by a Gaviota State Park sign.

A CAUTION

Be careful crossing the railroad tracks when walking to and from the beach. San Onofre is known as a "clothing optional" beach, which means you may encounter nudists here. If this offends you, there are many other beaches from which to choose.

THE WALK

San Onofre Beach gets more use than other beaches along the

Gaviota coastline, so it isn't as uncrowded as some of the other beaches; nevertheless it rarely has more than 15 or 20 people here at any time. There are wonderful walks in either direction at low tide, and it is three miles in either direction to Arroyo Hondo or Gaviota State Park. At times in the winter after storms there isn't much sand on the beach, but at other times, San Onofre has a half-mile-long stretch of sandy beach on which to relax.

Often I choose the San Onofre beach when the tide is about at medium level. This means there are some points in either direction I may not make it around, but I like walking along the edge of the cliffs with the surf pounding near me. To the east, a series of boulder fields make the walking seem uninviting, but they last for only a hundred yards or so and after that is a long section of almost perfect beach with hard-packed sand to walk on and soft fluffy sand to kick back on. Three-fourths mile brings you to a point with more huge rocks to work your way through. From there on are smaller coves and more frequent points. At low tide the walk out and back to San Onofre is very, very nice.

To the west the beaches are much narrow and there are more ledges jutting out into the ocean which you will need to climb, making this a much more adventurous section of the coastline to walk. At low tide the walking is free and easy, but when the tide is in the medium range, dashing in and out to avoid the waves and clambering over the rocks is lots of fun. It is a half-mile down to Vista Del Mar, where you can climb up onto the cliffs and return via one of the many paths that wander in and out of the clifftop sagebrush.

26. Vista Del Mar

BEACH WALK INFORMATION
Distance—.5 miles east to San Onofre Beach; 2.5 miles west to Gaviota Beach
Topo—Gaviota
URL—http://www.sb-outdoors.org Keyword Search: Vista Del Mar

DIRECTIONS
The Vista Del Mar beach access is 7.6 miles west of Refugio Beach. Continue to the Mariposa Reina turnoff (8 miles from Refugio), cross the freeway, then head back toward Refugio on the freeway. The beach is a half-mile and is marked by a Gaviota State Park sign.

A CAUTION

Look carefully for the parking area, as it is hard to spot. Be careful crossing the railroad tracks when walking to and from the beach.

THE WALK

Vista Del Mar provides an access point to the beach between Gaviota and San Onofre. A narrow trail leads down to the bluffs. Below is a small quarter-mile-long beach that has a very remote feeling to it. The walk to (or from) Gaviota is a pleasant way to spend several hours. When you reach the bluffs and leave your car, go left (east) on the bluff trail for about a hundred yards to a rough dirt trail that leads down to the beach.

This is a great beach to come to with a beach chair, umbrella, and a good book. The trail down is a bit rough, but once you are down on the beach it is like having a small retreat all to yourself. It isn't as crowded as San Onofre Beach and somehow feels more rugged.

27. Gaviota State Park

BEACH WALK INFORMATION

Distance—2.5 miles east to the Vista Del Mar beach access; 3 miles east to San Onofre Beach

Topos—Gaviota & Sacate

Telephone—968-0019

URL—http://www.sb-outdoors.org Keyword Search: Gaviota

DIRECTIONS

From downtown Santa Barbara, follow Highway 101 west for 32 miles to the turnoff into Gaviota State Park. Follow the narrow road for .3 miles, cross Gaviota Creek, then bear left to the beach. There is a $3.00 fee for parking at the beach.

A CAUTION

The turnoff into the park is from the fast lane and isn't easy to spot because it is around a corner. Look for it as Highway 101 turns away from the coastline and heads into Gaviota Canyon.

THE WALK

Gaviota State Park is not just a beach access point; it extends several miles inland and on both sides of Highway 101. This provides a number of day hikes (which can be found in another section of this book) as well as beach walks. You can drive a mile west toward Hollister Ranch before you get to private property. There are several beach access points along here, as well as trailheads leading up into the hills. The Gaviota pier is a favorite of fishermen, and the boat hoist (when it is working) makes it possible to explore this part of the coastline from the ocean. It is 3 miles from here to San Onofre Beach, an excellent, short walk on which you'll rarely see anyone.

I have always found walking along the Gaviota beach to be a wonderful experience, and I try to do it at least three or four times a year, usually in the winter months, when it is much less crowded. West of the pier the coastline is rocky and you won't be able to get too far, but what you will discover as you walk to the east easily makes up for this.

The walk begins by crossing under the train bridge, which is very impressive both in size and looks. Combined with the canyon behind it, it makes for a great photo opportunity. Just beyond the bridge you will need to cross the creek. This doesn't usually involve any wading, but it might. Once beyond the creek, if the tide is low, you won't find any other obstacles all the way to Arroyo Hondo, six miles distant. This is a walk I encourage you to find time to do.

Rather than the typical cliffs, you will find steep layers of shale as you walk along, and in the light of the later day these can turn a golden yellow. On the beach itself you will find thin edges of shale protruding from the sand like a series of fins, creating a very picturesque setting. There is one that has the shape of a young girl. Fringed with barnacles for hair, it looks exactly like Little Orphan Annie to me. See if you can find it.

The walking continues through similar geology, with lots of rock outcroppings at the edge of the ocean and plenty of places for sea stars and other creatures to find homes. I usually continue on past Vista Del Mar until I can see the tall yellow-colored formation that marks the mouth of San Onofre Canyon, a bit more than two miles from Gaviota. Then it is back to the state park for a quick walk out to the end of the pier for the sunset before I head home for the evening.

Douglas Family Preserve

Town Walks

Viewed from above, the open spaces along the ocean bluffs and foothills are easy to spot: in the springtime they are like emeralds, the rich green colors sparkling in the afternoon light. There are many of them: Ellwood Bluffs, Santa Barbara Shores, More Mesa, Lake Los Carneros, the Douglas Family Preserve, and the Carpinteria Bluffs.

These are places you can go to spend a few minutes or an hour or two, depending on the time available to you. More important than what these areas provide for us is the wilderness corridor they offer for the animals, birds, and especially migratory species with which we share the land. We have changed much, and it is important that we preserve as much as possible of what we have left.

Walker Tompkins, in his wonderful book, *Goleta the Good Land,* provides a glimpse of what the past might have been like:

> . . . Golden poppies made flame-colored patches on the rounded foothills; between them and the mountain chaparral line, in the mile-wide frost-free belt, wildflowers were blooming in riotous profusion. Lupin, verbena, and Castilian roses made a rainbow-hued blanket on the overflow lands closer to the slough. Daniel Hill, reveling in the clouds of ducks and geese, the herds of antelope and deer glimpsed through the live oaks, was convinced he had stumbled onto the Garden of Eden.

There are still a few of these sylvan retreats left in the Goleta Valley and in the Montecito and Summerland areas as well. Here are a few of them.

1. San Antonio Creek

WALK INFORMATION
Distance—1.5 miles
Elevation Gain—148' to intersection with Highway 154
Difficulty—Easy
Topo—Santa Barbara
URL—http://www.sb-outdoors.org Keyword Search: San Antonio

HIGHLIGHTS
Though this is a relatively short hike, and not terribly wild, San Antonio Creek is a wonderful place to take children. Tucker's Grove is perfect for a picnic, and it has the best playground equipment for kids anywhere in Santa Barbara. The hike is level, so you can take even the littlest tots on the trail. The riparian community found along the way is excellent for teaching kids about the local environment.

DIRECTIONS
From Santa Barbara, drive north on Highway 101 to the Turnpike Road exit in Goleta. Turn right and drive .6 miles north to Cathedral Oaks Road. Drive straight through the intersection into Tucker's Grove County Park. Curve right and continue through the park and across San Antonio Creek to the last parking lot. You can pick up the trail there near a small sign that says "Bridle Path" or walk through Kiwanis Meadows.

SETTING THE SCENE

The San Antonio Creek Trail begins at Tucker's Grove. In the late 1800s this sheltered oak grove served as a favorite picnic area for Santa Barbara's Scottish-American population. It was privately owned by Charlie Tucker, a popular valley resident who maintained the sylvan retreat for public use free of charge until he died in 1912. Shortly thereafter it was purchased by rancher George S. Edwards, who deeded it to the county, thus allowing it to become one of the valley's first public parks.

This is one of the most pleasant of the short hikes, especially for those of you who want to take younger children along with you. In the spring, with the cascading waters of the creek flowing cool and clear, the oak woodland and canyon vegetation provide just the touch of color, richness, and variety for an hour or two of relaxed hiking.

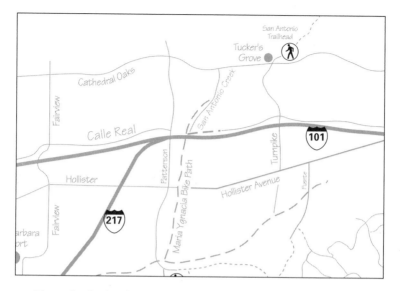

If you look closely, in most places you will still see the effects of wildfire in the canyon, though after a decade of regrowth the canyon has returned to what it looked like before the fire. The Painted Cave Fire began about 6 P.M. on June 27, 1990, near the intersection of Painted Cave Road and Highway 154. Though high in the mountains, thundering Santa Ana winds caused the flames to roar down the mountainside and across San Antonio Creek in less than 45 minutes. More than 600 houses and apartments were destroyed by the fire, and with the exception of the larger trees, the oaks and sycamores, the canyon was reduced to a barren condition.

THE WALK

The trailhead is near the rear of Tucker's Grove at the end of an area known as Kiwanis Meadows. Although you can begin immediately by taking the bridle path across the creek (it recrosses in a hundred yards), most hikers continue through Kiwanis Meadows because this eliminates a stream crossing.

Though the trail is unmarked, the well-used path is relatively easy to follow. Just past Kiwanis Meadow a canyon section begins. The hillside is covered with ferns and sorrel and is shaded by numerous oaks. There is poison oak along here as well, so take care, especially with children.

The trail follows the east side of the creek for a quarter-mile to a large oak meadow that has numerous trails radiating through it. The air has the sweet smell of bay and sage, and in the early morning, light filtering through the trees gives this grove a cathedral-like atmosphere.

From here the trail opens for a while, then closes back in. In places the path is not much more than shoulder-width wide and is rutted a foot deep in the sandy soil. The tunnel-like enclosure hems one in with the aroma of the soft chaparral. Nearby are the sounds of the hidden creek and numerous birds.

The trail reaches an opening once more, this one filled primarily with sycamore, and the canyon makes several lazy S curves. The trail crosses and recrosses the creek several times. There is a farm along the back side of one of the curves that looks like it must be a wonderful place to live. Immediately beyond the farm the trail crosses the creek and heads up onto a bench, which leads to a large flood-control dam.

There the trail crosses the dam and turns upstream along the left side of a large flood-control basin. Above the basin, several trails appear to lead upstream, but the main path turns right, crosses the creek, and passes by a long chain-link fence, which you can see before you make the crossing. The other trails lead up onto San Antonio Creek Road to provide horse riders access to the canyon.

Once on the east side of the creek, the trail wanders through a most enjoyable section, thick with oaks, thistles, and blackberries. Here and there large cream-colored boulders provide a very color-ful accent to the greenery. In a half-mile the trail intersects with Highway 154, where the trail ends under the bridge, near the beginning of the Vista del Mundo Ranch.

2. Lake Los Carneros

WALK INFORMATION
Distance—.5 to 1.5 miles
Topo—Goleta
Difficulty—Easy
URL—http://www.sb-outdoors.org Keyword Search: Los Carneros

HIGHLIGHTS
The stroll around the lake provides a wonderful early morning or afternoon walk. The lake and its mountain backdrop make you feel like you are out in the country. This is a great place to watch birds, including many varieties of ducks that migrate here in the winter. The historic Goleta Depot and Stow House are nearby, where you can find out more about Goleta Valley history.

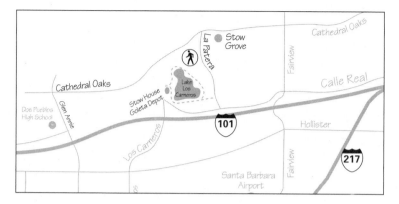

DIRECTIONS

From Santa Barbara drive, north on Highway 101 to the Los Carneros Road exit in Goleta. Turn right and drive 0.4 miles north to the parking lot for Stowe House and the South Coast Railroad Museum. Follow the paved path past Stow House to the trails which lead around the lake.

SETTING THE SCENE

In the summer of 1871, William Whitney Stow, a former speaker of the California State Assembly, visited the Goleta Valley. He was looking for farming property for his son, Sherman Stow. Colonel W.W. Hollister entertained the well-known politician at his Glen Annie home and during the visit suggested Stow consider purchasing the nearby La Patera Ranch, which he did in July 1871.

One of the most important landmarks included on the property was the original duck pond—or *la patera*. This small body of water was called Stow Lake or Stow Pond by the owners, but the Spanish word quickly became attached to the name of the ranching enterprise, and thereafter it was known as La Patera Ranch.

After securing water rights in the upper canyon through what was most likely a bit of dubious lobbying, the Stow family began building its agricultural fortune. The first crop planted was tobacco, which failed due to both grasshoppers and a climate that was too mellow to produce good quality leaves.

However, in the spring of 1974 Sherman Stow planted the first of several thousand lemon trees on thirty acres of rolling foothills, which had been cleared of the once-predominant oak trees by hardworking ranch crews. The orchards and the valley lemon industry continued to prosper under the management of Sherman's younger brother, Edgar, who cleared even more land using the first tractors seen in the Goleta Valley.

Lake Los Carneros

Edgar Stow also developed an extensive irrigation system by raising the dam on Stow Lake to impound more water and building three other permanent reservoirs on the property. Thus, he assured both an adequate supply of water for the orchards, which comprised nearly 300 acres now, as well as the survival of the original *patera*, so that it might become what is today—one of the hidden jewels of the Goleta Valley.

Much of what was the historic La Patera Ranch is now part of the public park system. In 1964, the Stow company deeded Stow Grove to the county as a public park, and in 1967, when the county acquired an additional three acres around the Stow House, the heirs donated the two-story house, thus creating the initial parts of what would become the park which is now known as Stow Grove County Park.

The balance of the 136 acres of the park was purchased in 1975 from Boise Cascade with $1.25 million of state money. Initially, the county had plans to construct baseball fields and other developed facilities, but neighbors protested. "Leave it the way it is," they said. "It doesn't need any improvement." Fortunately, the county heeded this wise advice.

THE HIKE

From the parking lot there are a number of options. The historic Goleta Depot is nearby, and it is well worth visiting, as is the Stow House, if you are interested in learning more about the history of the Goleta Valley. The Depot store is open Wednesday through Sunday from 1 to 4 P.M. throughout the year. If you would like more information about the depot you can find it at the South Coast Railroad Museum web site (http://www.goletadepot.org).

For me, however, the main attraction is Lake Los Carneros, the old *patera*. This is a beautiful place for a relaxed walk, and the views from the benches located on the south side of the lake are wonderful. You can head in either direction.

To walk around the lake in a clockwise direction, look for a side trail on the left side of the road just after you pass Stow House. The trail is unmarked and narrow but it leads to a very pretty wooden bridge and across the upper inlet, the main water source for Lake Los Carneros. You will discover beautiful views along this section through the cattail and tule reeds into the upper lake. Often you can stand on the bridge and spot different types of ducks, egrets, and other birds right below you as they search of morsels of food. After you cross the bridge the trail begins to rise up onto the surrounding open space. If you want to continue along the edge of the lake, turn right on the first path and follow it.

Most people head off to the right for the walk around the lower part of the reservoir. There are benches along the way to sit and watch the birds and enjoy the mountain views. Usually there are plenty of ducks, and often there are geese along the southern part of the lake. As you continue around the lower part of the lake you'll eventually reach a network of trails leading around and along the eastern side of Lake Los Carneros. The paths seem to meander here and there rather than head in any specific direction, and there are routes down through the eucalyptus trees to the water's edge and out onto the open meadows. This is a very peaceful part of the park, and the trees are very pretty to walk in and out of. You'll know Stow House is just around the corner as you cross over the last bluff and drop down across the wooden bridge marking the upper inlet.

3. More Mesa Bluffs

WALK INFORMATION
Distance—0.25 miles to the bluffs; 0.75 miles to the ocean overlook; 1 to 2
   miles beyond this, depending on how far you go
Difficulty—Easy
Topo—Dos Pueblos Canyon
URL—http://www.sb-outdoors.org Keyword Search: More Mesa

DIRECTIONS
From Santa Barbara, drive north on Highway 101 to the Patterson Avenue
exit in Goleta. Turn left, cross over the freeway and drive 0.3 miles to
Hollister Avenue. Continue on Patterson 1 mile to the start of the trail,
which is located just before the road turns sharply to the right and heads
up a steep hill. You will need to turn around in order to park.

A CAUTION
Be very careful when you cross the bike path (.6 miles from Patterson) and
when you turn around to park on the side of the road near the trailhead.
There is lots of poison oak on either side of the trail in the first half-mile.

SETTING THE SCENE

One of the major milestones in the history of the Goleta Valley
occurred when T. Wallace More completed a 900-foot-long, 35-
foot-wide wharf at what is now the More Mesa bluffs. It was located approximately a half-mile east of the Goleta Slough, and provided a major economic boost to the community.

More was the grandfather of the late *News-Press* publisher
Thomas M. Storke (the M. stands for More). T. Wallace and his
brother John energetically developed the wharf business, mining
asphaltum themselves from the nearby cliffs for export and ship-
ping cattle and produce for ranchers and farmers who lived nearby.

Unfortunately for the More brothers, their days of prosperity
were not long lived. T. Wallace was ambushed and killed at his
ranch in Ventura County not too long afterward, and when the railroad was completed through the Santa Barbara area in 1887 the
wharf business was doomed. When a fierce storm destroyed a portion of the wharf in March 1889, John quickly repaired it, but as
business diminished so did the effort to maintain the structure.

Today, if you are waking on the beach at the lowest of low tides
you may be lucky enough to spy some of the old pilings, but otherwise the last remains of the old wharf have disappeared.

THE WALK

The trail leading from Patterson Avenue to More Mesa follows and old Edison right-of-way. Over the years the dirt road has become more and more overgrown until today it has become a very nice trail. The route leads through oaks for a half-mile, and along the way there are several routes leading up onto the bluffs.

The first of these is just a few hundred yards from the trailhead and it is the way I usually go. The opening is easy to spot, though the first twenty yards is steep as you climb up out of the creek bottom. Once you're on top, views out over the valley open up to you, and the walking is almost level from here on out.

There are just over 300 acres of bluffs up on the mesa, most owned by Sun Oil, though the county purchased 35 acres at the west end in 1991, thus preserving some of it. Mostly what is here is grassland, with some wetlands and oak woodlands. Much of the mesa has been designated as environmentally sensitive habitat, which may help ensure that the balance of the property not be developed in the future.

The path follows the edge of the bluff for a short while, providing even nicer views of the valley and mountains, and then begins curving to the right and out to the cliffs, where you can look almost directly down on the area where the wharf was located. There is a very primitive trail leading down to the beach here, which can be negotiated fairly easily if you are careful.

Most will turn east and follow the cliffs in the direction of Hope Ranch. There are great views of the coast all the way to Arroyo Burro Beach, as well as lots of side trails leading back toward the creek, mak-

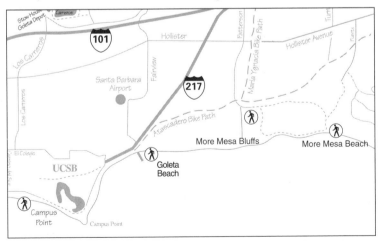

ing it possible to loop back whenever you've gone far enough. It is a half-mile from the western edge of the bluffs to the eastern end, where the main trail leading down to the More Mesa beach is located. Beware: this is considered a clothing-optional beach by many.

4. West Campus Loop

WALK INFORMATION
Distance—0.75 miles to Coal Oil Point; 1.5 to 3 miles along the bluffs, depending how far you go
Difficulty—Easy
Topo—Dos Pueblos Canyon
URL—http://www.sb-outdoors.org Keyword Search: West Campus

HIGHLIGHTS
Walking toward the beach from the West Campus entrance provides a number of possibilities. Continuing on the paved road will take you along the Devereux Slough, which is very pretty, to the beach near Coal Oil Point. You can also walk for miles and miles along the bluffs toward Sandpiper Golf Course and, if you wish, make this a loop walk by returning along the beach.

DIRECTIONS
From Santa Barbara, drive north on Highway 101 to the Glen Annie/Storke Road exit in Goleta. Turn left, cross over the freeway, and drive 0.3 miles to Hollister Avenue. Continue on Storke 1 mile to the entrance to the West Campus of UCSB, which is at the point where Storke Road turns sharply to the left. Park along the street, or on weekends you should be able to park in the IV School parking lot.

THE WALK
As you walk into the entrance of UCSB's West Campus, the long driveway flanked by tall trees makes you feel like you are entering someplace special. You are. The road leads down along the edge of the Devereux Slough, a serene body of water and tidal flats that is home to many species of birds and most likely many hundreds of small animals that are hidden by the brush that surrounds the slough.

In the morning and evening light, especially when the air is calm, the water is mirror smooth, reflecting the colors of both the sky and of the nearby trees. It is a beautiful setting. Out on the water, the birds—herons, grebes, kingfishers, egrets, teals, gulls, and an assortment of ducks seem oblivious to your presence as you as you walk by.

The easiest walk is simply to continue on the paved road around the edge of the slough to Coal Oil Point, where you can enjoy the views from the edge of the bluff, or drop down for a walk on the beach or a few moments of tidepooling. If you head west on the beach it is three-fourths mile to the path leading up onto the open meadows on the Ellwood and Santa Barbara Shores blufftops.

My favorite walk, though, takes me along the upper edge of Devereux Slough alongside the Ocean Meadows Golf Course. This leads out to a series of more primitive trails on the west side of the slough or, if you continue straight ahead on the dirt road past the large oil tank, hundreds of acres of open bluffs through which you can meander to your heart's content.

After you walk through the West Campus entrance, continue for several hundred yards until the road begins to drop down to the slough. Look for a path leading off to the right, which will take you down a small hill and around the upper end of the slough. This leads to an open dirt road leading due west and slightly uphill. The golf course is on your right.

If you prefer a more rustic walk, there are several small trails leading around the western side of the slough to the beach. If you continue straight ahead, as you walk past the large oil tank the road curves left, and this, too, leads to the beach or the bluffs overlooking the coastline. This is one of the nicest walks you will find anywhere.

It is also possible to continue straight ahead and through the eucalyptus trees. You'll find a network of trails leading here and there on the bluffs, all of them eventually taking you either toward the ocean or the long stands of eucalyptus trees marking the northern boundary of the bluffs. There are very enchanting paths leading in and out of the eucalyptus trees, as well as a very nice trail leading in a westerly direction along the edge of the trees. You will find the monarch butterfly sanctuary in these groves.

5. Monarch Groves

WALK INFORMATION
Distance—Two hundred yards to the Monarch reserve; a quarter-mile to the bluffs; 1 mile to Coal Oil Point; 1.5 miles to Haskell's Beach
Difficulty—Easy
Topo—Dos Pueblos Canyon

URL—http://www.sb-outdoors.org Keyword Search: Monarch Groves or Santa Barbara Shores

DIRECTIONS

From Santa Barbara, drive north on Highway 101 to the Glen Annie/Storke Road exit in Goleta. Turn left, cross over the freeway, and drive 0.3 miles to Hollister. Turn right and continue 1.1 miles to Coronado Drive, just past the 7-Eleven store. Turn left on Coronado and park near the Coronado Butterfly Reserve sign or at the end of the street.

A CAUTION

Observe all of the do's and don't that are posted on the reserve sign. The Ellwood overwintering site is very fragile, and the butterflies need to be treated with respect.

HIGHLIGHTS

From the end of Coronado Drive you can enjoy the mesmerizing beauty of monarch butterflies fluttering through the tall eucalyptus trees during the winter months, then walk out over the open meadows to the blufftops. Small trails lead in and out of the eucalyptus trees and a network of paths crisscross the bluffs, allowing you to walk for miles. Several trails lead down to the mile-long beach.

SETTING THE SCENE

When I lived on Coronado Drive in the 1960s we would head out to the eucalyptus groves whenever it was a warm, sunny day in late February or March. What made it so beautiful wasn't the puffy clouds or the green hills; it was the sight of the skies filled with butterflies, often hundreds and hundreds of them.

Later, when I taught an environmental education class at UCSB, I would bring my classes here every winter to experience the wonder of seeing the monarchs hanging in thick clusters from the tops of the eucalyptus trees in what is now called the "Ellwood Main." This short gully is surrounded by tall eucalyptus trees, and is the overwintering site for thousands of monarch butterflies every year.

Before we would come I would tell my students to bring bandannas large enough to be used as blindfolds. We would meet at the bottom end of Coronado Drive and talk a bit, but I wouldn't tell them anything about the monarchs or what we were going to see. I would have the students form a long line just on the other side of the barrier, and we would create a caterpillar by having each of the students place his hands on the shoulders of the person in front of him.

Once they got the idea, they would blindfold themselves, place their hands on the students in front of them, and I would lead them in caterpillar fashion down into the creekbed and over into the ravine. It would take a while, and there was always lots of laughing as the students stumbled, but we would go slowly and they would warn each other about upcoming obstacles.

Finally, when we were in the ravine, I would help the students lie down on their backs in a comfortable place, blindfolds still in place. As we were doing this I would tell them to imagine something beautiful and magical, something that would be so powerful it would leave them breathless. One by one all of them would get in position until finally all of them were lying there, heads resting on the ground, eyes facing straight up.

At this point I would ask them to take a few deep breaths and to let me know when they were ready to take off their blindfolds. Then, perhaps a minute or two later, I would lie down beside them so I was looking up as well and lead the countdown. On "three" all of them would take off their blindfolds.

All I can say is this an incredible experience, looking up toward the sky, with the silhouettes of the eucalyptus trees all around, the butterflies floating about you, and the incredible silence. At first there would be lots of words, but then inevitably the students would all lapse into silence, mesmerized by the experience of watching the butterflies flying everywhere.

In a minute or two the really amazing thing would occur to them. In the silence they would begin to realize that it was not completely quiet. You could hear the sound of the butterfly wings as the monarchs moved through the air. It is an amazing sound.

THE WALK

As you drive down Coronado Drive, you will notice the large sign that marks the beginning of the Coronado Butterfly Reserve, which is owned and managed by the Land Trust for Santa Barbara County. It is possible to begin walking from this point. The trail through the reserve leads over a small hill and then down a very pretty creek to the Ellwood Main, where you can observe the monarch butterflies during the winter months.

You can also continue down to the end of Coronado. Devereux Creek is on the other side of the barrier, and the ravine where the Ellwood Main is located is just 50 yards to the right. There are really no established trails in this area, but rather a network of paths that will take you through the eucalyptus groves or up along the bluffs.

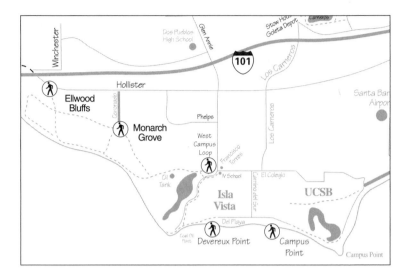

Historically, monarch butterflies have used many of the eucalyptus groves along the Goleta and Gaviota coasts as either temporary bivouacs or permanent winter aggregation sites.

The butterflies begin to arrive around the beginning of fall in late September, but the largest numbers of them arrive in December and January. This is the period when they are the most concentrated and viewing them is the best. A good time to enjoy the monarchs is midday on a warm sunny afternoon when there may be thousands of them in the air as well as thousands of others forming long tendrils of spiky brown clumps on the leaves and trunks of the eucalyptus trees.

If it is really warm you may see them fluttering about quite a way from their home site in the ravine, sunning or collecting nectar along the trails. When it is cooler you may spot them in long clusters high in the trees. When they cluster they fold their brilliant orange-and-black wings so that only their brown undersides show, making them appear more like clusters of leaves than butterflies—great for camouflage but making it hard to spot them unless you look closely.

The monarchs cluster to stay warm and conserve energy during the winter so that enough energy is left to mate and reproduce in the spring. This is why it is important to enjoy them quietly and not disturb them. Dogs should be on leashes and their barking kept to a minimum. Children should be watched carefully to ensure they don't shake the trees or throw anything at the butterflies. Making the butterflies fly and use up precious energy reserves could cause their premature death and diminish the population of the next generation.

In February and March you may see pairs of butterflies mating. This is their major activity once the cold winter is over and before they begin dispersing inland. As the days grow longer and warmer, the females begin moving inland in search of milkweed plants on which to deposit their eggs. The butterflies consume leaves from the milkweed, which turns out to be a very good defensive tactic. The milky white sap contains a chemical toxin to which the monarchs are immune, but which is sickening to birds and other potential predators.

During the late spring and summer months, subsequent generations of monarchs will be born as these butterflies travel further east and north away from the coast, following the available milkweed. By fall, amazingly, monarch butterflies many generations removed from the ones that left the Ellwood Main will begin to migrate back in our direction in search of overwintering sites with favorable conditions for them—like Ellwood.

Once you have had an opportunity to experience the monarchs, there are numerous possibilities for walks through the eucalyptus groves, out into the meadows, or on the beach. Try walking in and out of the eucalyptus trees for a while and you will be mesmerized by the peaceful feeling they exude. There are plenty of down trees to use as benches, and the way the light filters down through the upper branches creates very nice effects.

One of my favorite loops leads over to the Ellwood Bluffs and back along the cliffs. To take this walk, continue west beyond the Ellwood Main along the side of Devereux Creek in the direction of Sandpiper Golf Course. The trail continues all the way to the golf course boundary, then curves left and takes you along the edge of several of the greens to the cliffs.

There is a very overgrown trail here that will take you down to the beach, or you can head back in an easterly direction along the top of the bluffs until you reach one of several easier-to-use beach access points. In any case, there is no prescribed route; sometimes I drop down and walk along the beach for a while, and at other times I just wander along the blufftop until I feel like circling back to the eucalyptus groves. No matter which route you chose, you'll have a great time.

6. Ellwood Bluffs

WALK INFORMATION
Distance—1 to 3 miles or more
Difficulty—Easy
Topo—Dos Pueblos Canyon
URL—http://www.sb-outdoors.org Keyword Search: Ellwood Bluffs

HIGHLIGHTS
This is a very nice place to go for an afternoon walk. Paths lead out to the blufftops overlooking the beach and along the edge of Sandpiper Golf Course, as well as through the eucalyptus groves to the monarch butterfly groves.

DIRECTIONS
From Santa Barbara, drive north on Highway 101 to the Glen Annie/Storke Road exit in Goleta. Turn left, cross over the freeway, and drive 0.3 miles to Hollister Avenue. Turn right and continue 1.7 miles to the Ellwood Bluffs parking lot.

SETTING THE SCENE

When Ellwood Cooper first visited Santa Barbara as a tourist in 1868, he was impressed by the olive trees that had been planted along Los Olivos Street by the mission padres. Quickly, he became convinced that the olive oil produced in Santa Barbara's mild Mediterranean climate could compete with that produced in Italy.

By coincidence, Cooper later met Colonel W.W. Hollister in northern California and began corresponding with him. When Hollister moved to the Goleta Valley in 1869 and built his fabulous Glen Annie retreat, he began singing the praises of the "Good Land" to Cooper and convinced him to move to the area in 1870.

When he arrived in the Goleta Valley, looking at the property on which he would soon locate his olive trees, Cooper wrote:

> The appearance of the Goleta Valley is perfectly lovely, the prospect grand and sublime, mountains on the one side, the great ocean on the other. The building sites on our ranch cannot be surpassed anywhere. I can have wild ravine views, rugged mountains, the ocean and look all over the country between me and Santa Barbara 12 miles distant, the west view being of equal beauty.

Cooper, being the industrious person he was, had 400 acres of his canyon holdings (what is now known as Ellwood Canyon) planted with 7,000 olive trees and 12,500 walnut trees within two years. For many years he was the largest producer of walnuts in California, and Cooper's olive mill eventually became the largest in the United States. He was hailed as America's olive oil king, but ironically, the olive oil business that brought him to Santa Barbara ended up being a failure; Cooper could not compete with the cheaper (and inferior) oil being produced in Sicily at a fraction of the cost.

The olive trees are gone, as are the walnut groves; nevertheless Cooper's mark has been left indelibly on the Goleta countryside and in areas like Ellwood Bluffs County Park. It is he who was responsible for bringing the eucalyptus tree to Santa Barbara. Cooper was the first grower in the United States to begin commercial propagation and distribution of eucalyptus trees. The main plantation was just across from Ellwood Bluffs County Park, near Ellwood Union School.

Today, as you walk down through the park you will notice the long rows of eucalyptus that line Hollister Avenue and in places separate the open fields from one another. These are the legacy of Ellwood Cooper.

THE WALK

From the Ellwood Bluffs parking lot the main trail leads through the middle of a long corridor of open grass meadows. This is the first of a series of very lovely fields that you can walk through on your way to the bluffs overlooking a very long and beautiful stretch of coastline.

On your left you will pass a narrow trail meandering off into a long grove of eucalyptus trees. This is one of a number of trails that lead, here and there, in some cases brief detours through lovely forests of the eucalyptus or, in other cases, to another trail that then connects with another and still another.

After you've walked a few hundred yards from the parking lot and just before crossing the upper end of Devereux Creek, you will come to a trail intersection. Turning left on the intersecting trail leads along the side of the creek to the monarch reserve. Continuing ahead will take you directly to the blufftop and a wide trail that leads east along the edge of the bluff for more than a mile.

I like turning right and heading west, perhaps because fewer people go that way. This takes you to the edge of Sandpiper Golf

Course, where the trail crosses the creek and then follows the side of the golf course out toward the ocean. Once you are at the bluff's edge, an overgrown but serviceable trail leads down to the beach. Often I just meander along the bluffs, stopping here and there to admire the views toward Coal Oil Point before heading across the meadows to the monarch reserve. This is one of the most wonderful loops you can make and I never tire of it, especially just after a storm, when the vernal pools are full of water, the clouds puffy, and the sunsets perfect.

SANTA BARBARA

7. Elings Park

WALK INFORMATION
Distance—1.3 miles for the Sierra Club loop
Elevation Gain—300' to the top of the knoll
URL—http://www.sb-outdoors.org Keyword Search: Elings

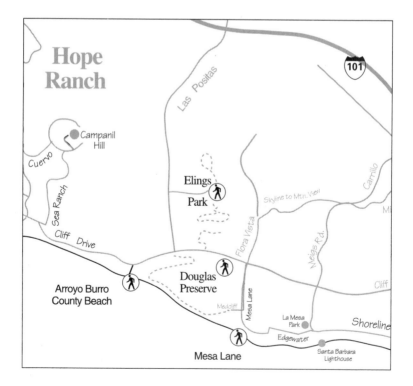

HIGHLIGHTS

The 236-acre park has baseball and soccer fields for the kids and plenty of places for a wonderful picnic at one of the many sites overlooking the city. From the developed part of the park you can hike up onto the top of the hills, where you'll have views in all directions. The Memorial Walk and Terrace of Remembrance, honoring the county residents who have died in hostilities, is very special. There is more rustic hiking on the south side of the park. From Cliff Drive you can hike up and watch the paragliders take off.

DIRECTIONS

From Highway 101 in Santa Barbara, exit on Las Positas Road. Drive 1.2 miles south toward the ocean to the entrance to Elings Park. Turn left and take the park road .4 miles to the parking area near the soccer fields. The rustic trail leads up from the ocean side of the road. To reach the paragliding area, continue on Las Positas to Cliff Drive. Turn left and then left again in .2 miles onto a dirt turnoff, which leads up to an open field where you can park your car.

SETTING THE SCENE

Elings Park is named after Dr. Virgil Elings and his family, who contributed $1.5 million in February 1999 to help support the long-term financial stability of the park. Formerly the park was known as the Las Positas Friendship Park.

THE WALK

For most people, Elings Park serves as a destination for more traditional recreational activities such as soccer or softball. There is even a BMX track in the park for younger kids, and plenty of places for a very nice weekend picnic. But there is also a number of opportunities for walks.

As you drive up the steep hill leading into the park you will pass the BMX track and the soccer and softball fields. Near the top of the park the road ends in a large saddle where you have a number of choices, all of them nice.

To reach the upper pavilions, the city overlooks, and the Memorial Walk, turn left and follow the narrow road leading to the upper parking area. You'll spot the Memorial Walk on the left just before you reach the parking lot. My preference is to walk up the road from the saddle rather than drive up, as this extends the walk and the views along the way are very nice.

Once you reach the turnoff to the Memorial Walk, follow the paved path around the west side of the knoll. This leads past plaques honoring those who died in Vietnam to the Terrace of Remembrance, where county residents are honored who died in hostilities dating all of the way back to the Civil War. This is a very powerful and moving walk. To reach the upper pavilions and the city overlooks, continue on and loop back through them to the parking area.

For a more rustic hike, park near the soccer fields or in the saddle. The 1.3-mile-long Sierra Club loop trail leads onto a knoll that has very nice views in all directions. The trailhead is almost directly across from the narrow road leading up to the Memorial Walk. The trail heads steeply up at first to a junction. My preference is to take the right fork and follow the switchbacks up to the top of the knoll. Once you are up on top, the trail turns east and follows the ridge-top up to the stunning views. Continuing a bit farther, you will find the trail turning left and back to the west, where more switchbacks will take you down to your car.

Another option, though not really a formal hiking trail, will take you to the top of another knoll, where you can watch the hang gliders and paragliders taking off. This area is known as South Park. The land here has just been acquired and is now part of Elings Park. There are plans to develop this area in the next few years.

The South Park can be reached from a small side road just a few hundred yards up Cliff Drive from Las Positas Road. The side road is dirt and a bit bumpy, but passable except after rain. Park in the open meadows and walk up the dirt road to the take-off area. The views looking across Cliff Drive toward the Douglas Family Preserve are great, and it is quite something watching the gliders soaring off the top of the hill.

8. Douglas Family Preserve

WALK INFORMATION
Distance—1 to 3 miles
Elevation Gain—200' to the blufftops where the preserve is located.
Difficulty—Easy
URL—http://www.sb-outdoors.org Keyword Search: Douglas Family
    Preserve or Wilcox

HIGHLIGHTS
Several hundred acres of almost level blufftop overlook the coastline near Arroyo Burro Beach. The preserve has a very relaxed atmosphere with no formal trails. The walk along the edge of the cliff at sunset is one of the

nicest you will find anywhere. The steps leading down to the beach at the end of Mesa Lane are nearby, making a very nice loop walk.

DIRECTIONS
From Highway 101 in Santa Barbara, exit on Las Positas Road. Drive 1.75 miles south toward the ocean to Cliff Drive. Turn right and continue 0.2 miles to the Arroyo Burro Beach parking lot and park.

SETTING THE SCENE

What is now known as the Douglas Family Preserve is at the heart of a number of battles to preserve the coastal blufftops and maintain wildlife corridors along the south coast for birds and mammals. Ironically, what has made much of this possible is the oil companies. The county collects about $1 million annually from companies with offshore operations, which it uses through its Coastal Resource Enhancement Fund to buy local properties for preservation.

Historically, the 69-acre blufftop was a plant nursery owned by Roy Wilcox until the 1950s. There have been efforts to develop this land since the 1960s, when surviving members of the Wilcox family sold it to developers. Ballot measures in 1987 and 1988 would have authorized the city to purchase the land for a public park, but both were narrowly defeated. In 1993, a proposal to subdivide the land into 45 lots was rejected by the city Planning Commission, but it appeared that the Wilcox property might be developed soon.

However, in 1996, armed with a $1 million challenge grant from the Santa Barbara County Board of Supervisors, the Small Wilderness Area Preserves (SWAP) organization began a major campaign to find an additional $2.6 million to buy the land. The organization's efforts were successful, thanks to the contributions of thousands of local citizens and one large grant from the Douglas family.

THE WALK

Though there is no direct access to the beach from the preserve, a wonderful loop hike can be made by combining a stroll through the 69-acre parcel, walking a few blocks to the steps at the end of Mesa Lane, and returning back to the Arroyo Burro Beach parking area along the water's edge. In the late afternoon, often I do this walk in the opposite direction, following the beach and then making my way up to the park. The eucalyptus and fir trees along the top of the bluffs are perfect places to sit and watch the sun go down.

If you come often and take the time to sit for periods of time you are likely to see a variety of wildlife here: monarch butterflies in the winter months, great-horned owls, and red-tail hawks, and if you are really lucky, perhaps a glimpse of a fox darting off into the bushes.

The easiest starting point for the walk is from the parking lot at Arroyo Burro Beach. Most people park near the beach, but the lot extends quite a way east along Cliff Drive. Follow this along the edge of Cliff Drive to the actual trailhead, which is right across the street from the end of Las Positas Road.

The trail leads up an old road to the bluffs through a delightful series of oak forests. Several hundred yards of climbing lead you up onto the mesa and one of the prettiest areas you will find in Santa Barbara. There are no "established" trails; rather, there is an assortment of old roads, mostly overgrown now, which at one time lead through the Wilcox Nursery. However, if you stay to the right you will find yourself at the westernmost edge of the park, looking almost directly down on Arroyo Burro Beach.

The views are incredible as you continue along the edge of the bluff. There are openings in the fir and eucalyptus trees here and there, and an assortment of places to sit on the trunks of downed trees and watch the sunset. If you would like to make this a loop trip, continue east along the bluffs until you reach the end of the property and the start of the residential area. It is a half-block to Mesa Lane and the steps that will take you down to the beach.

MONTECITO

9. San Ysidro Creek Preserve

WALK INFORMATION
Distance—1 mile
Elevation Gain—Almost level
Difficulty—Easy
URL—http://www.sb-outdoors.org Keyword Search: San Ysidro Creek
    Preserve

HIGHLIGHTS
This is one of the most beautiful strolls through an oak woodland environment, and it is almost entirely level. The oak forests are deep in the heart of Montecito and provide a glimpse of why this area received its name, which means "little forest" or "little woods" in Spanish.

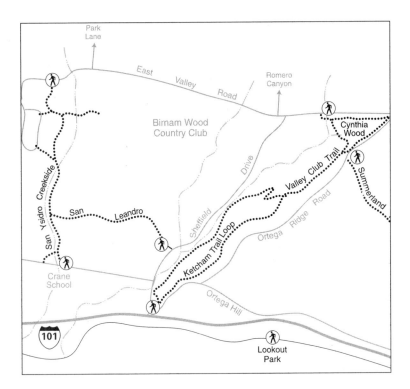

DIRECTIONS

From Santa Barbara, drive south on Highway 101 and exit on San Ysidro Road in Montecito. Turn left, cross Highway 101, and continue one block to San Leandro Lane. Turn right on San Leandro and drive 0.7 miles to the parking area near the white picket fence (1710 San Leandro Lane). Along the way, San Leandro is slightly offset, forcing you to turn left and then back to the right to stay on it.

THE WALK

When you start the hike it almost feels like you are walking onto private property; the 44-acre preserve is surrounded by large estates. However, as soon as you begin your walk through the beautiful forests you will feel as if you have stepped into another world. San Ysidro Creek flows through it, adding an even more enchanting feeling.

You can start on either the east or west side of the creek but I prefer beginning on the west side by the small white picket fence. Immediately you will find yourself under a canopy of oaks, with the huge trees providing a filtered light that is very pretty. In a hundred yards you will reach a very charming stone bridge. The trail crosses it and meanders along the right side of the creek for a bit.

In a half-mile the trail comes out of the trees and parallels Ennisbrook Drive for a hundred yards before dropping back down into the forest. After a few hundred yards of more creekside walking you will come to a second stone bridge, just as pretty as the first. The trail crosses the bridge, then wanders through more forested area. Beyond this point there are several trail junctions. A left turn on any of them will take you to a cul-de-sac on East Valley Lane.

My preference is to turn right at the first junction. This takes you across a small tributary of San Ysidro Creek through even more lush forests. At the second trail junction, turning right, leads through a very pretty eucalyptus creek, but dead-ends on private property.

By turning left you can make a short loop out of this upper section of the preserve. The trail re-crosses the tributary and joins East Valley Lane. You can then follow this back to the cul-de-sac and then a short connector until you rejoin the main trail. From here retrace your steps back to the car.

10. Valley Club Loop

WALK INFORMATION
Distance—1 to 2 miles
Elevation Gain—300′ to the high point as it parallels Ortega Ridge Road
Difficulty—Easy
Topo—Carpinteria
URL—http://www.sb-outdoors.org Keyword Search: Montecito Walks

HIGHLIGHTS
Thanks to the efforts of the Montecito Trails Foundation (MTF), which maintains the trails in this area, there is a network of trails, some of them hidden, throughout the Montecito area. In the area between Sheffield Drive, Ortega Ridge Road, and East Valley Road there are several of the most exclusive riding clubs to be found here, as well as a combination of trails that allow you a glimpse of Montecito you won't see any other way.

DIRECTIONS
From Santa Barbara, drive south on Highway 101 and exit north on Sheffield Drive in Montecito. Turn left, cross under Highway 101, then curve right to the start of Sheffield Drive. To start your walk from the Valley Club, park off the road near the entrance to the club. The trailhead is just to the right of the entrance. To begin at the other end of the trail network,

when you reach Sheffield Drive, bear to the right on Ortega Ridge Road and continue uphill to the stop sign. Turn left on Ortega Ridge Road and drive 1 mile north. Park along the side of the road.

SETTING THE SCENE

My first hint of the Montecito trails system came a number of years ago when I began perusing a map designed by the MTF that the organization provides to each new member. I was amazed to see the number of trails that exist in Montecito between the freeway and East Valley Road. Many of them are short and of benefit only to nearby residents, but there are a number that anyone will find delightful.

One of the nicest areas to walk more or less traces the interior borders of the area between Sheffield Drive, Ortega Ridge Road, and East Valley Road. Within this area you will find three trails that can be combined to create a wonderful walk. These include the Ketcham Loop, the Valley Club Trail, and the Cynthia Wood Trail.

THE WALK

The easiest way to begin your walk is from the intersection of Sheffield Drive and Ortega Hill Road, just after you have exited the freeway. Look for the small parking area on the right side of the road opposite the turn onto Sheffield. Though it isn't easy to spot when you are driving by, the Ketcham Loop begins just to the right of the entrance into the riding club.

The first several hundred yards of the trail heads uphill and parallels Ortega Hill Road but just below it. As you rise you begin to get your first glimpses of the Montecito Valley and the mountains behind them. The trail gradually turns to the north and for the next half-mile contours along the side of Ortega Ridge, gaining elevation slightly. The views are better and better as you near the north end of the riding club and the start of the Birnam Wood Golf Course.

As you near an open area that is relatively flat the trail splits. The Ketcham Trail drops down an old road into an open area between the riding club and the golf course and then follows Romero Creek back to your starting point. Continuing on takes you onto the Valley Club Trail. This part of the walk brings you to the highest point and the best views. You can spot many of the holes on the Birnam Wood course, as well as the homes situated along many of the fairways.

For the next quarter-mile the trail is almost level and takes you just under several of the homes on Ortega Ridge. One has one of the best tree forts I've ever seen. Just beyond this point the trail comes to the edge of Ortega Ridge Road at the point where the road begins to drop down toward East Valley Road. Across the road in a small draw, the Summerland Trail will take you down into the upper end of Greenwell Avenue (see Town Walk #11).

Often I begin my hike from this point, following the Valley Club Trail to the Ketcham intersection and back. It is about a mile out and back and is especially nice in the evening light, when the views out over the Montecito area are especially beautiful.

To continue all the way to East Valley Road on the trail, look for the Cynthia Wood Trail intersection. This trail leads sharply down the hill, over a series of steps created from railroad ties, to Romero Creek, where the trail splits. The left fork meanders a bit through the oaks and along one of the Birnam Wood greens then crosses Romero Creek and ends on East Valley Road near the Romero bridge.

The right fork follows the creek upstream past the riding club, which you could see from above on the Valley Club Trail. It, too, exits onto East Valley Road, near the intersection of Ortega Ridge Road. You can retrace your steps from here or cross Ortega Ridge Road and continue on the Cynthia Wood Trail. This will take you up a steep hill several hundred feet high. Near the top of the hill the trail splits, with the left fork dropping down into Summerland and the right fork heading back to the west across the hill near several nurseries to Ortega Ridge Road. Cross and reconnect with the Valley Club Trail and follow it back to your car.

SUMMERLAND

11. Summerland Trail

WALK INFORMATION
Distance—0.5 to 2.5 miles
Elevation Gain—300' to Ortega Ridge Road
Difficulty—Easy to moderate
Topo—Carpinteria
URL—http://www.sb-outdoors.org Keyword Search: Summerland Trail

HIGHLIGHTS
The Summerland Trail provides access to the hills surrounding the Summerland area. You can follow the Summerland Trail across Ortega Ridge

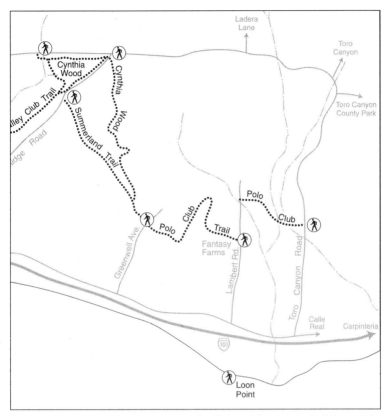

Road and extend your walk on the Valley Club and Ketcham trails. It is possible to make this a long loop hike by returning on the Cynthia Wood connector.

DIRECTIONS
From Santa Barbara, drive south on Highway 101 to Summerland and exit north on Padaro Lane. Cross over the freeway and turn left onto Via Real. Follow this 0.5 miles to Greenwell Road. Turn right and continue .4 miles north to the Greenwell Preserve parking lot.

THE WALK
The Summerland Trail is part of a complex that was created primarily to provide horseback riders with a route extending from Toro Canyon on the east to the Montecito riding clubs on the west. However, these trails also provide hikers with several very nice routes leading from the Summerland area.

As you drive up Greenwell Road you will notice a large parking area near the preserve sign. The Summerland Trail leads directly out of the parking area, following an old dirt road up a small side canyon for a half-mile to Ortega Ridge Road. A hundred yards along the way you will notice a trail on the right that crosses the creek through an opening in the willow thickets. In the winter, after it has rained, the crossing can be more of a bog, and you are likely to get your shoes muddy making it across. The side trail leads up a half-mile-long ridge to the Cynthia Wood Trail. This makes it possible to do a loop walk.

A few hundred yards past the side trail you will notice an old gravel pit just before the elevation begins to increase. Once you reach Ortega Ridge, the Valley Club Trail is just on the other side of the road. Following this to the left takes you along the west side of Ortega Ridge. The views are great, and in the morning or evening this makes a wonderful out-and-back walk.

To create a loop hike, turn right on the Valley Club Trail and follow it a short distance to the Cynthia Wood Trail. Head downhill on the Wood Trail and bear right past the riding club to the East Valley–Ortega Ridge intersection. Cross Ortega Ridge Road and continue on the Cynthia Wood Trail. This will take you up a steep hill several hundred feet high. Near the top of the hill, the trail splits. The left fork drops down to the Summerland Trail and crosses the creek at the trail intersection you saw on the way up. The right fork heads back to the west to Ortega Ridge Road near the top of the Summerland Trail. Take this route back to avoid any problem with the lower creek crossing.

From the Greenwell Road parking area, it is also possible to head toward Toro Canyon on the Polo Club Trail. The trail begins along the right side a private lane. There is a gate across the road, but there is an opening on the right side of it you can use. Follow the side of the road due east as it rises to a saddle. Directly in front of you is a large lemon orchard. From here on out the route-finding is somewhat difficult.

Basically the trail skirts the boundary of the orchard, then cuts through the middle of a horse ranch on the other side of the saddle. The route follows the orchard road to the left and then to the right once you've reached the top of the orchard. Bear left on the first dirt road and cross over the ridge. You'll spot the huge riding stable almost immediately below you. The trail drops down from the ridge a short distance, then turns immediately to the right at the bottom of the east side of the lemon orchard. Continue a hundred yards in a southerly direction until you spot the 8-foot-wide trail corridor that leads through the stables to Lambert Road.

To reach Toro Canyon Road, head up Lambert Road across a

small bridge and look for the trail on the right side of the road just beyond a beautiful old wooden house. The remainder of the route leads through a thick forest of oak and eucalyptus trees.

12. Polo Club Trail

WALK INFORMATION
Distance—1 to 2 miles
Elevation Gain—300' to the high point overlooking Greenwell Road
Difficulty—Easy to moderately easy
Topo—Carpinteria
URL—http://www.sb-outdoors.org Keyword Search: Polo Club

DIRECTIONS
From Santa Barbara, drive south on Highway 101 to Summerland and exit north on Padaro Lane. Cross over the freeway and turn right on Via Real. Follow this 0.5 miles to Toro Canyon Road and turn north (left). Drive up Toro Canyon for 0.5 miles to the trailhead. Look for the trail sign (which is easy to miss) on the left near a private driveway.

THE WALK

This part of Toro Canyon is like much of the Montecito area: the rolling hills are interspersed with flatlands covered with oak forests. In between Toro Canyon and Greenwell roads there are several magnificent horse ranches. You can get an intimate glimpse as you make your way along the trail. One—called Fantasy Farms—is especially magnificent.

The trailhead is tough to spot but is almost exactly .5 miles up Toro Canyon Road, not too far after you cross Toro Creek. Ironically, there is a sign on the side of one private lane that says "NOT THE TRAIL," which you will most likely see first. The trail is just to the left of this private lane. The first several hundred yards lead along a narrow pathway that feels like you are entering a forested tunnel. The oak forests and thick vines covering the ground on your left create the feeling of being in an enchanted forest.

As you walk past the end of the private lane you will find a delightful creek crossing and then more forests as you meander past a series of ranches and houses. Lambert Road is not too far ahead. When you reach it, turn left and walk south until you've crossed the narrow stone bridge, then look for an opening in the Fantasy Farms complex. The corridor is barely 8 feet wide and easy to miss.

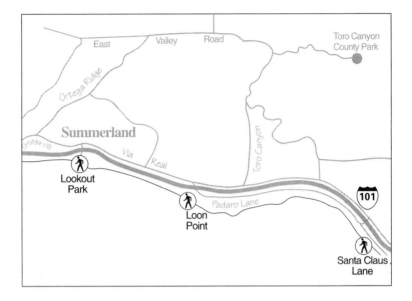

This takes you through the farm and up to the edge of a large lemon orchard. Turn right when you reach the orchard and then follow the trail in a clockwise direction around the lemon trees. The trail passes over a small ridge and down into the Greenwell area.

13. Toro Canyon County Park

WALK INFORMATION
Distance—1 mile
Elevation Gain—300' to the top of the knoll, where a small gazebo is located
Difficulty—Easy
Topo—Carpinteria
URL—http://www.sb-outdoors.org Keyword Search: Toro Canyon

HIGHLIGHTS
Though this is a short hike and doesn't really head up into wild country, I can't say enough about this little-known county park. It is a great place for families to take their children for the afternoon. The setting is very picturesque, there's lots of play equipment for the kids, and the trail is short and not too steep. It's romantic, too. A small gazebo is situated in a perfect spot for sunset views to the east and west.

DIRECTIONS

From Santa Barbara, drive south on Highway 101 to Summerland and exit north on Padaro Lane. Cross over the freeway and turn right on Via Real. Follow this 0.5 miles to Toro Canyon Road and turn north (left). Drive up Toro Canyon for 1.3 miles to the park entrance and turn right. Proceed one mile to Toro Canyon Park. Turn left and drive to the upper end of the parking lot.

SETTING THE SCENE

The drive to Toro Canyon County Park is almost as worthwhile as the park itself, which is actually not in Toro Canyon, but the upper end of Arroyo Paredon, a beautiful oak-filled canyon that drops down into the Carpinteria Valley not too far from the polo fields.

Toro Canyon Road leads steadily uphill, then at the point where Foothill Road intersects from the right, becomes a narrow, twisty canyon that is as pretty as any in Santa Barbara. A half-mile beyond Foothill Road you'll find the entrance to the park. The entrance sign is actually a bit premature as the park is actually a mile further up this side road, which winds up through more twisty canyon and avocado farms to a high point. On the way back stop here. The views across the Montecito foothills are spectacular. Once you reach the high point, the road drops sharply downhill into a large bowl where the park is located.

Along the way through the 0.2-mile drive to the trailhead you'll find ample picnic areas, playground equipment, a great sand volleyball court (who says the only place to play volleyball on the sand is at East Beach?), and several hiking trails.

THE WALK

Though there are several short loops, the nicest leads up to the right to a knoll where there is a gazebo with an Oriental feeling to it. At the upper end of the park, look for a large sandstone rock outcropping. The hikes start here. As you hike past the rock outcropping, you will almost immediately spot the route up to the gazebo on the right. A short distance up the trail (actually a bulldozed path) you can see the silhouette of the gazebo. The path circles both the knoll and the gazebo. At the top is a surprising view. To the west you are looking across the upper part of Montecito. To the east the view is across the Carpinteria plain. Not only can you see Rincon Mountain, but also Ventura and the Point Hueneme area. At sunset, this is indescribable.

Tangerine Falls

Foothill Hikes

"I cannot describe my feelings as I stood on that ridge, that shore of an ancient ocean. How lonely and desolate! Who shall tell how many centuries, how many decades of centuries, have elapsed since these rocks resounded to the roar of breakers, and these animals sported in their foam? I picked up a bone, cemented in the rock with shells. A feeling of awe came over me. Around me rose rugged mountains; no human being was within miles of me to break the silence. And then I felt overwhelmed. . . ."

WILLIAM BREWER
Up and Down California

INTRODUCTION

Hiking wasn't something that came naturally to me; exploring, yes, that did. Running up and down the cliffs, crashing down creeks, and heading off into the hills—all these things I did when I was a kid, and still do. When I was in third grade in Cincinnati, Ohio, I went off on one of my typical adventures, trudging off down the street, not sure quite where I was going.

There was a lot more open space then, and it was easy to find fields here and there between the clusters of houses and to make your own routes through the neighborhoods. I found an old deserted firehouse, then a large meadow, and a small creek after that. Before long I was thoroughly lost and had no idea how to get home. Simple, I thought. I knew my address. So I found a house, knocked on the door confidently and asked the woman who opened it to call me a cab, which she did.

Boy, was my mom mad when I got home and she had to pay the fare. I don't think I've ever gotten lost since then, though I've tried enough times (I always see to keep finding myself). But when I came to Santa Barbara I didn't think too much about going hiking. Why, when the beach was right there and the surf was great? Then, too, when I looked up toward the mountains, they were very impressive to me in size and shape, but they didn't look very inviting. Was I ever wrong.

It wasn't until after nearly six years of living in Santa Barbara that I took my first walk in these woods (can you call the chaparral "woods"?). Some of you may remember Dunall's, the outdoor store, if you've been here for a while. There was one in Santa Barbara and another in Goleta. One day I was in there looking for a knife when I spotted a collection of books. I found one there that completely changed the way I thought about the mountains. It was by Dick Smith and the title was *Exploring the Santa Barbara backcountry*. The book was filled with pictures and descriptions of each of the ranges and valleys.

I remember one picture best, of a place called Lion Canyon. The reason I liked it so much was the sandstone, huge walls of stone and shapes that seemed to defy description. There were other places like this, so many that I was overwhelmed, not sure which of them I would try to find first. I bought the book and have had a copy ever since. Not too long after that I began my hiking career in the Santa Barbara mountains, though it was to the far backcountry I went first.

Do you remember your first day hike here? Mine was an all-day trip down the Arroyo Burro Trail. In places we went straight down the creek, and I must confess I know we went across a little bit of private property to reach Foothill Road. But who knew better then?

Since then I have hiked the foothill trails hundreds of times and it never seems to get tiring. There are different seasons and so many hidden places. Each time I update my day hikes book I seem to find a new place or something unusual or unique.

It is the springtime when I love this area the most. The ceanothus comes into bloom, and the thick clusters of white flowers turn the mountainsides a dusky white. Green shoots begin to appear along the trail sides and cover the foothills. Then come the golden poppies and the colorful lupine, the shooting stars, the blue-eyed grass, the intensely yellow mayflowers, and the rich reds of the hummingbird sage, and I fall in love with these mountains all over again.

In the mountains there is magic, the kind that awakens all of your senses, vibrations of the good kind that make life seem worth living. In them is the antidote for what ails the soul. There is one sure cure when the spirits flag. Head to the mountains. Go often, stay as long as you like, and return again and again.

"If you take the San Roque Canyon trail northward from Stevens Park, a half-mile beyond the twin-arched Foothill Road bridge you will come to a grove of ancient oaks and sycamores where Chumash Indians gathered long before Columbus discovered our continent. Alongside the trail you will see an outcropping of sandstone which is polka-dotted with deep, funnel-shaped mortars.

"Here Chumash squaws, using stone pestles, ground their acorn harvest to obtain a powdery meal which, when leached to rid it of its lye content, produced a tasty gruel to go with their seafood and wild game diet.

"When the first white men arrived in 1769 with Governor Portolá, they camped at the mouth of San Roque Creek, which they named to memorialize the patron saint of invalids, Saint Roque, a Carmelite friar of the 14th century. Thus our neighborhood got its name."

WALKER TOMPKINS
Neighborhood Series No. 1, San Roque, 1977

The San Roque area has known the tread of all of those who have come before: the Chumash Indians whose camps dotted the open grasslands; the Franciscan padres who sought to convert them to a pastoral way of life; the Mexican rancheros who supplanted the Chumash when this disastrous experiment was ended in the 1820s; and the soldiers of John C. Frémont, who "liberated" Santa Barbara from Mexico in the 1840s.

Today there are large homes jutting out on both sides of San Roque Canyon, and what is left of the pastoral life consists mainly of avocado ranching. But as you enter the canyon and begin to walk along the creek's edge, the feeling of being in a very special place still remains.

1. Stevens Park

TRAIL INFORMATION:
Distance—1 mile
Elevation Gain—100' to Jesusita Trail
Difficulty—Very easy
Topo—Santa Barbara
URL—http://www.sb-outdoors.org Keyword Search: Stevens Park

HIGHLIGHTS

The trail beyond Stevens Park wanders through a beautiful oak-filled canyon whose combination of picturesque scenery and easy hiking is perfect for children. There are lots of places to stop by the creek, and there are mortars cut into the rock by the Chumash when they once used this area. This a perfect place to go for an afternoon picnic, game of volleyball, or canyon hike.

DIRECTIONS

From Highway 101 drive 1.5 miles north on Las Positas to Calle Fresno, which is just below Foothill Road (Las Positas becomes San Roque Road at the top). Turn left on Calle Fresno, then right on Canon Drive to reach the park entrance.

THE HIKE

The hike begins at the upper end of the park, where the grass gives way to a wide dirt path that is very easy for even the youngest of children to walk on. Almost immediately you are immersed in canyon vegetation, with oak trees and sycamore trees your companions.

A hundred yards takes you under the Foothill Road bridge, which is high overhead. The path continues along the creek and for the next quarter-mile is wide, rising slightly, but still easy walking. There are several spots where you can reach the creek, and on the right an absolutely beautiful grass meadow with excellent views of Cathedral Peak.

Beyond the meadow, the trail rises steeply over a small ridge, then drops back down to the creek. The path is much narrower here. The creek jogs to the right and then back to the left just ahead. There are several great places for kids to play at the edge of the creek and a fabulous oak forest on top of a hill to the right. There are paths leading up into the forest, and a beautiful place to sit on top of the rocks and look down on the creek from the shade of a gnarly old oak tree. But you are better off leaving this area alone: there is poison oak everywhere.

As the path turns to the right and follows the canyon, you will reach a creek crossing and a small pool. Just across the creek is a second oak forest and a ring of truck-sized boulders that form a very peaceful and secluded glen.

Beyond the glen the trail splits. One path leads back to the creek; the other up over a hill to a spillway. This is a good spot to end the lower canyon hike. However, if you would like to continue further you can. The Jesusita Trail is just a bit past the upper end of

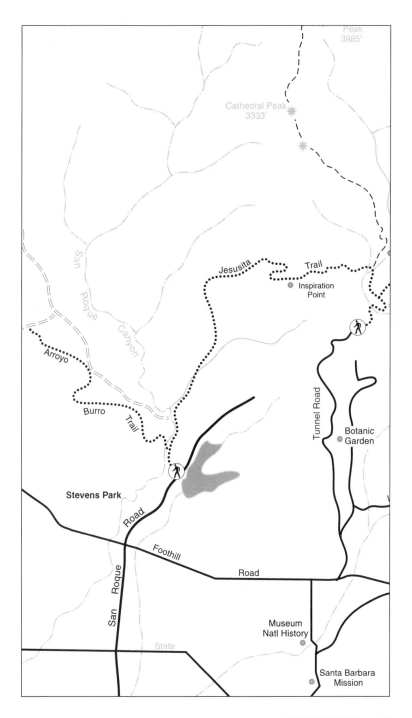

Peak
3985'

Cathedral Peak
3333'

San
Roque

Canyon

Jesusita   Trail

Inspiration
Point

Arroyo

Burro   Trail

Tunnel Road

Botanic
Garden

Stevens Park

Road

Foothill

Road

San Roque Road

State

Museum
Natl History

Santa Barbara
Mission

Jesusita Trail

the spillway. Stay on the left side of the basin and follow the path through an opening in the brush, then across the creek. The Jesusita Trail is a hundred yards beyond the crossing.

2. Jesusita Trail

TRAIL INFORMATION:
Distance—4 .5 miles
Elevation Gain—100' to end of canyon; 1225' to Inspiration Point
Difficulty—Very easy to moderately strenuous, depending on the distance
    Topo—Santa Barbara
URL—http://www.sb-outdoors.org Keyword Search: Jesusita

HIGHLIGHTS
Jesusita Trail wanders through a beautiful oak-filled canyon whose combination of picturesque scenery and easy hiking is perfect for children. The hike to Inspiration Point provides views that make the ascent worthwhile. Along the way you will find a cutoff trail leading up to the historic Arroyo Burro Trail. Stevens Park is at the lower trailhead, making this a perfect place to go for an afternoon picnic, game of volleyball, or canyon hike.

DIRECTIONS
From Highway 101 drive 2 miles north on Las Positas to the posted trailhead, which is just beyond the Cater Filtration Plant. The trail begins .5 miles above Foothill Road.

THE HIKE

Unlike other foothill trails, which begin in the lower canyons and extend upward through the chaparral to East Camino Cielo Road or Gibraltar Road, Jesusita Trail is a loop of sorts, connecting San Roque and Mission canyons via Inspiration Point and its awe-inspiring panoramas.

The Jesusita isn't a historic trail but was built in 1964 as part of an $8,000 project financed by the State Division of Beaches and Parks after an exchange of easements between the county and the Marion Moreno family, who owned most of the upper canyon.

The first section of the trail drops down into the canyon and follows a lazy course along the right side of the creek with one small exception—there is a steep knoll which you will need to go up over. This detour was created when the main trail washed out in the 1995 floods. There is a creek crossing or two along the way, which the kids will like, and lots of sycamore trees and huge old oaks to shade you. Look for the old picnic table along the way, which was buried by silt in 1995.

In a half-mile the trail turns right, heads up onto a long plateau covered with annual grasses, then retreats back into the canyon. You should see a trail sign under a large oak. The left fork leads up to the Arroyo Burro Trail and the right one up to the grass plateau.

A half-mile of hiking takes you in and out of a series of oak forests and back and forth across the creek several times to the Moreno Ranch, marked by a horse corral. This is the end of the lower canyon section of the trail.

The upper chaparral section begins just above the point where the creek branches. Turn right just beyond the fenced corral and follow the dirt past a gate into the east fork of the canyon. Just as you cross the creek you will spot a trail sign and the well-worn trail. The owners would be extremely grateful if you would keep to the trail rather than meander onto their property.

The next several hundred yards leads along the creek through an oak forest and grassy openings, then begins to climb much more rapidly as you make your way through a thin but spectacular layer of Vaqueros sandstone. The sandstone marks your final exit from the canyon vegetation and the start of the hard chaparral.

This area is dominated by chamise, ceanothus, holly-leaf cherry, and manzanita. The trail winds back and forth up a set of switchbacks and then levels somewhat, turns east, and continues along the Sespe redbeds before widening to become a power line road. This signals the start of another section of bedrock—the Coldwater sandstone. Towering overhead are the precipitous Mission Crags. The toothlike shape of Cathedral Peak can be seen a thousand feet above.

At the base of the 300-foot-tall spire is an enormous cave, almost 60 feet in length and more than 30 feet deep, which, according to legend, harbored stolen horses during the early 1800s. It is seldom visited now because of the thick chaparral. In 1966, two years after the Coyote Fire, *News-Press* writer Dick Smith made the trek when the more open landscape made it possible. "The view from Cathedral Peak is truly sensational, much closer and equally as high as that from La Cumbre Peak," he noted. "One can look down on the entire city, unobstructed by any foreground ridge.

"Getting to take a look at this fabulous view is not an easy task," he mused afterwards. "In fact it took . . . nearly two hours of rock hopping to gain the end of the ridge. . . . There's no trail. You must pick your way across the brush." Today, thanks to the efforts of climbers and other trail enthusiasts who have carved routes through the chaparral up to Cathedral Peak, it is possible to gain the summits Dick Smith once sat upon.

Another few hundred yards along, Jesusita Trail leads to Inspiration Point, which is actually not at the highest point but rather at the east end of the knoll where the power line road ends. To find it, rather than dropping down into Mission Canyon on the trail, walk east on the dirt road and look for a small trail that leads to a series of boulders that marks the view point. You'll know you are there if you spy the initials carved a half-century ago in the bedrock.

From Inspiration Point, Jesusita Trail continues another three-fourths mile, winding down into the west fork of Mission Creek and the beginning of Tunnel Trail. For a refreshing dip before the hike back, Seven Falls is but a half-mile up the creek.

You can return to your starting point by retracing your steps back along Jesusita Trail, or you might consider bringing another car along and parking it beforehand at the Tunnel Road trailhead to use for a shuttle. Consider carrying a flashlight so you can stay for sunset at the point before heading down.

3. Arroyo Burro Trail

TRAIL INFORMATION

Distance—1.5 to 5 miles

Elevation Gain—350' to top of knolls; 850' to end of powerlines; 1550' to top of the main ridgeline; 2700' to East Camino Cielo

Difficulty—Moderate to Very strenuous

Topo—Santa Barbara, Little Pine and San Marcos Pass

URL—http://www.sb-outdoors.org Keyword Search: Arroyo Burro

HIGHLIGHTS

Provides an opportunity to re-visit one of Santa Barbara's most historic trails, great views from the upper knolls above Barger Canyon, a rugged and more remote experience than most since the trail is used much less than others. Just above the power lines a series of rocky ridges jut out of the chaparral creating the best viewpoint on the Goleta coastline, which is evident from the number of people who have carved their names in the soft, red Sespe Formation.

DIRECTIONS

The trail splits off from the Jesusita Trail. From the freeway drive 2 miles north on Las Positas to the posted Jesusita trailhead, which is just beyond the Cater Filtration Plant.

SETTING THE SCENE

There's just a wisp of a line across the ridgeline nowadays, a long thread of a line that suggests more of the past than it does the future. This is the Arroyo Burro Trail, once the main passageway into the backcountry for the Chumash. It is a trail rich with history. Countless hunting parties used it heading into the San Rafael Mountains. Prospectors walked along the rutted path on the way to quicksilver mines. Later the Forest Service improved it as use of the backcountry increased.

Yet for many years the Arroyo Burro Trail was off limits to the public because a three-mile section of it lay on private property, part of it running through Rancho San Roque. In 1972, despite hundreds of years of trail use, the ranch fenced off the property and posted NO TRESPASSING signs at the trailhead.

Recently, due to the development of the ridgeline on which the Arroyo Burro Trail is located, an easement has been negotiated, making it possible to hike up this once forbidden trail.

THE HIKE

The trail begins slightly more than a half-mile after you begin your hike up the Jesusita Trail. The trail sign is under a large oak and is situated right before you would head up onto a long plateau if you were continuing on the Jesusita.

I noticed the sign for the first time in fall 1999. Curious about what was beyond, I abandoned my planned hike, which was up to Inspiration Point, and began to investigate. The Arroyo Burro Trail was the first I ever hiked in these mountains, and I was very interested to discover where it would lead me.

The trail crosses the creek and heads up the west side of the canyon wall. A decade ago an old bulldozed path could be followed up to a higher crest, where you could then continue along, yo-yo'ing up and down on the ridgeline until you reached the end of the power lines and the beginning of the upper trail.

A hundred yards up the hill the trail disappeared at a wide asphalt driveway. I was at a bit of a loss where to head next; then I spotted another trail sign up the road. I headed over to it, thinking there must be a path hidden in the brush just beyond it, but when I got there I couldn't find the trail. Slowly it dawned on me that the driveway, which headed steeply up the hill, was the trail—or at least that's what you were supposed to follow.

As I trudged up the hill I questioned whether this was the route but sure enough, when I reached the top there was another trail sign, a reminder that, indeed, the trail easement did go this way.

I've come back several times since, exploring more of the upper trail. The route from here on isn't what it used to be, and the necessity of having to follow the asphalt takes a lot away from the experience, but I like it up here. But then, I am prejudiced: getting up onto the upper Arroyo Burro Trail is like coming home, and it evokes very special memories.

The ridgeline you reach, once you have gotten up this extremely steep road, separates San Roque and Barger canyons. There are sweeping views in all directions, and I can see why the road leads here. Were I rich enough, I would want to have my home perched on one of the knolls that dot the ridge.

The route continues to follow the asphalt for several hundred more yards, and is level, so you have time to catch your breath and look out on the coastline. Just as the road starts to drop down into Barger Canyon there is another trail sign. Here you will finally get back on a real trail. This cuts across the west side of the ridgeline, leading to a large, open meadow. What you will be doing is paralleling the ridge but just off it. There is a dirt road that goes straight up the ridge, and I suppose you could just follow that, but I don't think you are supposed to, even though no signs tell you not to. (That could change.)

Beyond the meadow, the trail heads up into the chaparral until it reaches a dirt road. You turn right and follow this a hundred yards to a point where you are back on the main ridge. From there you go left, and until you reach the end of the power lines, you go up and down a series of short, steep hills leading up the main ridge.

By the time you've reached the end of the powerlines your legs will probably be pretty tired. There are a lot of ups and downs. But there is a great rest stop just ahead of you. The upper trail begins right after the last tower. There are several switchbacks leading to an outcropping of Sespe redbeds and a perfect place to take a break. You can tell plenty of others have rested here too. There are carvings everywhere. This is also a good spot to end your hike—unless, of course, you can't resist more switchbacks and lots more uphill.

The trail moves from the Sespe into layers of Coldwater sandstone and really begins to gain elevation. Seven hundred feet of switchbacks bring you to a second series of outcroppings, several of which make good rest spots. Right after this the trail levels out, goes through several meadows, then begins cutting west across the mountainside until it reaches the east fork of San Antonio Creek. The trail drops down into the canyon, follows it upstream for a bit, then crosses to the west side of the canyon and rises rapidly for 800 feet to East Camino Cielo Road. Unfortunately, the canyon section is private property, making it illegal for you to hike all the way up to the crest.

MISSION CANYON

Mission Canyon. The name stirs the imagination. There are numerous canyons to be found in these mountains, but none quite like this one. Flanked on either side by twin towers of sandstone, Mission Canyon leads up into the very bedrock of these mountains.

Along the way there are artfully sculptured formations, etched by millions of years of relentless weathering, the wind and water working their magic, until just right—the results of which are to be found in the cascading pools of Seven Falls, the boulder-filled escarpment of La Cumbre Peak, and the jumble of rocks that my friend Bob Hardy has so aptly titled "the Rock Garden."

This is magic country. Most people will be drawn to the pools and the joy of sliding off the edge of the final pool at Seven Falls, plunging deep into the water, and the excitement of the moment; but I find magic in the bedrock above, clambering my way up the razor-edged sandstone leading skyward to the edge of heaven: Cathedral Peak on the left flank, the Rock Garden on the right.

This is not Forest Service-"approved" country. No trail leads to either place and none ever will. The irony is immense: in the canyon most visible to the eye from the heart of the city, the secrets hidden are still numerous, worthy of discovery, but only available to those who make the effort, which is large.

In Mission Canyon you will discover a larger variety of opportunities than anywhere else in the Santa Barbara area. Whether it is the hike up to Mission Falls for lunch, the awesome views from Inspiration Point, a quick dip in the pools at Seven Falls, or one of many off-trail challenges, you will find this country well worth your time.

The history of this canyon is as immense as its beauty. I am sure Chumash Indians sat near the foot of the fabled Seven Falls, just as many of us have in past years, and felt the magic we have.

WATER HISTORY

More recently it has been the need for water, and for a place to get away from the hectic pace of city life, that has drawn people into the canyon. The most famous route to the top of the mountains is Tunnel Trail, built at the turn of the century as a link between a tunnel being bored in the south side of the Santa Ynez Mountains and a dam to be built on the Santa Ynez River at Gibraltar Narrows.

In 1900, with a population of barely 6,000, Santa Barbara was already experiencing its first water crisis, although earlier Chumash populations must have approached 8,000 in the South Coast area without severely taxing food or water resources. The water shortage was brought on partly because of the increased numbers of people coming to the area after the Southern Pacific Railroad completed a branch line here from Los Angeles in 1887. Droughts in the late 1890s also contributed to the problem.

As early as 1870, when the population was about 2,900, Santa Barbarans had begun to feel the need to develop water supplies. In 1872, local investors organized the Mission Water Company, which tapped the Mission Creek water supply. In 1887, the De la Guerra Water Company was formed, and seven artesian wells were drilled to a depth of 200 feet to begin capturing underground supplies.

Several years later the two companies were consolidated and became the Santa Barbara Water Company. This company proceeded to buy a 17,000-acre tract on the upper Santa Ynez River, which embraced all potential reservoir sites along this section. Impetus toward using the Santa Ynez River as a source of water for Santa Barbara grew gradually. A series of dry years in the mid-1890s and a donation to the city of 320 acres in Cold Springs Canyon by Eugene Sheffield helped the process.

The eyes of city engineers first turned to the Santa Ynez Mountains in January 1896, when, at an elevation of 1,400 feet, Cold Springs Tunnel was carved a mile into the mountain wall, adding some 290 acre-feet of water to the city's annual supply.

After the years 1898, 1899, and 1900 proved to be ones of sustained drought, the city hired J.B. Lippincott, head of the hydrological branch of the U.S. Geological Survey, to investigate the possibility of developing water storage facilities on the Santa Ynez River. His recommendation was to construct a tunnel from Mission Canyon through the Santa Ynez Mountains to the Santa Ynez River near the Gibraltar Narrows.

Work began in 1904, when Santa Barbara entered a contract with the water company to build the tunnel. Workers on both sides burrowed deep into the mountain flanks for eight long years, encountering many obstacles before they finished.

The tunneling began from the south portal on April 29, 1904. After the excavation crew had progressed 1700 feet into the mountain, they encountered quicksand. Sulfur water was the next obstacle, and it was heavily charged with hydrogen gas, which affected the eyes of the workers, who were forced to work in one-hour shifts. Then these and other gases caused a fungus to attack the supporting timbers, destroying them and forcing the use of concrete to shore up the walls.

These difficulties, which incapacitated several workers, caused the city to release the contractor and proceeded with the work itself. On the north side of the mountain, pockets of marsh gas were found from time to time, and safety lanterns were carried by workers as the gas would ignite otherwise. According to Lee Hyde, whose father was chosen by Lippincott to engineer the project, "On one occasion, two brave men, while literally taking their lives in their hands, went into the tunnel, ignited the gas by torch, then lay prone beneath the body of the flame. The heat was, of course, terrific, and the men survived by turning over and over in the water that was flowing below."

A small electric train was used to carry men into the tunnel and excavated material out. In 1912 another potential disaster was averted when a cave-in was discovered. The train operator then reversed his direction and picked up eight men who were farther on in the tunnel. At the point where they encountered the cave-in the men were forced to wade armpit-deep through the mucky water to escape. Though the men were saved, it was necessary to detour around the spot and wait a year for it to dry out enough that the tunnel could be straightened at that point.

From 1912 until Gibraltar Dam was completed in 1921, supplies went through the tunnel on the miniature electric train. In 1915, a $590,000 bond issue was passed that authorized the construction of Gibraltar Dam, which began in 1918. Materials were transported by a narrow-gauge electrical railroad through the tunnel. The dam was completed in 1920, initiating Santa Barbara's dependence on the backcountry for water.

4. Tunnel Trail

TRAIL INFORMATION
Distance—4 miles to the crest; an additional mile to La Cumbre Peak
Elevation Gain—2350' to the intersection with East Camino Cielo (La Cumbre Peak is an additional 600' gain)
Difficulty—Easy to Seven Falls; strenuous to crest
Topo—Santa Barbara
URL—http://www.sb-outdoors.org Keyword Search: Tunnel Trail

HIGHLIGHTS
Mission Canyon provides a variety of outdoor experiences ranging from a sunset hike to Inspiration Point to a refreshing dip in the pools at Seven Falls,

to a picnic on the lip of Mission Falls, or the awe-inspiring views from the top of La Cumbre Peak. You can hike from Mission Canyon to Stevens Park in San Roque Canyon or over and into Rattlesnake Canyon. You can even drop down to Fern Falls and work your way down Mission Creek to the Botanic Garden.

DIRECTIONS
From the Santa Barbara Mission drive up Mission Canyon Road to Foothill Road and turn right, then turn left several hundred yards later (by the fire station). Continue up Mission Canyon to the Tunnel Road turnoff, a half-mile before the Botanic Garden. Continue several miles to the end. Park properly; the police frequently ticket illegally parked cars. The trail begins about three-quarters mile beyond the locked gate.

THE HIKE
The trailhead begins three-fourths mile beyond the end of Tunnel Road. Walk up the paved road, which continues steadily uphill. A hundred yards before Mission Tunnel the road turns sharply to the left and then curves past the west fork of Mission Creek. If you look carefully beneath and to the right of the bridge you can see the tunnel.

The Tunnel trailhead begins a bit past Mission Tunnel. Fifty yards after the paved road ends (marked by a California Riding and Hiking Trail sign) Tunnel Trail begins. To hike up it, turn right. You will find the next half hour or so of hiking a challenge to the legs and your lungs.

Tunnel Trail proper passes through the four geologic formations of the Eocene epoch on its three-and-a-half-mile length. At the trailhead Coldwater Sandstone predominates, and the steeply-tilted slabs of this stone are what make this section such an effort.

The trail switches back and forth through rocky outcroppings of this rock, finally heading straight up the ridgeline separating the two main forks of Mission Creek. Views across the west fork canyon to Cathedral and La Cumbre peaks help soften the effort. In three-quarters mile the path turns right, then heads up a rocky section fortified with railroad ties and around a large knoll that marks the end of this formation. A large peace symbol painted on the face of the cliff in the 1960s will provide notice that you are about almost at the end of the tough hiking. I have often wondered who painted this 30-foot-high sign and just how they were able to get there to do it. Perhaps one of you might know.

There is one last steep climb, then suddenly you round a corner and Mission Falls comes into view, a half-mile away across the canyon. Rarely does water flow over its wide lip, but it is the per-

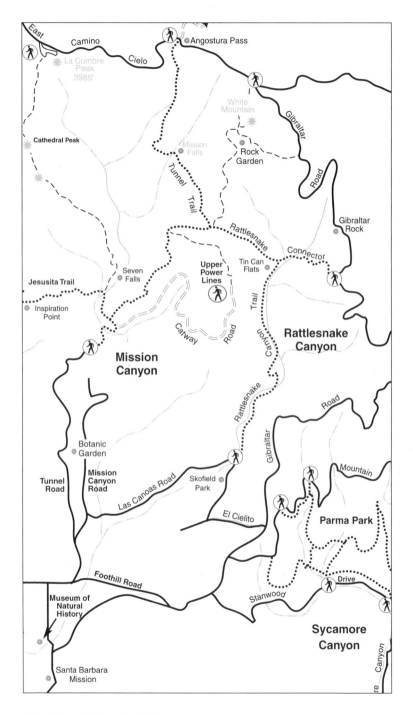

East Camino Cielo

Angostura Pass

La Cumbre Peak 3985'

White Mountain

Gibraltar Road

Cathedral Peak

Mission Falls

Rock Garden

Gibraltar Rock

Tunnel Trail

Rattlesnake

Connector

Seven Falls

Upper Power Lines

Tin Can Flats

Jesusita Trail

Catway Road

Trail

Rattlesnake Canyon

Inspiration Point

Mission Canyon

Rattlesnake Canyon

Botanic Garden

Gibraltar Road

Mountain

Tunnel Road

Mission Canyon Road

Las Canoas Road

Skofield Park

Parma Park

El Cielito

Drive

Foothill Road

Stanwood

Museum of Natural History

Sycamore Canyon

re Canyon

Santa Barbara Mission

fect place for a lunch stop. From here it is 20 minutes of very easy hiking around the upper end of the canyon to the falls.

If you look closely on the right you will spy a small, almost unnoticeable path leading up to the right. This off-trail route will take you directly up and over the thin ridgeline on which the peace symbol is painted. It is a scramble getting up and over the ridge, but the views are spectacular, there are numerous perches upon which to spend a bit of time, and most importantly it will take you across and down to the power lines, allowing you to make a loop out of your hike up Tunnel Trail. I often head up to the falls for lunch, drop back down to this point, and then make my way across the ridge and back down via the power line road.

Continuing up Tunnel Trail on your way to the falls you will encounter a large saddle where a second geological formation is encountered—the easily weathered Cozy Dell Shale. Here you will find a connector trail leading down into the upper end of Rattlesnake Canyon.

A quarter-mile beyond the connector trail large walls of tawny sandstone begin to appear, marking the end of the shale and the beginning of a third layer of rock, the rugged and highly scenic crags of Matilija Sandstone. A half-mile farther along, look for the short path leading over to the falls. There you'll find a sandstone bench marking the upper edge of the 200-foot-high Mission Falls. In springtime, with the creek flowing at its maximum, the spot is an ideal sunbathing and picnicking area. The view is breathtaking. It is also a wonderful place to view the sunset, but if you stay late be sure to bring a flashlight along for the trip back to the car.

After crossing the creek, the trail wanders for a half-mile through the sandstone. Then, as the canyon narrows, you enter the fourth layer, the Juncal Formation, a shale which weathers readily to form clay hills. After this, the trail then meanders back and forth around small rounded knolls formed by the easily weathered rock to a saddle at East Camino Cielo known as Angostura Pass. La Cumbre Peak is an additional three-quarters mile (and 600 feet of elevation gain) to the west on the paved road.

Hardcore hikers will make it all the way up to the top of La Cumbre Peak. Those who are just a little bit crazy make the return trip via Cathedral Peak. The route down is off-trail and requires quite a bit of effort along the way, but at day's end, savoring the magnificence of what you have accomplished, you will be well pleased with yourself. A caution: this is hardcore. Make sure you allow yourself plenty of time to make it all the way down. The Cathedral ridgeline is not where you want to be after dark.

5. Seven Falls

TRAIL INFORMATION
Distance—1.5 miles to Seven Falls; 1.5 miles to Mission Falls
Elevation Gain—400' to Seven Falls; 1750' to the intersection Tunnel Trail at
    Mission Falls
Difficulty—Easy to Seven Falls; hardcore to Mission Falls
Topo—Santa Barbara
URL—http://www.sb-outdoors.org Keyword Search: Seven Falls

HIGHLIGHTS
Both the east and west forks of Mission Creek have eroded through the
highly resistant Coldwater Sandstone, forming in the upper off-trail
sections a series of narrows with deep pools, steep falls, and rich green
fern coverings—the fabled Seven Falls. For hundreds of thousands of
years erosive forces have eaten away at the Matilija Sandstone that forms
the bulk of La Cumbre Peak, and the grinding power of the sand and water
as they tumble downhill has etched magical shapes in the rock formations
below. One of these is a series of small falls and deep potholes known for
more than a century as Seven Falls.

DIRECTIONS
See directions for Tunnel Trail.

SETTING THE SCENE

Seven Falls was as much admired in the 1800s as it is now. In
Geography of Santa Barbara (1899), Francis W. Conrad wrote:

The music of falling water comes at intervals upon the ear.
The uneven trail winding around huge rocks, upon the edge
of precipitous banks or plying through the slippery stones at
the bottom of the creek, gives just enough elements of
beauty, danger, grandeur and loneliness to make a ride here
thoroughly enjoyable. Near the head of the canyon is what is
known as "Seven Falls." The water here falls into seven stone
basins in succession. The rocky banks are broadcast with
delicate maiden hair ferns and are green with moss. This is a
favorite resort. At the head of the canyon is a large rock
[Mission Falls] over which the water leaps with considerable
force in the rainy season. This fall can be seen from the city.

THE HIKE

To reach this beautiful glen, continue past the turnoff to Tunnel Trail and follow Jesusita Trail for two hundred yards until it drops down into the west fork of Mission Canyon. The falls are a quarter-mile up this fork.

The easiest route to the falls is via the creek. Rock hopping, a bit of scrambling, and a few creek crossings lead to the falls. Just as you start upstream there is also a trail of sorts on the left. This will take you through the chaparral partway up to Seven Falls, but at some point you will need to follow the creek.

In the spring, and usually the summer months too, the water will be flowing at the falls, allowing you to swim in the deeper pools or—if conditions are right—slide off the edge of the last fall. The pool below is usually plenty deep, but those of us who are cautious check the pool first for any hidden obstacles.

If you are adventurous you might consider hiking up into the upper canyon. The biggest challenge will be getting past the falls. Make your way around what is now a large orange tree (how many of you remember when it was a small seedling?) and look for the toeholds chipped into the rock to help you up the first ten-foot wall. From the small apron on top it may seem impossible to get any farther, but a few short maneuvers will get you past the last two pools and allow you to hike on. A caution: don't try to make it past by climbing up the rock. It is easy to get stuck, and extremely dangerous.

There are several waterfalls in the next few hundred yards, and at some point you will run into flowing water no matter how dry or late in the season it is. Prior to the early 1900s Seven Falls always flowed year round, but not so after the tunnel was cut through the Santa Ynez Mountains, diverting much of the water that would have otherwise percolated downward.

A quarter-mile will bring you to another set of pools. These are formed by a last upthrust layer of Coldwater Sandstone, and they are well worth the hike up to them.

It is also possible to scramble up the creek and eventually reach Tunnel Trail at Mission Falls, creating a strenuous but exciting loop. Look for a fork in the creek leading off to the right next to the large stand of prickly pear. The route is straight up the creekbed, steeply up and over lots boulders that choke the creek all the way to Mission Falls. A brush-choked path leads up the right side of the 200-foot waterfall.

6. Inspiration Point

TRAIL INFORMATION
Distance—.75 miles to the bridge; 1.25 miles to the creek crossing; 2 miles
to Inspiration Point
Elevation Gain—800'
Difficulty—moderately strenuous
Topo—Santa Barbara
URL—http://www.sb-outdoors.org Keyword Search: Inspiration Point

HIGHLIGHTS
Inspiration Point is formed by the extension of the ridgeline leading off the
southeast side of Cathedral Peak. Near the bottom the ridgeline flattens
out, forming a promontory from which you can enjoy excellent views over
the city. The vista across the western flank of the Santa Ynez Mountains is
particularly enchanting.

DIRECTIONS
See directions for Tunnel Trail.

THE HIKE

As you continue past the turnoff to Tunnel Trail, though there
are no trail signs marking its beginning, you are just about to start
up the eastern end of the Jesusita Trail. Look for the turnoff on the
left, which officially marks the trail's beginning.

A short section of trail leads down and across the west fork of
Mission Canyon. Along the way you get quick peeks up the canyon
to Cathedral Peak and, if you look closely, the canyon walls that
form Seven Falls.

Many hikers head up toward Inspiration Point in the later afternoon, both because of the lighting, which turns golden in the later
part of the day, and the cool shade. Much of the 600-foot climb to
the top of the ridge is in the shade by then.

Most of the hiking is relatively easy, with plenty of switchbacks
to help you gain elevation without gaining too much horizontal distance. For most of the way you'll find yourself immersed in chaparral, although the occasional view back across Mission Canyon and
up toward Tunnel Trail provides relief from the canopy of chaparral
overhead.

Then, at what seems like it might be the high point, you cross a
small saddle that provides a hint of what the views up on top will be
like. Ahead of you are the power lines and, just beyond, the high

point. Suddenly you come out of the chaparral and onto a wide dirt road. Across the road you will see the continuation of the Jesusita Trail. Fifty yards will take you to one of Santa Barbara's nicest viewpoints. Exclamations of delight, the feeling of joy at being here, and many moments of quiet contemplation are sure to greet you here.

Though you might think you've made it to Inspiration Point, you haven't actually gotten there quite yet. Head back down the trail to the road, turn right (toward Santa Barbara), and look for a narrow trail leading off into the chaparral. It looks more like a game trail, but actually it is quite nice. A hundred yards of meandering, at times with head ducked to avoid the overhanging ceanothus, will bring you to a series of boulder fields where you will find the actual point. You will know you are there if you find the initials that have been carved into the sandstone.

7. Upper Power Lines

TRAIL INFORMATION
Distance—1.75 miles to power lines; 2.25 to intersection with Tunnel Trail
Elevation Gain—1250' to power lines; 1600' to intersection with Tunnel Trail
Difficulty—moderately strenuous to strenuous
Topo—Santa Barbara
URL—http://www.sb-outdoors.org Keyword Search: Power Lines

HIGHLIGHTS
A must hike for power walkers. The dirt road is open and fairly easily traversed by most hikers. The route continues around the upper end of the east fork of Mission Canyon, bringing you high up on the mountain within a relatively short distance. There are excellent views across Rattlesnake Canyon and the Montecito coastline. An off-trail route continues across a high ridgeline to Tunnel Trail, making a loop possible. Mountain bikers make use of the road quite frequently as a conditioning ride.

DIRECTIONS
See directions for Tunnel Trail.

THE HIKE
The first time I was asked if I wanted to hike up to the power lines I thought my friend was crazy. After all, he knew I'd rather be out on a rock scramble or busting through the brush than hiking on a dirt road. But that was before. Now I know what it is really like.

Hiking on the dirt road is fairly pleasant, and though it gains elevation quite rapidly, it isn't nearly as steep as the roads you'll find in the San Ysidro and Romero areas. Not having to worry about your footing also makes it easier to enjoy the views, and the higher you go the nicer and nicer the views get. This is a great walk for those who like walking and talking with a friend or two, and you can actually walk side by side, which is pretty hard to do when you are on a narrow trail, having to watch your every step.

The road ends abruptly near the upper power line, and there are plenty of places to stop for a while, catch your breath, and sample the sights and minty chaparral aromas. The surprise for me was what lay in store just beyond the road's edge. Cut into the thicker ceanothus, chamise, and manzanita is an almost-hidden trail, which I discovered leads up over the high ridgeline right above the power lines to Tunnel Trail.

Without a moment's hesitation I quickly headed up the trail. A switchback or two brought me up on the ridgeline proper, which became more of a knifeblade, a thin, rocky edge leading west to a high point a hundred feet or so higher than my current location. By this time the trail had ended, turning into more of a goats' path but always open enough to get through pretty easily, and never hard to follow.

What views! Like most rocky ridges, this one had plenty of ups and downs, though mostly ups, leading me to the high point, which I found out later was almost directly above the peace symbol painted on the cliffs just off Tunnel Trail on one side and the Rattlesnake connector on the other.

I sat near the high point for a while; the views weren't that much different from the ones back down near the power lines, but what a difference. Sitting in the middle of the mountain, perched on my own piece of the rock, I knew I had found my place.

Continuing on I found myself dropping quickly. Using the chaparral on either side for handholds made the down climbing much easier. Before I knew it I found myself sliding out onto Tunnel Trail at the Mission Falls viewpoint.

8. Cathedral Peak

TRAIL INFORMATION
Distance—2 miles to Cathedral Peak; 2.75 miles to La Cumbre Peak
Elevation Gain—2350′ to Cathedral Peak; 2950′ to La Cumbre Peak
Difficulty—hardcore

Topo—Santa Barbara
URL—http://www.sb-outdoors.org Keyword Search: Cathedral Peak

HIGHLIGHTS

From Santa Barbara, the Mission Crags dominate the skyline. On the left side of Mission Canyon a rocky shoulder rises from its depths, forming a long, steep, and picturesque profile. If you can imagine yourself climbing up that ridgeline, leaping from boulder to boulder, you will have a sense of the feeling you will get. Climbs such as this are for those who do not mind the hard effort that comes before the well-earned reward. It is hard to imagine what it is like to be there atop Cathedral Peak, unless, of course, you have already been there.

DIRECTIONS

See Tunnel Trail for directions.

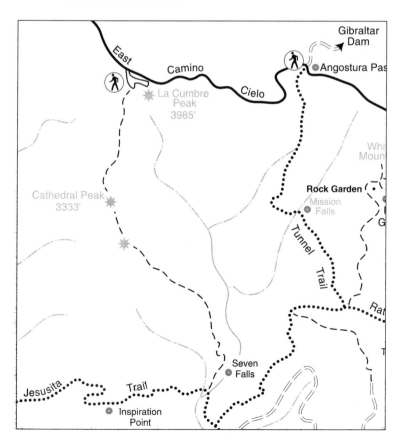

SETTING THE SCENE

For many millions of years, as erosion from the high interior mountains brought huge loads of sand down the rivers to the sea, a massive layer of sand began to form, more than 500 feet thick. Successive layers of other material covered this rock and as the earth began to buckle under the force of the movement of monumental pieces of the earth's crust, the pressure solidified this sand into a series of thick layers and began to turn them skyward.

The process of erosion continued, breaking down the sandstone. Along the mountain wall, cracks began to appear in its flanks and perhaps a million years afterward, the first creeks began to carve out the canyons. For unknown reasons, portions of the bedrock remained intact, resisting erosion. While on either side of them the canyons began to take on more defined shapes, the peaks seemed to rise even higher, thousands of feet above the coastline.

This is how we come to have these peaks: La Cumbre, Cathedral, Montecito, and White Mountain. High above us, they are sentinels, beacons of yellowish white light that draw many of us to them. And so we climb them.

THE HIKE

To reach the start of the hike to Cathedral Peak continue past the turnoff to Tunnel Trail and follow Jesusita Trail for 200 yards until it drops down into the west fork of Mission Canyon.

Just as you start upstream, a trail of sorts leads up into the chaparral on the left side of the creek. Follow this for about 50 yards until you come to a six-foot-high wall. Instead of climbing it, look to the left. You will spot a small opening that appears to be going straight up a chute. It does, but quickly opens to become a more of a hiker's trail. Nevertheless, from here on the route is more of a scramble than a hike.

The narrow route is almost completely covered by chaparral and is very steep. You will find yourself using branches to help you over the boulders and up the hill. After a few minutes of hard climbing the trail levels out and turns up the canyon. Look for a small trail leading off to the right to a promontory. You will find yourself looking almost directly down on Seven Falls and the best views of the pools from anywhere but a helicopter.

The trail you have been on thus far is actually a route up and around Seven Falls. If you should continue straight ahead on it you would find yourself dropping down into the upper canyon, beyond the narrow gorge.

Look for a small trail leading up to the left just after the promontory. This is the Cathedral Peak trail. The first part continues in the chaparral and gets even steeper in places. What you are still doing is making your way up the side of the ridge. Just when your legs need a break you will find yourself coming out onto the ridge itself. It is quite a feeling to step onto the sandstone boulders of the ridge and look directly across at the Tunnel Trail or down into the upper end of the canyon.

Now the adventure really begins. Below you on the right you are looking almost directly down at the upper pools in Mission Canyon. Your eyes can trace the route from there up the right fork of the canyon to Mission Falls and to La Cumbre Peak looming well overhead.

From here the route is nothing less than spectacular. The ridge is about fifty feet wide, filled with huge, beautiful sandstone boulders all the way to the top, and plenty of places where you will use your hands to get up and over or around them. Along the way you will find lots of places to sit and relax and, magically, graceful Coulter pines here and there growing out of the rocky recesses.

It is a grind to the top—no doubt. If you aren't in shape you will regret it, and even if you are you will still find this route challenging. Finally, after several hours of climbing you will be nearing the top. The last section is extremely steep, which makes the views even more spectacular. Then, 2,300 vertical feet later, you will suddenly find yourself topping out on the Mission Crags, and glad for the chance to rest for a while.

Once your breath has returned to a semblance of normal and some of the rubbery feeling has gone from your legs, look for the register tucked away in the recesses of one of the rocks. It is worth reading what others have had to say.

You are almost, but not quite, at Cathedral Peak at this point. Standing on one of the higher rocks you can see its toothy point just off to the north. The trail continues on to it. As you approach the peak be very careful. The ridge becomes very sharp, and at places, if you slipped the fall would be much longer than you would ever want. The drop off the peak itself is 300 feet.

Should you want to continue on, it is possible to do so. The route is sketchy but makeable all the way to the top of La Cumbre Peak. Drop down off the back side of Cathedral Peak and then make your way across the rocky ledges you can see ahead of you. Once you reach the last of these outcroppings look for a rough trail leading several hundred feet almost directly down to the saddle between Cathedral and La Cumbre Peaks. From there it is a 900-foot gain to the top of La Cumbre. If you watch for cut branches and footprints you should be able to find your way up without too much difficulty.

A warning: This is perhaps the most hardcore route in the front country. Make sure you have plenty of time if you attempt to make it all the way. Even once you're at the top, it is still a long way down Tunnel Trail if you loop back that way.

9. The Rock Garden

TRAIL INFORMATION
Distance—2 miles to the Rattlesnake connector; 2.75 miles to the Rock Garden
Elevation Gain—1600' to Rattlesnake Connector; 2850' to the Rock Garden
Difficulty—hardcore
Topo—Santa Barbara
URL—http://www.sb-outdoors.org Keyword Search: Rock Garden

HIGHLIGHTS
Those of you who have been to the Playground you will understand what is meant by a garden of rocks. There are no trails but many small openings that lead throughout the hundred acres or so of bedrock. There are all sorts of shapes and sizes and lots of nooks and crannies and caves and tunnels to keep you busy for quite a while. The hike getting there is not easy, but that is as it should be.

DIRECTIONS
See Tunnel Trail for directions.

SETTING THE SCENE
My friend Bob Hardy told me I should hike up Tunnel Trail, then up across the ridgeline leading over to the power lines.

"When you are at the top of the ridge look up to the north," he told me. "Right below you will be the Rattlesnake connector and beyond that a ridge leading up to a series of high rocks. I think there's a trail going up that ridge. See if you can find it."

Several weeks later I hiked up to the high point Bob had described and sat there studying the upper ridge and the rocks up at the top. I thought I could make out a trail going up through the thick chaparral-covered ridge, but I wasn't quite sure if it was my imagination or wishful thinking. A week later Bob and I hiked up to Mission Falls, and on the way back we ventured a way out onto

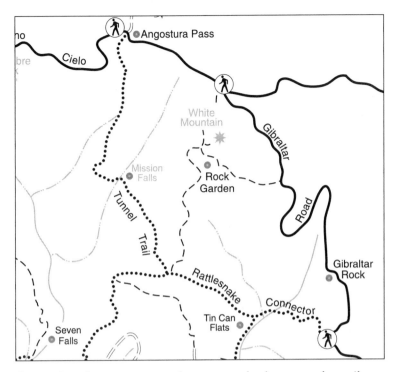

the Rattlesnake connector and sure enough, there was the trail, cut so you could barely see it. We followed it a way, verifying its existence, then decided to come back another time, determined to see where it would lead.

THE HIKE

Though it is 1,600 feet of elevation gain to the Rattlesnake Connector, getting there is the easy part. Bob and I had spotted the trail on an earlier hike. Now was the time to find out what it was like, or if it even went where we thought it did.

The route up the ridgeline we had found the week before was just 50 feet up from Tunnel Trail, hidden enough so you wouldn't spot it if you weren't looking for it. Bent over, we made our way under the low-hanging brush and started up the trail. The first part goes through a narrow opening and over a small knoll. This part was easy. But then the work began, a steep uphill climb directly up the ridge and completely covered with chaparral, a gain of about 400 feet straight up.

Finally we reached a knoll. Still surrounded by chamise, but only waist high here, we could take measure of where we were.

Directly in front and above us we could see where the Matilija Sandstone began, steep headwalls. Unlike the Cathedral Peak hike, which proceeds directly up the thin ridgeline, what was in front of us was more like a wall. Rather than assaulting this from the side, as at Cathedral Peak, we were coming at it from the front, head on.

Here the real climbing began, in and out of the boulders, up over rocky ledges, the route-finding a little bit more difficult— almost but not quite rock climbing. There are places along the way that you will really appreciate, slabs of rock jumbled on top of each other with little openings and beautifully sculpted sides. There is one I liked the best. Fifteen feet long, ten feet wide, and perhaps three feet thick, it lay atop a series of others, nearly level, a great spot to rest and take in the views. What was most impressive to me was the eye-level view I had from there of Cathedral Peak.

I looked up, a bit dismayed. We were still nowhere near the top! I was getting pretty tired but I trudged on, knowing it wasn't much farther. The trail continued to wind its way to the top, and manzanita began to predominate as we reached the 3,500-foot foot level, its wonderfully green leaves and rich red limbs a perfect contrast to the orange-reds and yellows of the rock. A final climb brought us to the top.

In front of us was a huge field, boulders that seemed to go on and on. The pine forests were everywhere, providing a distinctly different character from that of the Playground. My first thought was of a fairyland, like that in Bryce Canyon, spires of enchanting colors and shapes and thin openings leading in and out of them.

As we neared the top of one of the many formations, Bob and I sat for a while and looked out on what lay below us. There were rocks everywhere, huge ones, thirty to fifty feet high. The pines were almost as numerous, rising out from the spaces between the boulders. Manzanita clung to the fringes of the rock, covering the ground in front of us like a garden.

"It's a rock garden," Bob said after a while.

"Yes it is," I thought, and this is how it got its name.

RATTLESNAKE CANYON

Rattlesnake Canyon serpentines its way up into the Santa Ynez Mountains, its name appropriate: the gently curving canyon has the shape of a rattler sunbathing on a deserted sand bar. Though Rattlesnake Creek is actually a tributary of Mission Creek, it has a character and a history all its own.

I have always loved the drive up Las Canoas to the Rattlesnake trailhead. The houses are beautiful, and the countryside has a wildness unusual for its close proximity to the city. Situated on the back side of the Riviera, thick oaks are found on the shady hillsides, in sharp contrast to the open wildflower- and grass-covered slopes of the sunny side of the hill.

Arriving at the entrance to the canyon is a treat in itself. The narrow, sandstone-block bridge is quaint, a reminder of times when this was truly wild country. Skofield Park is on one side of the bridge, thirty-five acres with activities ranging from overnight camping to volleyball and barbecues. The wilderness park is across the road on the north side of the bridge. Its hiking trail will lead you into the upper end of the canyon, and if your legs are willing, routes lead over into Mission Canyon or up onto Gibraltar Road for a bit of relaxation at the edge of the ice-cube shaped rock, where climbers can usually be found clinging to the wall.

Rattlesnake Canyon has seen constant activity since early Mission days. In the 1790s, water was supplied to the Mission and the presidio through a ditch from Mission Creek—thus giving Las Canoas it name: *canoas* in Spanish means "flumes." These flumes funneled the precious water flowing down Rattlesnake Canyon into Mission Creek for use during periods of scarcity. Chumash helped dig the channel and lay the tiles lining the flumes and constructed a temporary dam of brush, earth, and rocks to store the water.

Eventually, in the years 1790 to 1795, artisans were sent from Mexico to assist in the building of houses and more permanent water storage facilities. Initially a large stone dam and an aqueduct were built in Mission Creek, and in 1808 another dam was added in Rattlesnake Canyon. With Indian labor the fieldstone-and-mortar structure was built across the creek about a half-mile up from Las Canoas Road.

While remnants of the dam still exist, sediments have filled in behind, eliminating the reservoir and carving a V-shaped notch in the middle of the dam. However, the pool below, shaded by alder and bay and surrounded by wood ferns and the colorful tiger lily, still provides welcome relief from the hot afternoon sun.

Rattlesnake Canyon's more recent history is the product of a single family: the Skofields. Once the entire canyon was owned by Ray Skofield, a wealthy New Yorker who moved to Santa Barbara in the 1920s with his family, including son Hobart.

Hobart took on the role of caretaker for the canyon wilderness area. In the early 1930s he planted a number of pines and, placing rawhide baskets on either side of his palomino horse, Hobart packed the young trees in them and started up to the meadow. But apparently the horse bucked part way up the trail when it caught sight of the trees waving from its backside. In the end Hobart secured the aid of a friend, and together they carried the trees the rest of the way, using an old ladder as a carrying platform.

During the next few years Hobart watered the pines faithfully until they were able to persist on their own. Unfortunately, these trees burned in the Coyote Fire. However, in 1966 the Sierra Club took on the project of replanting them. On two February weekends 100 holes were dug and six-inch Aleppo pines were planted. Water was carried up from the creek in one-gallon containers throughout the spring, summer, and fall until the following rainy season. As you walk past them when you are hiking in the upper canyon, say thanks to Hobart and the Sierra Clubbers, whose work made their existence possible.

In 1970, Hobart Skofield helped complete the transformation of the canyon by offering the upper 450 acres of the canyon for $150,000, less than half its appraised value, on condition it be made into a wilderness park.

That is why, when you visit the canyon today, you will see a sign prominently displayed that proclaims this area to be the Rattlesnake Canyon Wilderness Area. In keeping with this tradition of wildness, mountain bikes have been banned from the park, though you may occasionally see an outlaw rider flash by.

10. Rattlesnake Canyon

TRAIL INFORMATION

Distance—.75 to the first creek crossing; 2.5 miles to the connector trail leading to Tunnel Trail; 3 miles to the intersection with Gibraltar Road

Elevation Gain—200' to the first creek crossing; 1000' to the connector trail leading to Tunnel Trail; 1550' to the intersection with Gibraltar Road

Difficulty—Moderate

Topo—Santa Barbara

URL—http://www.sb-outdoors.org Keyword Search: Rattlesnake Canyon

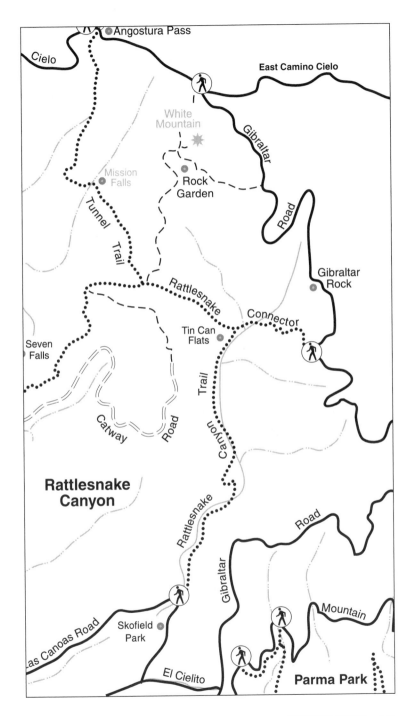

HIGHLIGHTS

Rattlesnake Canyon is filled with cascading waterfalls and deep pools. The alder cover provides shade and a lovely green canopy. If you hike up the creek from the trailhead or take one of the many side trails leading down to the creek, you'll find the remains of a dam built in the early 1800s to serve the Mission. Within just a few minutes' drive from downtown Santa Barbara you can be hiking up this picturesque canyon, lost in its wilderness beauty. A connector leading to Tunnel Trail makes it possible to hike all the way to the crest.

DIRECTIONS

From the Santa Barbara Mission, drive up Mission Canyon Road to Foothill Road. Turn right, then left several hundred yards later (by the fire station). Continue up Mission Canyon past Tunnel Road to Las Canoas. Turn right and continue a mile and a half to an open area immediately preceding a narrow bridge. You'll find a large sign there noting the start of the Rattlesnake Canyon Trail.

THE HIKE

The trail begins just before the entrance to Skofield Park, near a delicately shaped stone bridge. From there, cross the creek and follow a short connector trail to a wider dirt road. For many decades this was a buggy road, running alongside the creek to a point about three-quarters of a mile upstream where a prominent layer of sandstone crosses the creek. This was the location of a stone quarry from which much of the stonework in Montecito was derived.

The old buggy road rises gradually through rolling sage-covered hills and the Sespe Formation, then heads back to the creek and the first of a series of narrows created as the stream eroded through successive layers of Coldwater Sandstone during the Pleistocene mountain-building process.

Numerous side trails lead off the main path through the sage to small oak meadows, and they provide access to waterfalls as well as to the old Mission Dam. Beware of the poison oak, though!

After the narrows, the trail crosses the creek and follows a set of switchbacks up a steep hill that opens to a large grass meadow marked by a series of Hobart Skofield's scattered pines. Above the meadow, the trail switches back and forth several more times to a point about 200 feet above the canyon floor. From there it levels for three-quarters of a mile through chaparral shrubs that form a pleasant corridor.

A short drop down to the creek brings you to a cluster of bigleaf maple that seems to guard the entrance to the second of the

Coldwater narrows. The walls are vertical and the sunlight generally indirect, as alder and maple crowns filter the sun's rays, creating a cool, verdant feeling. This is an enchanting place and a worthy spot for lunch or a few minutes' rest.

The next several hundred yards take you through the narrows and one of the most beautiful canyon sections in the Santa Barbara foothills. Cascading waterfalls, pools, the canopy of alder above you, and the sound of the rushing water make this very special.

A half-mile more walking brings you to a large triangular meadow known as Tin Can Flat, for many years a familiar landmark. There, a small cabin was built by a man named William O'Connor.

"The homesteading laws required that a dwelling be erected on each section," according to Public Historian Gregory King, so "O'Connor went into town, collected empty five-gallon kerosene cans, flattened them, and had them carried back on a mule to a site he liked. Cutting branches from the nearby chaparral, O'Connor quickly put together a frame constructed from the branches and used the flattened kerosene tins to shingle the roof and tack up walls. The floor was provided by Mother Nature—the ground."

Years later, adventurous boys used Tin Can Shack as an overnight retreat, and it was even mentioned in several of the early-day guide books. But shortly after the 1925 earthquake a forest fire burned through the canyon and destroyed the structure. If you are keen-eyed you may still spot some of the tin scattered out in the meadow.

County records show that a 160-acre section was also home-steaded in the canyon. John Stewart built a rough adobe on the side of a steep hill, where he lived for several years. This changed in the 1920s when New York millionaire Ray Skofield moved to Santa Barbara and began to buy up the property in Rattlesnake Canyon, 456 acres in total, from Las Canoas Road to Tin Can Flat. He then started construction of a mansion overlooking the canyon. The work ceased after the Depression began. Later the villa was developed into the Mt. Calvary Retreat.

From Tin Can Flat, which marks the beginning of the Cozy Dell Shale, you can either follow the trail through the meadow, cross the creek to the east side, and hike three-quarters mile up to Gibraltar Road, or you can turn left and follow the connector trail up to its intersection with Tunnel Trail, which provides a full day's loop.

FOR THE ADVENTUROUS

For those who are adventurous, several other options are available. After hiking to the upper end of the meadows, instead of continuing up to Gibraltar Road, turn upstream. In a short distance you will enter a third set of narrows formed in the most dense of the mountain rock, Matilija Sandstone. The hike isn't easy, but the effort is rewarded. For a half-mile a series of waterfalls and pools cascade down the slender channel one after the other.

Eventually you will find yourself climbing up onto Gibraltar Road near Flores Flats, once the home of the Brotherhood of the Sun and now a private residence. To return the easy way, walk down Gibraltar Road past the climbing area and then take the connector trail back down into the canyon.

Once you reach the narrow canyon below Tin Can Flat, you can head straight down the creek rather than taking the trail. This isn't particularly difficult, though it is slower and involves a lot of scrambling. The reward for your efforts will be quiet solitude and the exhilaration of boulder-hopping, my favorite creekside activity. Take care climbing down the many boulders and, of course, watch out for poison oak. There is plenty of it.

Eventually you will come upon a trail leading down the east side of Rattlesnake Canyon. It is narrower and not as well maintained, but it is abundantly shaded—more a tunnel through the chaparral than an opening, thus providing a touch of coolness on warm afternoons.

11. Skofield Park

HIGHLIGHTS
A beautiful set of meadows and oak forests provide the setting for one of Santa Barbara's most beautiful picnic and group camping areas. The 35-acre retreat provides all of the facilities for a great afternoon barbecue. The Rattlesnake Canyon Wilderness Area is not far away, and kids will love exploring in the creek. The road leading into the park also makes a loop around the park. This provides a great short hike for younger kids, leading past large boulders and through wonderfully sculpted oaks.

DIRECTIONS
See directions for Rattlesnake Canyon.

PARK HISTORY
In the 1930s Skofield Park was first used by Rancheros Visitadores as a staging ground for their annual trip from Santa Barbara Mission to Mission Santa Ínes. The men's riding group was founded in 1930 by Ray Skofield, Ed Borein, Dwight Murphy,

T. M. Storke, and others as a celebration of Santa Barbara's Spanish history. The riders began their annual pilgrimage from the mission, riding up over the Santa Ynez Mountains to a series of camps in the Santa Ynez Valley.

The riders needed a staging area from which they could depart and Ray Skofield had the perfect place in Rattlesnake Canyon. Hobart built a road to the meadow area, along with other facilities, and in 1937 the Rancheros used portions of the Skofield property before heading out on the ride.

Use of the camp by the Visitadores was suspended during World War II, but was resumed in 1946 and thereafter was used each year until 1964. In 1950 the group asked Hobart if he would be willing to sell the property, which he did for $15,000. More campsites were built, utilities were added, and a parking area was constructed on the north side of the creek, developing the site into a very comfortable campground. Not too long after, the Rancheros also began permitting youth groups to use the camp.

The individual campsites were tucked away on the edges of the main meadow, areas which now constitute the picturesque picnic sites hundreds of Santa Barbara families use each year. Los Amigos, The Mavericks, Los Vaqueros, Los Borrachos, Los Flojos, and The Vigilantes were among some of the camp names used by the riders.

By the early 1960s, however, traffic due to the increase in nearby residences was making it more and more difficult for the riders to make it down to the Mission. In 1964 the group offered the land to the city. After a brief study the Parks Commission recommended the purchase and that it be named "Skofield Camp."

The area is now known as Skofield Park. It is still the most beautiful park you will find for a picnic, a walk by the creek, and a hike up into the mountain wall. Perhaps, if you listen carefully, you will hear the laughter of the Rancheros Visitadores and the smell of their steaks sizzling on charcoal grates as they shared tales over the campfire and readied themselves for the next morning's ride.

If you would like more information about picnicking or overnight camping, please call (805) 564-5418.

12. Rock Garden Loop

TRAIL INFORMATION

Distance—.5 mile to the Rattlesnake Connector; 1.25 miles to the Tin Can Flat; 2.25 to the intersection with Tunnel Trail; 3.0 to the Rock Garden; 5.0 back to the car

Elevation Gain—800' loss to Tin CanFlat; 600' gain to the intersection with Tunnel Trail; 1950' to the Rock Garden; 1150' loss back to the car

Difficulty—Strenuous to the Tunnel Connector; hardcore for the loop

Topo—Santa Barbara

URL—http://www.sb-outdoors.org Keyword Search: Rock Garden

HIGHLIGHTS

This hike provides one of the most challenging and spectacular loops you will find anywhere in the Santa Ynez Mountains. It combines both trail hiking and off-trail scrambling, taking you down into Rattlesnake Canyon to the historic Tin Can Flat, then sharply up the connector to Tunnel Trail. An off-trail route takes you straight up a ridgeline to one of the most spectacular boulder fields in these mountains.

DIRECTIONS

From the Santa Barbara Mission drive up Mission Canyon Road to Foothill and turn right. Continue past the fire station. At the stop sign turn left onto Mountain Drive, follow it up to Sheffield Reservoir, turn left again and head straight uphill, continuing on until you reach Gibraltar Road. Park at the Gibraltar Rock climbing area, approximately 5 miles up the road.

SETTING THE SCENE

While most hikers tend to start their hikes in either Rattlesnake or Mission canyons from the lower trailheads, an often overlooked route into the upper ends of both of these canyons can be made from Gibraltar Road. Whether you are visiting the upper meadows in Rattlesnake Canyon or continuing up the connector to Tunnel Trail, this is a very pleasant starting point and most likely you will see far fewer people. I find this a nice alternate route to Mission Falls. One of the bonuses, too, is the opportunity for watching the evening sunset from atop Gibraltar Rock at the end of your hike.

When my friend Bob Hardy and I drove up Gibraltar Road one fine winter morning, we weren't heading to the falls, however. We were looking to see if it would be possible to make a loop hike via the Rock Garden, which we had discovered on a previous trip. The description which follows chronicles the hike.

THE HIKE

It was 8:30 A.M. and cold but that was okay—we both knew we would be doing a lot of uphill climbing, and we didn't want to lose any more perspiration than we had to. Gibraltar Rock was deserted when we pulled off the road and parked. We had decided to park here because it would allow us to split up the road walking.

We knew it was possible to hike down into Rattlesnake Canyon, take the connector up to Tunnel Trail, then make our way up to the Rock Garden, but we weren't sure if we could find a way from the garden over to the upper end of Gibraltar Road. In our minds we were sure we could, but there were no guarantees.

In any case, we would have to walk at least a mile or so back down the road. Rather than parking right by the Rattlesnake Connector, we decided to park further up, allowing us to do a little road walking at the start and another stretch of it at the end, rather than all of it at the end. Afterwards we both agreed this was the nicest way to do it.

Ten years ago you would have seen a trail sign marking the start of the Rattlesnake Connector, but there isn't one there now. Most likely you'll miss it when driving by, but we didn't have any problem spotting the trailhead as we walked down the road. We were still in the shade, and the air was crisp. However, the three-quarter-mile walk from the climbing area down to the connector didn't take too long.

The trail switched back and forth on the shady side of a small ridge, dropping several hundred feet. At the end of each of the turns Gibraltar Rock and the upper canyon were clearly visible. A half-mile of hiking brought us down into the canyon. Crossing the creek, we headed down the right side of Rattlesnake Canyon, and within a few minutes we were at the connector leading up to Tunnel Trail. What a nice way to visit this part of the Rattlesnake Wilderness area. Tin Can Flat is just a few yards around the corner.

We stopped for a few minutes under the oak canopy, resting on one of the large boulders there, stretching our legs for the uphill that faced us. The connector is short and sweet, steadily uphill, and takes you up 600 feet in just over a half-mile of walking. A half hour later we were up at the saddle, taking another rest break and getting ready for the big climb up the ridgeline to the Rock Garden.

The climb up to the top was tough, though not nearly as difficult as we thought it might be. Ducking under the chaparral that nearly covered the hidden trail, we were soon working our way almost directly up the ridge. An hour later we were in the boulders, having lunch, admiring the views, and sharing a few thoughts about the hike up.

The Rock Garden is at the apex of the high peaks on the right side of Mission Canyon, separating it from the Rattlesnake area. From town, its craggy face isn't quite as impressive as the pyramid-shaped peak leading up to Cathedral Peak; nevertheless, once you are up here at the top it is spectacular. The crest here has weathered more, forming a wider, more open area, several hundred acres in size, with all sorts of shapes formed in the sandstone.

As we explored in and out of the cracks and crevices I spotted one thin, 30-foot-high slab with bolts attached to it. The climbers had been here. It was a fairyland of mazes. The manzanita was waist high, making travel through it relatively easy, and there had been enough people up here to create small paths.

Bob and I spent an hour exploring the garden before we came to the moment we had been wondering about: the time when we would find out if we could make it over to Gibraltar Road without having to go back the way we had come. It turned out not to be too difficult.

As we headed east through the boulder- and manzanita-covered hillsides we began gaining elevation. The Rock Garden is not the high point of this peak; the high point is a quarter-mile away on a nondescript chaparral hill. As we made our way toward the hill we discovered the problem wasn't whether we could find a trail, it was that there were too many. Within a short distance we passed several intersections with small trails leading off into the chaparral.

Confused, we decided to try the trail leading to the high point, thinking it might continue over to the road. A surprise awaited us at the peak, where the trail suddenly ended. Attached by a four-by-four pole anchored solidly in the ground was a beautiful wooden sign proclaiming this to be WHITE MOUNTAIN.

Tracing our way back down, we finally found a small trail leading in the direction of Gibraltar Road. The route dropped quickly, the first half switching back and forth through the rocks and manzanita, the second half a tunnel of taller chaparral. Within twenty minutes we were on the road, at a point not too far from the area where hang gliders and parasailers begin their precipitous drops off the mountain wall.

The walk back down to the car took about thirty minutes and, though quite different from the hardcore hiking we had been doing for the past four hours, it was actually quite a treat to walk along the road, stopping here and there, looking back up at what we'd done—and savoring those moments and reminiscing about them all the way back to the car.

PARMA PARK

It is a mystery of sorts—there are almost no trail signs telling you where Parma Park begins, nor are the routes seemingly planned out. As you head up a hill and down through a canyon, suddenly you find yourself looking over at another trail shooting off, cutting up over a knoll or heading over to another part of the canyon. Rarely will you go more than a few hundred yards without spotting another trail shooting off to who knows where.

Actually it is kind of refreshing to find it this way, more a maze of trails that will take you here or there, depending on your mood and the shape you're in. Surprisingly, the park is one of Santa Barbara's best kept secrets, yet it is the largest block of undeveloped green space you will find anywhere in the city. Bounded by Stanwood Drive, Mountain Drive, El Cielito Road, and Coyote Road, the 200 acres of thickly wooded canyons, rolling chaparral, and grass-covered hillsides form a great horseback riding and hiking area.

The acreage was once owned by the Parma family. G.B. Parma came to Santa Barbara more than 120 years ago, established a grocery store on State Street, and promptly bought the tract of land in what was then the "far hills." Parma raised goats on the property.

Parma Park

Apparently it was those animals, intent on foraging the hillsides, who decided where the trails would go.

In 1973 Harold and Jack Parma, sons of the elder Parma, gave the land to the city to establish a natural preserve. "The community has been nice to us," Harold reminisced, "and we've been here so long. Every community should have some open space. I think it's precious, something we could do in return for the community" *(Santa Barbara News-Press)*.

There are lots of ins and outs, and unlike most trails, which head up through the chaparral, there is more than one way in and out. You'll find yourself, as I often do, making spur-of-the-moments choices as to which way you'll turn when you reach this turnoff or that one, meaning that most times you come to Parma Park you never quite take the same route twice.

13. West Side Canyon Walk

TRAIL INFORMATION:
Distance—Varies from 1 to 2.5 miles
Elevation Gain—350′
Difficulty—Easy to moderate
Topo—Santa Barbara
URL—http://www.sb-outdoors.org Keyword Search: Parma Park

HIGHLIGHTS
An excellent area to bring kids for their first hikes. Close to the city, yet a very remote feeling. There are trails leading in a variety of directions, making it possible to take a short hike or combine sections to create a 3- to 4-mile hike. The canyon section is covered by a beautiful oak forest. It is possible to create a 2.5-mile loop by walking along a short stretch of Mountain Drive.

DIRECTIONS
Take Sycamore Canyon Road north to Stanwood Drive. Turn left and continue .7 miles on Stanwood to a sharp turn in the road, where you will see the Parma Park sign. Park on either side of Stanwood, but please do not block the park entrance. There are several entrances to the upper canyon on El Cielito Road and Mountain Drive. To reach the upper entrances follow Stanwood .5 miles to El Cielito. The entrance into the upper meadows where the paragliders land is .1 mile on El Cielito. Or continue a quarter-mile to Mountain Drive. Turn right. The first Mountain

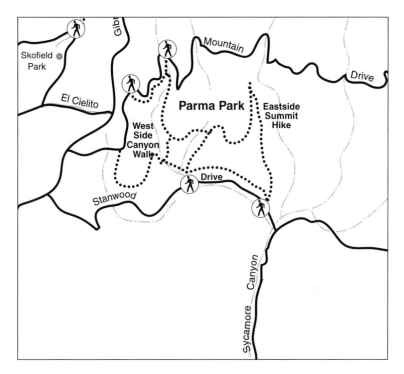

Drive trailhead is 50 yards along the way. It is .4 miles farther to a trailhead leading down into the west fork of Sycamore Creek.

THE HIKE

The first time I went hiking in Parma Park it had just finished raining and the water was cascading down Sycamore Creek. As I walked up the main road I noticed trails leading off to the east and west, but it was too wet to explore them so I continued up the road. It wasn't too long before I came to a fork in the road at the edge of a stand of tall eucalyptus trees. An owl, hidden somewhere in the upper branches, hooted again and again. I turned right and followed the road down to the creek, where I watched the water spill over the road. The owl continued to hoot, and the noise of the water provided a mesmerizing backdrop. The branches of the ancient oak trees along the path created fascinating patterns against the green hillsides. What a beautiful place, I thought as I retreated back to my car.

That was the first of many trips to the park. I especially like to go there in the springtime, when the creek is running, the hills are covered in green, and the flowers are in blossom. Though it is possible to wander almost anywhere, since there are so many intersecting trails, there are really two main sections to the park: the canyon section, which takes you up and around the west fork of Sycamore Creek, and the chaparral summit, which leads up the main ridge on the east side of Sycamore Creek to a vista point and then back down a secondary ridge through the chaparral-covered Rowe Trail.

From the locked gate at the bottom of Parma Park, a short walk up the main road leads to a picnic area. There are several tables under the oaks where you can enjoy a lunch, and your car is near enough that you can head out on a hike and then have lunch afterwards without having to take things with you.

From the picnic area there are three choices. To the right the Rowe Trail cuts across the creek and heads east to parallel Stanwood Drive. I usually follow this trail back from the summit loop hike rather than start out on it. The dirt road leads straight ahead up the east fork of Sycamore Creek. Two hundred yards lead you to the fork in the road I described previously. The right fork will take you up to the summit, the left fork up and around the hillsides to the west fork of the creek.

Immediately to the left, or west, of the picnic area is the route I prefer, which leads up into the canyon. (Perhaps there is something in me that prefers walking in a counter-clockwise direction when I make loop trips). The trail leads up into what appears to be a very narrow area, but as you go a bit farther into the canyon it opens into a very pretty oak-covered section. The creek is small, but the sound adds a very nice quality to place.

Off to the right a small trail veers up the hill. This leads up to the top of the hills and still another trail, which will take you into the upper canyon. This is the route back down if you continue all the way around on the loop.

Right beyond this you will cross to the left side of the creek, then start uphill and work your way out of the canyon. The trail turns back to the left as you climb, and then suddenly you come to a series of open meadows. From here the trail continues to climb through more and more meadows. There are houses on your left, but they are hidden enough to be not too intrusive.

You will begin to notice tall white poles in the meadows, some of them with flags attached. These are used by the paragliders to gauge the wind speed and direction as they come in for landings. The take-off point is on Gibraltar Road near the crest of the Santa Ynez Mountains.

As you continue up and around the edge of the meadows you will spy clusters of old, gnarled oaks and the dramatic shapes of beautifully-sculpted sandstone boulders. Near the top of the meadows the trail turns to the right toward the mountains and soon you will find yourself topping out on Mountain Drive. From this point you can return the way you came or, if you would like to make this a loop hike, follow Mountain Drive east for .4 miles until you reach a dirt road leading back down into the park. There is a cable across the road similar to what is down at the park entrance, and it is easy to spot.

The dirt road drops very gently down into the canyon, paralleling Mountain Drive (but just below it around the upper end of the canyon), then heading back south and down the left side of Sycamore Creek. A quarter-mile of walking brings you out onto the lower foothills, where you can take one of the short connector trails directly down to the picnic area or continue to the left until you reach the sycamore trees, where you will find the dirt road leading back to your car.

14. East Side Summit Hike

TRAIL INFORMATION:
Distance—Varies from a .5 mile to 3 miles
Elevation Gain—375'
Difficulty—Easy to moderate
Topo—Santa Barbara
URL—http://www.sb-outdoors.org Keyword Search: Parma Park

HIGHLIGHTS
An excellent area to bring kids for their first hikes. Close to the city, yet a very remote feeling. There are trails leading in a variety of directions, making it possible to take a short hike or combine sections to create a 3- to 4-mile hike. The summit hike follows a long ridge to a high point where there are views in all directions.

DIRECTIONS
Take Sycamore Canyon Road north to Stanwood Drive. Turn left and continue .7 miles on Stanwood to a sharp turn in the road, where you will see the Parma Park sign. Park on either side of Stanwood but please do not block the park entrance. There are several other smaller entry points into the park on Stanwood. The first is a hundred yards up Stanwood from Sycamore Canyon on the edge of a private driveway, the second .4 miles up Stanwood.

THE HIKE

From the picnic area near the park entrance you have two choices for the summit hike if you make it a loop trip. The Rowe Trail cuts through the picnic area and crosses the creek, then continues east, paralleling Stanwood Drive. As you near the Sycamore Canyon intersection the trail then turns north and heads steeply up a long ridgeline to the summit. You can then continue on down the next ridge back to your starting point.

However, I like to make this trek the other way around. Perhaps it is because I like to get up to the summit right away, enjoy my time there, and then putter my way back along the chaparral section via the Rowe Trail. In either case you will have a great hike.

To do the hike in the latter direction, continue on the dirt road straight up the east fork of Sycamore Creek. It isn't a long section but the oaks are beautiful and near the upper end the small forest of eucalyptus trees is very impressive. At the eucalyptus grove the trail splits. To the left is the west fork canyon section. To reach the summit turn right, drop down across the creek, then follow the road uphill. The road meanders alongside the creek for a bit then switches back to the right and climbs out of the canyon and up to a series of open, grassy meadows.

Gradually the road curves to the left around the hill and then heads straight for a quarter-mile, leading you up a series of undulating hills to the final knoll, which marks the summit. This is a great spot to stop for a while, and nearby you will find a marker.

The summit is an excellent spot to turn around and head back the way you came. An alternative is to make this a loop hike, which you can do by dropping back down the ridgeline that leads off to the side in the direction of Sycamore Canyon. The first drop down the fire break road is the steepest. As you get near the bottom of it, look for a trail on the right. Below here there are several trail sections that make the downhill much nicer. When you exit this first section of trail you'll spot another trail on the left leading off the ridge. This looks like the way to go, but it isn't. Continue along the right side of the ridge road. Just when it appears that you will have to go up a steep hill, you will see another trail section on the right. Continue on it.

As you near the bottom of the ridge, the Rowe Trail begins. The ridge route continues down to Stanwood Drive, almost directly across from Conejo Road. The Rowe Trail leads west and parallels Stanwood for a mile back to your starting point at the picnic area. This is a very pretty section, though there are quite a few ups and downs as you make you way along the hillside.

COLD SPRINGS CANYON

"Our favorite route to the main ridge was by a way called the Cold Springs Trail. . . . Beyond the apparent summit you found always other summits yet to be climbed. And all at once, like thrusting your shoulders out of a hatchway, you looked over the top.

"Then came the remarks. Some swore softly; some uttered appreciative ejaculation; some shouted aloud; some gasped; one man uttered three times the word 'Oh,'—once breathlessly, Oh! once in awakening appreciation, Oh! once in wild enthusiasm, OH! Then invariably they fell silent and looked.

"It left you breathless, wonder-stricken, awed. You could do nothing but look, and look, and look again, tongue-tied by the impossibility of doing justice to what you felt. And in the far distance, finally, your soul, grown big in a moment, came to rest on the great precipices and pines of the greatest mountains of all, close under the sky.

"In a little . . . the change had come to you, a change definite and enduring, which left your inner processes forever different from what they had been. . . . And often, perhaps a little wistfully . . . we spoke of how fine it would be to ride down into that land of mystery and enchantment, to penetrate one after the other the canons dimly outlined in the shadows cast by the westering sun . . . to see for ourselves what lay beyond."

STEWART EDWARD WHITE
The Mountains, 1904

The name "Cold Springs" conjures visions of emerald-green pools and enchanting waterfalls. I think of warm rocks on which I can rest after a quick dip into the refreshing waters, the cascading water splashing over the rocks deep into the summer months. It makes me think of when I was a kid and my friends and I would explore every little creek in search of the next great adventure.

If there is a canyon where the water runs clearer or lasts longer into the season that this, you must tell me where it is. Here, near the mountain crest, the upper walls of the Cold Springs canyons are formed by steep faces of shale. When it rains, the shaly clays absorb large quantities of water, slowly letting it percolate through the many layers until it reaches the canyon bottoms weeks—and even months—after the storms have passed.

But there is more to hiking in this canyon than the cool springs. The crest trail still leads to views which are as impressive as those seen by Stewart Edward White in 1904. Though the coastal area has changed considerably, once you reach Camino Cielo and gaze out over the backcountry you will find a land little changed since the Chumash roamed through it.

Thanks to the efforts of a few unknown trail builders, there are also several new routes that lead up into Cold Springs Canyon. On the east side it is now possible to make your trip up past the sandstone pools a loop hike, and a route around the west side of Tangerine Falls has also been opened up, providing access to the canyon above it. The trip up to the top of Montecito Peak is still one of the culminating experiences. No matter what your destination, you will find Cold Springs to be one of the very special places in these mountains.

15. Cold Springs East Fork

TRAIL INFORMATION

Distance—.75 miles to the pools; 1.5 miles to the loop trail; 1.75 to the Montecito overlook; 3.5 to Montecito Peak; 4.5 to Camino Cielo Road

Elevation Gain—350' to pools; 1100' to powerlines; 2450' to top of Montecito Peak; 2775' to the crest

Difficulty—Moderate to very strenuous, depending on the distance

Topo—Santa Barbara

URL—http://www.sb-outdoors.org Keyword Search: Cold Springs

HIGHLIGHTS

This is absolutely my very favorite trail. Within a few yards of your car the pools begin. Deep and shaded by alders, the perennial creek offers scores of places to spend an afternoon. Even the name suggests something special. Cold Springs represents the shortest distance you can travel to get the furthest away from Santa Barbara. Above the trailhead you will find bedrock pools and places to sunbathe, overlooks of the coastline, and a route to the mountain crest, the one memorialized by Stewart Edward White in his classic book, *The Mountains*. Though no trail leads to it, you'll find a beautiful waterfall hidden deep in the watershed.

DIRECTIONS

The trail is reached either from Sycamore Canyon Road near the Milpas Street area, or Hot Springs Road in Montecito. From Highway 101 drive up

Milpas to Montecito Street. Turn right and follow it to Sycamore Canyon Road and continue up Sycamore Canyon for 2 miles (it becomes Highway 192) to Cold Springs Road. Turn left (north), drive past Westmont College to Mountain Drive, and then turn right and go a half-mile east to the trailhead. Park near the point where the creek crosses the road. From Montecito, take the Hot Springs Road exit and follow that road until you reach the Highway 192 intersection. Turn left and follow this for a mile to Cold Springs Road. Turn right and continue up to Mountain Drive.

THE HIKE

From the parking area the path follows the east side of the creek, gradually rising through a forest of live oak before returning back to the creek and a profusion of alders. A very beautiful double-spouted waterfall and a bench from which to enjoy it can be spotted near the side of the creek. In a narrow opening, easily missed, you'll find the turnoff to the West Fork Trail.

Beyond here the East Fork Trail heads away from the creek, switching back and forth several times to a point where there is a nice view of the West Fork canyon. From there the trail is level. It is also narrow and a bit dangerous unless you are careful; the mountainside falls away rather precipitously. After a half-mile the trail rejoins the creek at a lovely grouping of alders, a small waterfall, and a pool.

The trail then crosses the stream, heads left up into a chaparral, then switches back to the right, bringing you to a bedrock canyon where there are a number of waterfalls and pools. The open sandstone ledges and sunning spots are very popular for afternoon lunches.

This also marks the end of the canyon section of the East Fork. A hundred yards beyond, the trail turns right, crosses the creek, and rises up a strike canyon into the chaparral. Continue up the creek if you like. Though it rises rather steeply, the hike up the canyon is worthwhile. Many surprises await you if you have the energy to travel far enough. Even if you don't get too far, there are plenty of places to stop and have a place all to yourself.

The main trail follows the side canyon, which was formed by the weathering of the easily-eroded Cozy Dell Shale. The path curves in a clockwise direction around the canyo,n then begins to switch back and forth up to a viewpoint where there are several power line towers and very nice vistas. The dirt road built to service these towers leads into Hot Springs Canyon and eventually over to San Ysidro Canyon.

Just before the last switchback leading up to the towers you'll notice a trail intersection. This marks the start of a new loop route,

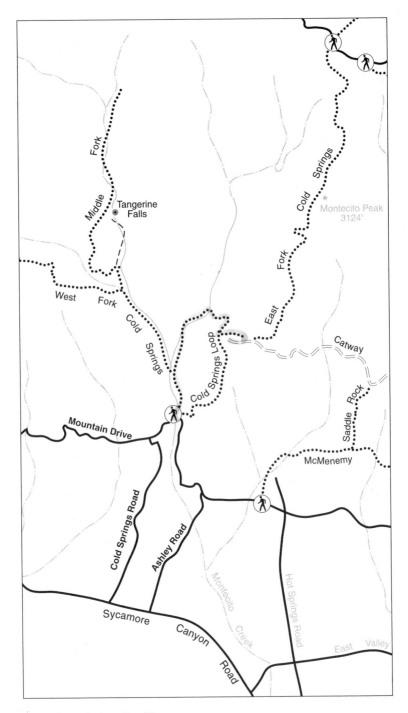

which will take you back down to Mountain Drive. This trail is actually a remnant of the original Forest Service trail, which was built nearly a hundred years ago when the Cold Springs Trail was rerouted from the Middle Fork to the East Fork. Ironically, this trail was then abandoned in favor of the present-day route.

Thanks to several local residents who believed the historic route should be reopened, it is now possible to follow it back down, creating a great loop hike. The trail isn't quite as well developed as the main trail, but it is very serviceable. Quickly you will find yourself coming out into the open, and you begin to descend from high on the east side of the canyon. There are spectacular views up the canyon and to the west. At one point you will find the remnants of a "hippie cabin"—a surprisingly large structure, considering how far it would have been to haul the lumber.

As you continue down, the trail passes through what is almost a tunnel of chaparral; then, as it nears the mouth of Cold Springs Canyon, the trail switches back and forth rapidly down to the road.

If you continue toward the crest you will reach the powerlines about a quarter-mile beyond the loop intersection. Follow the dirt road fifty yards east and you'll spot the start of the upper section of the Cold Springs Trail on the left. It rises quickly into the Matilija Sandstone. The route curves around the east side of a large knoll, which you will appreciate very much if you are hiking up in the afternoon, because the knoll shades this section, which is steep.

As you round the final curve you'll notice an intersection leading down into Hot Springs Canyon. There is a NO TRESPASSING sign posted at the entrance, and the trail hasn't been maintained for quite a while.

A mile further up, after a series of switchbacks, the solitary eucalyptus trees will tell you that Montecito Peak is not too far ahead. The trail crosses its western flank. If you want to hike to the top of the peak, continue on the trail until you are almost past it. The route leads very steeply up the north side of the 3,214-foot Montecito Peak. It is a 2,500-foot (a half-mile!) climb from the trailhead to the top, but what a feeling once you are there.

After this the trail continues upward along a ridgeline and then curves left into the upper end of Cold Springs Canyon. Gradually the steepness begins to lessen and the walking becomes easier as you enter the Juncal Formation. From here is it a half-mile of much more pleasant walking to the crest.

From here you can continue on down the back side of the Santa Ynez Mountains, either to Forbush Flats or all the way to the river (see the Forbush Trail description). Or you can turn right on Camino Cielo Road and walk east several hundred yards to the San Ysidro Trail and drop back down that way.

16. Cold Springs Middle Fork

TRAIL INFORMATION
Distance—.25 miles to West Fork intersection; 1 mile to Middle Fork intersection; 2 miles to the top of the falls; 2.5 miles to the remnants of the homestead
Elevation Gain—450' to Middle Fork intersection; 1075' to the top of the falls; 1300' to homestead
Difficulty—Moderate to strenuous
Topo—Santa Barbara
URL—http://www.sb-outdoors.org Keyword Search: Cold Springs

HIGHLIGHTS
Though not long or well-known this trail leads up to a series of beautiful cascades culminating in a 200-foot high waterfall. A small pool is at the base of the fall, making this a great place to hang out for the afternoon. A trail leads around the west side of the canyon to the top of the fall and into the upper canyon, where you can find remnants of an old homestead.

DIRECTIONS
Follow the directions for the East Fork of Cold Springs (Trail # 15)

SETTING THE SCENE
"Yesterday Mr. Shedd and two men, two donkeys, and two mules came over from the Los Prietos mines by a new trail in less than eight hours, two of which were used to clear the trail of brush to the top of the mountain on the other side," the *Santa Barbara Morning Press* reported on February 21, 1878. This is one of the earliest recorded accounts of the original Cold Springs Trail.

Originally, the main trail went up the Middle Fork of Cold Springs rather than following its current route. Passing the site of the Cold Springs water tunnel, bored into the mountain on land donated by Eugene Sheffield, the trail led up and around a 300-foot waterfall (now known as Tangerine Falls) and a large pointed rock at the top of the falls named "The Pinnacle" by E.M. Heath in his 1904 book, *A Guide to Rides and Drives in Santa Barbara*.

From there, it continued up the creek bottom through a narrows, then began to wind its way up shale slopes to the crest, where it crossed over and went down the head of Gidney Creek (where Forbush Flats is now located) to the Santa Ynez River.

When the Santa Ynez Forest Reserve was created in 1899, the Cold Springs Trail was improved by the forest rangers. Rather than having to split their efforts on trails up both branches of Cold Springs Creek, they decided to concentrate on the East Fork.

"It is considered advisable," Forest Inspector Louis A. Barrett wrote to his superiors in Washington in 1905, "to have one well-built main trail crossing the Reserve from the Coast to the desert side and one half of the field force will be at work on this trail all the spring."

THE HIKE

To reach the Middle Fork of Cold Springs Canyon you will need to hike up the West Fork trail for three-fourths mile to the turnoff to the falls. The lower canyon is extremely narrow, the creek flowing over solid bedrock. The upper part opens into a large semicircular valley, which is hidden from view until the last moment. (For more information about this part of the trail, see the description for Hike #17).

As you hike up the West Fork, look up across the canyon every so often. When you spot Tangerine Falls you will know you are close to the trail intersection. There is no sign marking the turnoff. The route up into the Middle Fork canyon isn't an official trail— even though the original route went this way. Drop down across a small canyon (containing the West Fork creek) then continue straight ahead up into the East Fork.

You will find yourself using your hands a lot, but because of the number of hikers who come up here the trail is becoming more and more developed. As you work your way up to the base of Tangerine Falls you will be scrambling most of the way. There are plenty of rocks to hop over, and lots of creek crossings. The route is steep, but the canyon is beautiful. Once you near the falls there is one last climb you will need to make to get to the actual waterfall. It can be slippery, so take care.

Though the hike up to the falls is hard work, once you're there you will be mesmerized by the cascades. Deposits from the mineralized water have created an apron of sorts, and there are little pockets in them in which you will find maidenhair ferns and thick green mosses. As the water drops down from the upper heights and hits the apron it turns into a fine mist, and it feels very good to stand under it and soak. The deposits have turned the rock a salmon—or what I think of as tangerine—color so that is what I named the falls for my last edition of this book.

Recently the same persons responsible for "rescuing" the historic East Fork Trail from Forest Service oblivion have restored the original route through the Middle Fork, and it is a real treat to be able to hike into the upper canyon.

After the Coyote Fire in 1977, Jim Blakely, the foremost authority on the Santa Barbara backcountry, located the remains of the old trail. Carefully tracing his way along it, he was able to discover the homestead of a member of the Romero family, after which Romero Canyon is named, and a few relics left behind when the homestead was abandoned—the blade of a rusted plow, a few bottles, and a scattering of tin cans, and the remains of an old root cellar.

At the time, however, no one seemed interested in re-establishing the trail, and the chaparral slowly began to creep back over it. Despite the thick stands of ceanothus and manzanita that made it impossible to navigate, the tread remained. Perhaps as a Year 2000 gift, the brush has been cut away, exposing the tread and making it possible to reach the upper canyon.

Look for the upper trail not too long after you've turned off the main trail and begun your hike up into the Middle Fork. It switches back and forth several times, heading up pretty steeply, then curves left and up until you are on the shoulder of the West Fork canyon, looking directly across at the trail leading up to Gibraltar Road.

Turning to the right, the trail leads away from the West Fork back to the east. Several hundred yards beyond, as you round a corner, Tangerine Falls comes into view, and you can see the route all of the way up past the Pinnacle. Once you reach this unique formation, the trail drops down into the shade of a narrow gorge, which is just upstream from the falls.

The route out to the Pinnacle requires using your hands, as there is a bit of scrambling to get over to it, but once you are there you will love both the perch and the views it affords. This is a very, very nice place to spend an afternoon.

You would expect that it would be easy to reach the top of the falls from here, but it isn't. There is a lot of poison oak in the creek and one ten-foot waterfall you would need to climb down to get there. With a rope you might be able to make it.

Hiking into the upper canyon is also a treat. It is narrow and filled with willows, sycamores, and oaks, creating a lot of shade, and the trail is almost level. There are lots of stream crossings, and you will find an assortment of small trails leading off the main one; but to reach the homestead area you should generally follow the trail that continues along the creek. If you are lucky you will find the old farm equipment, and a bit further up the old root cellar, which is an excellent place for lunch.

It appears that the old route up to the crest is also being restored as well. At one point before you reach the root cellar a trail leads very steeply up a hill on the right side of the creek. Should you explore this you will find yourself following a thin ridgeline directly uphill for a long distance. Eventually you will top out on a larger ridgeline that divides the Middle and East forks of Cold Springs.

The route up the main ridge is faint now, but this could change. There is one final knoll—marking the farthest I have been on this "trail"—on which I would love to spend the night if it weren't so hard to get here. The spot is open, with a fringe of chaparral all around, and there are 360-degree views. The hill drops off in all directions, and you can see Camino Cielo Road just above you, seemingly just a rock's throw away. But the 300-foot drop to a small saddle and the 900-foot climb to the road mean, in mountain terms, you are actually still a long way away.

If you would like to know where this spot is, look at the Santa Barbara topo: there is a marker on the map that says "2884" right below the "r" in "Forest." Perhaps we will meet there someday.

17. Cold Springs West Fork

TRAIL INFORMATION
Distance—1 mile to Middle Fork intersection; 1.75 miles to Gibraltar Road
Elevation Gain— 450′ to Middle Fork intersection; 1175′ to Gibraltar Road
Difficulty—Moderately strenuous
Topo—Santa Barbara
URL—http://www.sb-outdoors.org Keyword Search: Cold Springs

HIGHLIGHTS
Though not long or well-known, this trail leads up a very pretty canyon to Gibraltar Road. A side trip along the way leads to Tangerine Falls and the upper end of the Middle Fork canyon.

DIRECTIONS
Follow the directions for the East Fork of Cold Springs (Trail # 15)

THE HIKE

Unlike most frontcountry trails, which run north-south, the West Fork Trail follows an east-west course. The reason for this can be found in the geology of this particular area. Matilija Sandstone lies on the north side of the trail; Coldwater Sandstone is on the south side. Sandwiched in between is a layer known as Cozy Dell Shale. High along the crest the shale forms impressive saddles. As it dips across the ocean side of the Santa Ynez Mountains, it forms what are known as strike canyons, which run at right angles to the main canyons. The West Fork Trail winds its way up the largest of these strike canyons.

To reach the West Fork Trail, hike up the East Fork Trail a quarter-mile to a very pretty waterfall with a nearby bench. Cross the creek and look for the trail behind a series of large boulders. The trail climbs slowly, undulating up the left side of the narrow canyon. In the afternoon this section is shade-covered, making the hike pleasant on hot summer days.

The path wanders through dense green canyon vegetation for three-quarters of a mile before opening into the valley. Slightly to right of center is a magnificent waterfall 200 to 250 feet high. This is Tangerine Falls, and the trail leading up to it lies not too far beyond the viewpoint.

Just past the turnoff for Tangerine Falls, the main West Fork Trail crosses to the right side of the canyon and then, a hundred yards above this, crosses back and begins a series of switchbacks that takes you directly uphill for several hundred feet until you are no longer in the canyon but high up on the hillside.

Once you are at the end of the switchbacks, the trail climbs gradually until reaching Gibraltar Road at a hairpin turn that has been used for target practice in the past. Thanks to the efforts of the Sierra Club and other trail users, the Forest Service has closed this and other areas to "plinking," making it a much safer area for hiking.

If you would like to reach Rattlesnake Canyon, you can do so by walking up the road for a mile to the connector trail.

HOT SPRINGS CANYON

When Wilbur Curtiss came to Santa Barbara in the 1850s he was suffering from an incurable disease and doctors had given him only six months to live. Having lost his health in the mines, he was determined to spend his remaining days enjoying the scenery and wonderful climate of the Montecito hills. But he, too, would find an attraction in the mountain wall behind them.

One day while hiking in the foothills he noticed an old Indian bathing in Hot Springs Creek, who seemed to be in remarkable health. An Indian boy who accompanied Curtiss on his daily excursions explained that the secret behind the old man's lengthy years, which totaled 110, was his bathing in some hot springs that flowed from the base of a sandstone cliff farther up the canyon. After several hours of climbing, Curtiss reached the springs.

Hot Springs Canyon

There were four of these thermal pools, each heated to 116 degrees and containing a foul-smelling sulfur, as well as arsenic, iron, magnesium, and other minerals. Curtiss soaked himself in the soothing water, apparently even drinking from one of the pools. Perhaps the hot springs had nothing to do with it, but after repeated visits to them his health began to improve remarkably, enough so that six years later, still alive and doing well, Wilbur Curtiss filed a homestead claim for this part of Hot Springs Canyon.

Slowly the site evolved into a resort. First a rustic camp was built, and then more permanent tents were added. The springs proved to be so popular that a hut was added, and eventually a cottage was constructed not far from the miraculous pools. In 1873 the *Santa Barbara Morning Press* announced that a magnificent hotel costing $100,000 would be built at the mouth of the hot springs to accommodate the tourists flocking to the area.

One writer boasted, "Many a rheumatic and neuralgic cripple has left his crutches here as a memento to the healing touches of the waters, and gone down from the rocky mountain glen out into the gay world, shouting praises to the boiling fountain which has invested him with new life."

By 1877 there was a large plunge, a shower, and three bath houses, each containing large tubs—enough in all to handle forty people. In the early 1880s a three-story wooden hotel was finally completed on a bench above the springs. The rate for staying at the hotel was $2 per day or $10 per week, and included bathing in the hot spring water. There was a library, a well-stocked wine cellar, and even a billiards room. Hiking, of course, was a popular pastime as well.

By this time Curtiss's original homestead had become the property of a number of wealthy Montecitans, and the private club had become ritzy enough that anyone with a bank account containing less than seven digits was not considered substantial enough to apply for membership.

In 1920, a forest fire destroyed the hotel and most of the vegetation in the canyon. Thie hotel was rebuilt in 1923, but this time under the ownership of a corporation that contained but 17 members, all Montecito residents, who also controlled the Montecito Water Company. It is said that the members, when they wanted to partake of the hot baths, would simply call the caretaker and request that a bath be drawn, so that when they and their guests would arrive, the steaming water would be ready for them to slip into.

This structure stood until 1964, when it was destroyed in the Coyote Fire. For many years anyone who wanted to head up for a dip in the pools could do so, and I have done this on many an occasion. However, in the 1980s, perhaps because of fears that the land might become public through the process of adverse possession, NO TRESPASSING and PRIVATE PROPERTY signs were posted in Hot Springs Canyon, and access to the public has been restricted.

18. Saddle Rock Trail

TRAIL INFORMATION

Distance—.75 miles to Saddle Rock Trail; 1.5 miles to the powerlines; 2 miles to San Ysidro Canyon via the McMenemy Trail; 4.25 for the Girard loop

Elevation Gain—200' to the Saddle Rock Trail; 750' to the powerlines; 1100' total elevation for the Girard loop

Difficulty—Easy to moderately strenuous, depending on distance

Topo—Santa Barbara

URL—http://www.sb-outdoors.org Keyword Search: Hot Springs, Saddle Rock, McMenemy, or Girard

HIGHLIGHTS

The trail leads up onto a prominent ridgeline where there are several large rock outcroppings that provide nice spots to relax for the afternoon. This area is known as Saddle Rock. The ridge trail leads up to the powerlines, providing access to either Cold Springs Canyon or San Ysidro Canyon. A very nice loop can be made by following the powerlines to the Girard Trail and returning to your car via this and the McMenemy Trail.

DIRECTIONS

From Highway 101, exit on Olive Mill Road and follow this north. After crossing Alston Road, this becomes Hot Springs Road. Continue a mile past the beautiful southwestern-style church to Mountain Drive. Turn left and proceed .2 miles to the parking area. A Montecito Trails Foundation sign marks the starting point.

THE HIKE

In the three decades since my first day hikes book was published there have been quite a few changes in the Hot Springs area. The trailhead has been moved, new homes have been built, and the hot springs, which are on private property, have been posted with NO TRESPASSING signs. Nevertheless, the hike up the Saddle Rock Trail is still as enjoyable as ever.

The Hot Springs Trail follows the right side of a small creek for several hundred yards until it reaches a private lane. Turn left on the lane and follow it for several hundred yards more. There are no signs along this section, and at first glance it will appear as though you are walking up someone's driveway, but this is the right direction to go. The lane crosses a small creek before reaching a large gate. Stepping stones lead around the right side of the gate.

Continue along the lane to the point where the road swings left and heads up to a private home. You will find the trail just beyond, continuing straight up the canyon. Follow it up and across Hot Springs Creek. The turnoff to the McMenemy Trail is just a bit beyond the creek crossing and just before a locked gate barring access to the upper canyon.

Several hundred yards of switchbacks on the McMenemy Trail will bring you to a high point that marks the start of the Saddle Rock Trail. The McMenemy Trail continues east, dropping down into a canyon and then over a grass-covered ridge to San Ysidro Canyon. The Saddle Rock Trail follows the ridge and leads steadily uphill to the powerlines. Along the way you will find Saddle Rock, expansive views of the coastline, and, just before you reach the powerlines, a wide, open flattop that has a beautiful heart laid out in the middle of it, created from hundreds of small rocks.

From this point a small drop and then a brief climb under several towers leads to the power line road. Turning to the left will lead you down into upper Hot Springs Canyon in the vicinity of the former resort. The hot springs are not too far up the canyon, but they are on private property and it is possible you will be hassled if you go up to them.

Heading east on the power line road leads to San Ysidro Canyon. The road winds gradually uphill for a quarter-mile before descending precipitously into the canyon. However, just as you reach the drop-off, you'll see a new trail that is being constructed on the ocean side of the road, which will make it possible to loop back via the McMenemy Trail. This will be known as the Girard Trail, and should be finished sometime in 2000. It curves gradually downhill around the east side of a large peak and intersects the McMenemy Trail near the stone bench on the hilltop.

To make the loop, follow the Girard Trail for a half-mile to the McMenemy Trail and then continue back to the west on the Mc-Menemy Trail. The trail drops into a small canyon then climbs back up to the Saddle Rock intersection.

SAN YSIDRO CANYON

San Ysidro Canyon, like Cold Springs Canyon, begins high in the Juncal Formation, and thus the creek flows late in the summer when other creeks are nearly dry. It is a beautiful canyon and a nice one for taking trail novices because there is such a range of options.

Due to the tireless efforts of the Montecito Trails Foundation there is a large network of trails to be found in this area, and one new trail just about to be completed: the Girard Trail. It is named for Bud Girard, longtime volunteer and manager of the MTF trail system. If you see a new trail sign, a set of stairs that wasn't there last trip, or if the trail has been brushed out nicely—more than likely you should thank Bud and his crew.

If you would like more information about the Montecito Trails Foundation, call the MTF message line at (805) 969-3514, or write them at P.O. Box 5481, Santa Barbara, CA 93150. Family or individual memberships cost $25, and the money is well spent.

San Ysidro is a canyon of contrasts. In the lower canyon you pass by the San Ysidro Guest Ranch, where you can spy tennis courts, swimming pools, and cottages of all sorts, including one named for President John Kennedy when he stayed there after marrying Jacqueline. There are also several magnificent estates along the way, one of which is landscaped along either side of the Old Pueblo Trail.

Then suddenly the trail drops down into the canyon, and civilization is left behind. The road bobs up and down on the edge of the creek, and there are glimpses of the mountains that lie just ahead of you. Side trails lead off at regular intervals, and as you reach the top of one knoll a wall of sandstone appears on the west side of the canyon. Here you maybe able to sit and watch the climbers making their way like spiders up one of a number of routes.

Oddly, the canyon is much narrower where it passes through the Cozy Dell Shale than at this point, where it courses through the usually resistant Coldwater Sandstone. This is due to the peculiar nature of the geologic layers of the Santa Ynez Mountains, which do not run parallel to the crest, but pass obliquely over the crest and then dip to the east across the mountains and under the coastal plain.

The character of each layer changes as it descends from top to bottom. For instance, when crossing the top of the mountains, Coldwater Sandstone crops out as intricately worn boulder fields, such as those at Lizard's Mouth or the Playground. Closer to Santa Barbara this sandstone angles down to form the Mission Crags and the magnificent toothed shape of Cathedral Peak. At lower elevations the sandstone forms exquisite narrows such as those at Seven Falls and Rattlesnake Canyon.

As it dips under the coastal flood plain, as it does in San Ysidro Canyon, the sandstone is well eroded and the canyons are wider. This erosion began during the Pleistocene, a period of rapid uplift, when the canyons were much deeper and continued farther seaward, perhaps as much as three miles.

19. San Ysidro Canyon Trail

TRAIL INFORMATION
Distance—1.75 miles to the end of the canyon section; 4.5 to Camino Cielo Road
Elevation Gain—2970'
Difficulty—Moderate to strenuous, depending on distance
Topo—Santa Barbara and Carpinteria
URL—http://www.sb-outdoors.org Keyword Search: San Ysidro

HIGHLIGHTS
Though at first the trail winds past a home and then follows a graded dirt road for a half-mile, the upper end of the canyon is picturesque as it winds through a series of narrows formed by a thick layer of Matilija Sandstone. You'll find an 80-foot waterfall at the upper end of the canyon section. Several connector trails lead to the east and west, making several short scenic hikes possible, none of them too far from your car. A dirt road leads across the upper end of the canyon, providing access to Hot Springs Canyon on the west and Romero Canyon on the east. A great climbing wall can be found a mile up from the trailhead, with routes of varying difficulty.

DIRECTIONS
Take the San Ysidro exit off of Highway 101. Turn north on San Ysidro Road and continue a mile to East Valley Road. Turn right and follow East Valley another mile to Park Lane. Look for the eucalyptus-shrouded entrance to this narrow road just after crossing San Ysidro Creek. Turn left onto it, and then left again after a half-mile on Mountain Drive. Follow it several hundred yards to the trailhead.

THE HIKE
The trail begins just before the locked gate on San Ysidro Creek. A small sign marked with the San Ysidro Ranch brand is fastened to a nearby oak tree. The path continues along the driveway for a hun-

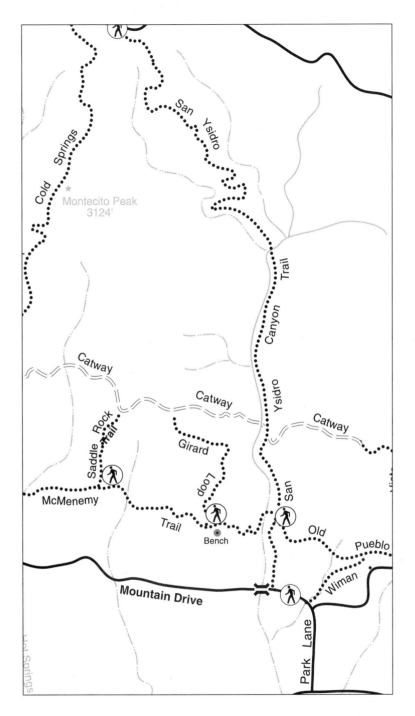

San Ysidro

Cold Springs

★ Montecito Peak
3124'

Canyon Trail

Catway

Catway

Ysidro

Catway

Saddle Rock Trail

Girard Loop

San

McMenemy

Trail

Old

Pueblo

● Bench

Mountain Drive

Wiman

Park Lane

Hot Springs

dred yards, then winds around the rear of a house and up onto a paved road. Follow this up to a wide dirt road that has a chain-link gate partially across it, and head up it. After a half-mile you will come to a thick sequence of Coldwater Sandstone forming a deep V, a gateway to the inner canyon beyond.

Just before this V several connector trails lead off to the east and west, providing access to the canyons on either side. The Old Pueblo Trail (Day Hike #21) is to the right, leading east, sharply uphill, and over a ridge to upper Park Lane and the Buena Vista Trail. The McMenemy Trail (Hike #20) is not too far beyond. This trail crosses San Ysidro Creek and leads up a grassy plateau above the San Ysidro Guest Ranch.

To reach the upper end of San Ysidro Canyon, follow the dirt road through the narrow V created by the Coldwater Sandstone. Look for a large sandstone wall on your left. This is a popular rock-climbing area.

The road continues bobbing up and down along the right side of the canyon for another third-mile through very pleasant forests of oak and sycamore. Occasionally there is an opening from which you can catch a glimpse of the upper canyon. The Buena Vista Catway (Day Hike #24) is on the right. It turns sharply back to the right and is easy to miss.

Eventually the road turns left, crosses the creek, and heads up to Hot Springs Canyon and the Girard Loop (Day Hike #25). If you've gotten to the creek crossing, you've just missed the trail turnoff leading into the upper canyon. Look for the trail just before the road turns left.

The path wanders for a mile through canyon vegetation and oak woodland before heading up into the chaparral. This one-mile section is the prettiest part of the canyon. Cozy Dell Shale dominates, and the canyon is filled with small waterfalls, numerous pools, and many short paths leading down to picturesque spots for relaxing or picnicking.

As you continue on, the canyon narrows and steepens as the trail passes into the Matilija sandstone. Along one section you'll find a pipe railing to aid the climb upward, though it is hardly needed. You might also follow the creek through the narrows if you are adventurous enough to brave the rock scrambling and occasional willow thickets. You won't find it easy going, but there are several waterfalls in the narrows that you can't see from the trail, which are very nice.

Eventually you will drop back down to the creek at a point where the canyon splits into east and west forks. The trail crosses the creek and begins a steep uphill climb. This marks the beginning of the Juncal Formation, as well as the point at which you will no longer have access to water. You'll need plenty if you plan to continue up to the crest.

The creek crossing is a favorite turnaround spot for many hikers. If you'd like to keep this a relaxing, cool, and moderately easy hike, stop here and explore each of the upper forks. You'll discover the 80-foot waterfall not too far up the west fork. You might also try exploring the east fork. There is no trail, but the rock hopping is fun and the creek is very pretty.

If you are heading to the crest, the trail begins to climb immediately beyond the creek crossing. Several switchbacks provide 300 feet of elevation gain, bringing you out on the side of the mountain and above the west fork of the creek. From here the trail contours above the west fork for three-fourths mile, then switches back and forth up a prominent ridgeline. Hiking to the crest adds another two miles, but the effort of making it to the top is well worth it.

From Camino Cielo Road, the Cold Springs Trail is only a short distance to the west, and it is tempting to make this a loop trip back down. This loop is one of my favorites. A good plan if you want to do the loop is to have a shuttle car at the Cold Springs trailhead to take you back to San Ysidro Canyon. That way you can enjoy a dip in the pools in lower Cold Springs Canyon.

To loop all the way back to the San Ysidro trailhead, continue down the Cold Springs Trail to the catway and follow this east back into the upper canyon. Alternate routes down the Saddle Rock and McMenemy trails or the Girard and McMenemy trails are also possible.

20. McMenemy Trail

TRAIL INFORMATION
Distance—.5 miles to McMenemy intersection; 1.2 miles to McMenemy bench; 1. 9 to Saddle Rock Trail; 1.7 to top of Girard Trail
Elevation Gain—650' to McMenemy bench; 200' elevation loss from bench into canyon and 250' elevation gain to Saddle Rock Trail; 350' elevation gain from bench to top of Girard Trail
Difficulty—Moderate to strenuous
Topo—Santa Barbara and Carpinteria
URL—http://www.sb-outdoors.org Keyword Search: McMenemy

HIGHLIGHTS
The trail leads across San Ysidro Creek and through a very pretty eucalyptus

grove. Views from the bench are some of the best. You can continue on to the Saddle Rock Trail and continue up it to create a longer loop hike, or follow the Girard Trail up to the Edison catway for a shorter loop.

DIRECTIONS
Follow the directions for Day Hike #19—the San Ysidro Canyon Trail. The McMenemy Trail begins a half-mile up the San Ysidro Canyon Trail. As you crest the hill leading past the huge estate there is a trail sign marking the Old Pueblo Trail. Look for the McMenemy turnoff on the left, not too far beyond the Old Pueblo turnoff.

THE HIKE
The hike up to the McMenemy bench for the morning or evening views is one of the great short hikes in the Santa Barbara area, but what I like most about this trail is the variety of two- to three-hour-long loops you can make by combining this with other sections of trail. Now that the Girard Trail is almost complete, there will be even more possibilities. Hiking over to Saddle Rock and back is another great trip.

To reach the start of the McMenemy Trail, walk up San Ysidro Canyon for a half-mile. It leads left across the creek and then through a wonderful eucalyptus grove before starting up a series of switchbacks winding back and forth through grass meadows and chaparral to the bench. It is a 500-foot elevation gain and will definitely get your heart pumping, but once you reach the shoulder on which the stone bench is located you will marvel at the views; they are spectacular.

For many, the hike up to this viewpoint will be enough, but if you would like to extend your hike for another hour or two there are several other possibilities. The McMenemy Trail continues west, dropping several hundred feet into a small canyon and then climbing back up to the far ridge, where the Saddle Rock Trail (Day Hike #18) is located. At the bottom of the small canyon look for a short path leading a few yards out onto the top of a 40-foot-high waterfall. It is a perfect place to sit for a spell.

From here it is a quarter-mile of gradual uphill to the Saddle Rock ridge. The McMenemy Trail continues over the saddle and ends a short distance later in Hot Springs Canyon. You will want to turn right and head up the ridge trail, even if only a short distance to Saddle Rock, which is *the* perfect place to sit and watch the sunset. From here you can return via the McMenemy Trail or continue up the ridge to make this a loop trip. Along the way you will find loads of impressive views and, just before the catway intersection, a flat hilltop where past visitors have created the outline a huge heart out of rocks.

Once you reach the catway, turn right and continue slightly uphill for several hundred yards to a high point. Here the catway begins to drop precipitously down into San Ysidro Canyon. The drop is short and sweet, and the walk back down along the creek is a very nice way to complete the loop.

Near the high point, the Girard Trail (when completed) will take you back to the bench. As of publication, the trail has been roughed out and it is possible to hike along it, but the hiking isn't easy.

21. Old Pueblo Trail

TRAIL INFORMATION
Distance—.4 miles to Old Pueblo junction; 1 mile to junction with Wiman Trail; 1.5 miles return to Park Lane via Wiman Trail
Elevation Gain—100' to Old Pueblo intersection; 250' to Wiman intersection; 200' elevation loss back down to Park Lane
Difficulty—Easy
Topo—Carpinteria (trail not shown on map)
URL—http://www.sb-outdoors.org Keyword Search: Old Pueblo

HIGHLIGHTS
This is a short loop hike, but it makes for a very pleasant walk when you want something that isn't too difficult. It can be combined with loops involving other trails for more strenuous hikes. Along the way you will get a glimpse of a few of Montecito's fine estates.

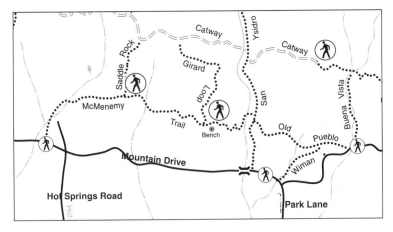

DIRECTIONS

Follow the directions for Day Hike #19—the San Ysidro Canyon Trail. The Old Pueblo Trail begins .4 miles up the San Ysidro Trail and actually cuts through the upper gardens of a very expensive estate.

THE HIKE

If you are looking for a hike that isn't too easy or too hard, has nice views, and can provide you with an hour or two of quiet relaxation, the Old Pueblo Trail is for you. It is a very nice trail for kids as well.

The trail is typical of those you will find in the Montecito foothills. Sandwiched between private property boundaries, the trails are a collection of short sections that have been patched together. It is to the credit of the Montecito Trails Foundation that the organization has been able to do such a great job of getting the easements and financing the trail construction to make them possible.

The Old Pueblo Trail's character seems to change as you round every bend. At one point you will find yourself immersed in a tunnel of chaparral; then around a corner or over the next hill you will be following a chain-link fence or gazing down into the backyard of a hillside estate. Then you will be back in the chaparral tunnel once again.

The trail begins not too far up San Ysidro Canyon. It is a pleasant .4-mile hike along the edges of several large houses and driveways to the trailhead. For those of you who have hiked here in the past, the first several hundred yards of the trail will look much different now.

As you walk up the hill past the last huge estate, at first glance you probably won't be able to find the route. The owners of the complex have extended the gardens—of which there are several acres—far up the hillsides and beyond the trail. The route now leads right through the gardens and around the top side of the house (mansion?) through a very pretty section of chaparral.

Several hundred yards of easy uphill bring you to a knoll and the beginning of the views out over the Montecito foothills. For the next half-mile you will find yourself dropping down along the edges of several estates, winding through another section of very enchanting chaparral and then more houses. At one point, as you begin to drop down into another canyon, you will find yourself looking almost directly down onto the patio area of a large Mediterranean-style house and one of the nicest pools you will find anywhere.

Not too far beyond this estate you will come to a long chain-link fence and what appears to be the end of the Old Pueblo Trail.

Turning right will take you down the Wiman Trail and a very pretty canyon back to Park Lane, not too far from the San Ysidro trailhead.

The Old Pueblo Trail angles to the left and climbs uphill next to the fence, then heads down across a small canyon and along an easement that parallels a private driveway. Several of my favorite homes are along this stretch. The driveway is a hundred yards long and drops you right onto the upper part of Park Lane. From here you can return back along the Old Pueblo Trail and take the Wiman Trail to your car. Or, if you don't mind walking along Park Lane, it is a very beautiful .7 miles back down to the San Ysidro trailhead.

It is also possible to make this a longer (and much more strenuous) loop hike by continuing up Park Lane two hundred yards to the Buena Vista trailhead. See Day Hike #23 for more information about this loop hike.

22. Wiman Trail

TRAIL INFORMATION

Distance—.5 miles to Old Pueblo Trail; .9 miles to upper Buena Vista Road; 1 mile to Buena Vista Trail intersection; 1.6 miles to upper end of Buena Vista Canyon

Elevation Gain—200' to Old Pueblo Trail; slight rises and drops to upper Buena Vista Road; 650' to upper end of Buena Vista Canyon; 1150' to Buena Vista lookout

Difficulty—Easy to Buena Vista trailhead; moderate to end of canyon; strenuous to Buena Vista lookout

Topo—Carpinteria (trail not shown on map)

URL—http://www.sb-outdoors.org Keyword Search: Wiman

HIGHLIGHTS

The Wiman Trail is a very short connector that leads up a narrow and beautiful canyon to the Old Pueblo Trail. This provides an easy loop possibility, or you can continue east on the Old Pueblo Trail to reach the Buena Vista Trail. The route leads past some very interesting Montecito homes that you won't see any other way.

DIRECTIONS

As you drive up Park Lane, look for the trailhead just after Park Lane splits. Curve left, as though you were heading to the San Ysidro trailhead, but just as you bear to the left look for the Wiman Trail sign on the right side of the road under a large oak tree.

THE HIKE

The Wiman Trail is short, just a half-mile in length, and as such probably isn't worth a separate trail description. Many of you might not even know it exists, even though you pass it every time you drive up to the San Ysidro Canyon trailhead. I know I missed it for quite a few years.

However, it does connect with other possibilities that I find well worth the effort. For those who are interested in a short hike, the Wiman Trail will take you up to the Old Pueblo Trail (Day Hike #21), from which you can loop over into San Ysidro Canyon or up into Buena Vista Canyon.

The canyon is narrow and heavily vegetated, making you feel almost as if you are hiking through a rainforest rather than in the Santa Barbara foothills. Huge oak and eucalyptus trees create a canopy, and the sunlight is mostly filtered, creating a much different kind of atmosphere.

There are a number of creek crossings along the way, and the backyards of a number of interesting houses come into views as you reach the upper end of the trail. A series of steps on the right side of the canyon leads you up into the sunlight and along a chain-link fence. Halfway up the hill, the Old Pueblo Trail intersects from the left.

23. Buena Vista Trail

TRAIL INFORMATION

Distance—.6 miles to end of canyon; 1 mile to Buena Vista catway; 1.1 to lookout on knoll; 1.8 to drop off into Romero Canyon

Elevation Gain—350' to upper end of Buena Vista Canyon; 850' to Buena Vista lookout; 950' to Romero overlook

Difficulty—Moderate to strenuous

Topo—Carpinteria (trail not shown on map)

URL—http://www.sb-outdoors.org Keyword Search: Buena Vista

HIGHLIGHTS

The Buena Vista Trail is the most colorful place to go in the fall. It is filled with sycamore trees whose leaves turn a delightful yellow in November and December. There are very interesting sandstone formations in the canyon, and you can combine the trail with a hike up to the lookout point or a loop via San Ysidro Canyon.

DIRECTIONS

As you drive up Park Lane, look for the split in the road. Turn right on Buena Vista and follow it uphill for .6 miles as it winds up through lovely estates. The trailhead is located on the right side of the upper canyon and is marked by a small trail sign.

THE HIKE

Driving up to the start of the Buena Vista Trail is a unique experience. The homes along the way are absolutely beautiful, and once you reach the trailhead you will discover you can see all the way up into the canyon right from your car.

Halfway up to where the mountain wall shoots high up into the sky, you can spot the narrows that makes Buena Vista Canyon so scenic. Bands of sandstone cut down across the canyon, creating a V that is like an entrance into another world.

My favorite way to reach the Buena Vista Trail is actually from the Wiman Trail. I like wandering through the backyards of the houses along the way and sampling the views out across the Montecito foothills. This provides a great warm-up before tackling the steeper mountain trails and allows me to loop back via the Buena Vista Catway if I feel like it later.

The first few hundred yards of the trail are steep. You are climbing up a series of sandstone ledges onto the shoulder of the foothills and there is a bit of effort involved. Once you near the V in the canyon the trail begins to level out and the hiking is much easier.

Geologically, you are moving through Coldwater Sandstone and into Cozy Dell Shale. The steeper hiking and the narrows take you through most of the Coldwater Sandstone while the upper canyon comprises mostly the shales.

The sandstone canyon is filled with sycamore trees and provides spectacular colors in the fall and a lush green canopy in the spring and summer. Once you reach the narrows you will find yourself immersed in the forest of trees, cutting back and forth across the creek and winding in and out of a series of beautiful sandstone outcroppings. The upper canyon is like a hidden jewel: thick green grasses and the pastels of myriad wildflowers in the springtime. Several hundred yards of very enchanting walking brings you to the end of the canyon and a fork in the trail. This offers two possibilities.

The Buena Vista Trail turns to the right. Switchbacks take you up through the chaparral to the catway road. It is 500 feet of climbing to reach the top, but worth the effort. Not too far beyond the end of the trail and the beginning of the catway, a small trail leads to a knoll that is marked on the Carpinteria topo with a small triangle and the elevation—1543 feet.

You will find a beautiful hand-carved bench here to sit on and enjoy the sunset views. You can thank the Montecito Trails Foundation for providing this magnificent bench. If you have time, you can also wander a half-mile farther on the catway to the Romero overlook before retracing your steps back to the Buena Vista trailhead.

The left fork trail will take you up to the Buena Vista Catway and then down into San Ysidro Canyon. The trail follows Cozy Dell Shale up into a side canyon and then switches back and forth up to the power line towers. From there the catway drops quickly down into the upper end of San Ysidro Canyon. It is a bit less than a mile down the canyon to the San Ysidro trailhead.

Those who parked at the Buena Vista trailhead can trace theirr way back to their car by taking the Old Pueblo Trail (Day Hike # 21). Look for the trail leading off to the left just after you climb a short hill and reach the large, well-landscaped estate.

24. Buena Vista Catway

TRAIL INFORMATION

Distance—.75 miles to catway intersection; 1.25 to top of ridge; 1.7 to Buena Vista Canyon; 2.2 miles to Buena Vista lookout

Elevation Gain—500' gain to top of ridge; 350' loss into Buena Vista canyon; 500' gain up to Buena Vista lookout

Difficulty—Moderate to strenuous, depending on distance

Topo—Carpinteria

URL—http://www.sb-outdoors.org Keyword Search: Buena Vista

HIGHLIGHTS

The loop provides a wonderful opportunity to combine the scenery in the upper parts of San Ysidro Canyon with the beauty of Buena Vista Canyon and the nearby lookout point. Continuing down the canyon and across the Old Pueblo Trail completes the loop.

DIRECTIONS

Follow the directions for Day Hike #19—the San Ysidro Canyon Trail. The Buena Vista Catway begins .75 miles up the San Ysidro Trail. The catway leads sharply back up to the right, making it easy to miss if you are not watching for it.

THE HIKE

In order to hike on any of the catway roads you have to be something of a masochist: rarely do they go up or down at an acceptable rate, and the dozer operators who built the catways obviously never had to walk up them. Nevertheless, in some cases they provide great opportunities for loop hikes where they would otherwise not exist.

This section of the catway leads over into Buena Vista Canyon and offers the possibility of a short side trip up to the Buena Vista overlook before returning down the canyon to Park Lane and across the Old Pueblo and Wiman trails.

The turnoff for the Buena Vista Catway is about three-fourths mile along the way and a few hundred yards before the upper San Ysidro Canyon Trail begins. The roadway turns back to the right beneath the shade of a large oak. The hiking seems pleasant enough until you reach the first turn and see where the catway is heading, which seems almost straight up. It isn't quite straight up, but close enough, and you will find your heart hammering most of the way up unless you go at a really slow pace.

It will take you about 20 minutes to a half-hour to make it up to the saddle, which is formed from easily weathered Cozy Dell Shale. Thankfully, once you are here most of the really hard work is out of the way. Just on the other side of the saddle the road ends and a very nice trail begins, taking you down several switchbacks into a small side canyon and then along the left side of this to the upper part of Buena Vista Canyon.

Just after you cross Buena Vista Creek you'll spot a trail sign. The trail splits here. Heading up to the left will take you to the Buena Vista overlook. Surprisingly, the road on the top is close to level for a half-mile or so. It is a 500-foot gain up to the overlook, but there are plenty of switchbacks and the trail climbs at a reasonable pitch, and somehow the hiking doesn't seem nearly as hard as it was on the catway.

If you've had enough uphill for the day, turn right and continue down Buena Vista Canyon. This is a beautiful canyon and leads though exquisite sandstone formations to Park Lane. The easiest route back to your car from here is to follow Park Lane downhill until you reach the San Ysidro trailhead. It is about .7 miles and the homes are worth checking out at a walker's pace.

However, if you would rather return by trail, head downhill for 200 yards to a private driveway, where you can connect with the Old Pueblo Trail. You'll know you're turning up the correct driveway if you can spot the signs marking 907 and 913 Park Lane attached to the sandstone wall on the right side of the private lane. Head up the driveway and then continue along the side of the roadway on the trail easement.

The Old Pueblo Trail passes several smaller houses, then drops down across a gully and continues over the next hill along a chain-link fence. Partway along this section the Old Pueblo Trail turns off to the right. Continue down along the chain-link fence and onto the Wiman Trail. This will take you into a very pretty canyon and to Park Lane about a hundred yards from the San Ysidro trailhead.

25. Girard Loop

TRAIL INFORMATION

Distance—.9 miles to the trail intersection where the road crosses the creek; 1.4 to top of ridge and intersection with Girard Trail; 1.9 to McMenemy bench; 3.1 miles back to Park Lane

Elevation Gain—400' to the trail intersection where the road crosses the creek; 1000' to top of ridge and intersection with Girard Trail; 350' loss to McMenemy bench; 650' elevation loss from bench back to Park Lane

Difficulty—Moderate to strenuous

Topo—Santa Barbara and Carpinteria

URL—http://www.sb-outdoors.org Keyword Search: Girard

DIRECTIONS

Follow the directions for Day Hike #19—the San Ysidro Canyon Trail. The Girard Trail connects the McMenemy Trail near the bench with the Edison catway.

THE HIKE

When Bud Girard finished hiking down the Cold Springs Trail on his seventieth birthday, he got a present from his daughter he would never forget: a new trail named in his honor. With the help of other family members his daughter, Mia, has raised more than $10,000 to make this a reality. The half-mile connector winds down around the west side of San Ysidro Canyon and links the Edison catway with the McMenemy Trail.

The toughest part wasn't getting the funds, though; it was securing the 15-foot easement though a patch of private property on the lower end and convincing the Forest Service to do the needed work

on their end. Currently, the trail has been roughed out and is walkable, though there isn't much of a tread and there are plenty of stumps to trip those who are too busy admiring the great views. This will change once the final details have been ironed out and the trail work is done, which should be by the end of 2000.

From the McMenemy Trail, the Girard connector takes off from an open meadow near the bench on the upper trail. You should be able to spot where it begins to curve around the hillside without too much difficulty. If you are coming from the Edison catway, the connector drops down and around the canyon from the top of the catway road near the towers.

Here are two of the hikes made possible by the Girard Trail: a longer loop hike from Hot Springs Canyon heading east on the McMenemy Trail out to the bench, continuing up the Girard Trail to the catway, and returning via the Saddle Rock Ridge Trail; and a shorter loop via San Ysidro Canyon and up the Edison catway followed by a return trip down the Girard and McMenemy trails.

Once the trail has been completed, perhaps the nicest place of all will be the stone-and-mortar bench that Bud's son Daniel is planning to build. It will be placed along the trail near the high point of the sandstone ridge that leads down to the climbing area. This will be a fitting tribute to the man who has worked so hard to make the Montecito trails what they are today.

The first time I come up after it is done I know what I will bring with me, the perfect complement to a warm afternoon—a Bud— and I will think as I gaze out over the long coastline stretching into the infinity of the southern horizon, Bud, this Bud's for you.

If you would like to support this or other local trails, you can do so by joining the Montecito Trails Foundation or, better yet, accompany your membership application with a check made out to MTF in care of The Bud Girard Trail, P.O. Box 5481, Santa Barbara, CA 93150.

ROMERO CANYON

Romero Canyon is named for the Romero family, whose ties to the Santa Barbara area are long and illustrious. Juan Romero was a soldier under Governor Felipe de Neve, the first resident governor of California, and Captain José Francisco Ortega, who helped found the presidio. Juan's descendants later homesteaded various locations in the Santa Ynez Mountains, including what is now Romero Canyon and the Middle Fork of Cold Springs Canyon.

Prior to 1978, Romero Road was the last remaining vestige of the primitive system of roads leading up to the top of the Santa Ynez Mountains. Built in the early part of the century, it was the only automobile route to the mountain crest that hadn't been paved.

My first experience on Romero Road was in the late 1960s. When I was younger (I had a 1965 Mustang convertible then) I would often jump in the car and meander through the Montecito area. The huge estates, the grandiose stone mansions, and the long sandstone walls make a kind of fairyland, and I love driving in and around them.

On one of the trips we happened upon the Romero roadway and decided to see where it would lead. It was foggy, and as we got higher and higher the mist closed in about us so that all we could see was a few feet in front of us. We were terrified that someone else would come down from above and hit us, and equally afraid to try to turn around on the narrow road in the pea-soup fog, so we kept going, on and on.

Then, just before we reached the top, I could feel the air getting brighter and the fog lifting. Before any of us knew it we were in the sunshine, the clouds below us lying on the horizon like a gauzy white blanket. As I have discovered many times later, when the fog hangs over the coast you can usually find the sun up on the crest.

Later, when I started to do more hiking in the backcountry, whenever I was returning from the upper Santa Ynez recreation area, if the gate were open I would take Romero Road back down to town. This rugged and extremely narrow dirt road was still available for public travel as late as the mid-'70s, when forty-two inches of rain in 1978 caused massive mud- and rockslides. Because it was too expensive to repair the old road, it has been closed to vehicle travel since then.

Subsequently, nature has reclaimed most of Romero Road, making the upper part of it more trail than road. Southern California Edison still keeps the lower portion of the road open for servicing the power lines, but once you are beyond the towers the only evidence of the road are retaining walls here and there and concrete aprons covering the places where small creeks cross the old road bed.

26. Romero Canyon Trail

TRAIL INFORMATION
Distance—.4 miles to Romero power line trail; .5 to canyon trail; 2 miles to intersection with upper road; 4 miles to crest via the upper trail or 3.5 miles to Romero Saddle via the upper road
Elevation Gain—1100' to intersection with Romero Road; 2175' to the top of the trail; 2000' to Romero Saddle
Difficulty—Moderate to strenuous
Topo—Carpinteria (trail not shown on map)
URL—http://www.sb-outdoors.org Keyword Search: Romero Canyon

HIGHLIGHTS
The Romero Canyon Trail is one of the few frontcountry trails that actually constitutes a loop. This is because the canyon trail starts at the bottom of Romero Road, now abandoned, and then intersects it again about two-thirds of the way to the crest. Though the creek is small, the canyon is very picturesque. Because it is a bit out of the way, the trail doesn't enjoy the popularity of those directly behind Santa Barbara, meaning you will often have it all to yourself. The upper end of the trail leads to the summit at one of the highest elevations of any of the crest trails, thus providing wonderful views. For more information about the upper trail look, at the description for Romero Saddle listed under Mountain Crest Trails.

DIRECTIONS
From Highway 101 take the Sheffield Drive exit. Follow Sheffield Drive 1.5 miles to East Valley Road. Turn left, then almost immediately turn right on Romero Canyon Road and continue another 1.5 miles to Buena Vista Road and turn right on it. The trailhead is about .3 miles farther. You will find a locked red steel gate marking the trail's beginning.

THE HIKE
Once you pass the locked gate you will find yourself walking up remnants of the old Romero Road. The canyon is relatively narrow, and the oak trees lining the creek side of the road make this part of the walk very nice. The road levels out a bit at the point where you cross an old concrete bridge, and just beyond this it splits. The left fork goes steeply up and over a ridge, eventually leading to San

Romero Canyon

Ysidro Canyon. (For more information about this hike see Day Hike #28—the Romero Catway.)

Follow the right fork across the creek and then up a very pretty section of the old road to a second crossing .1 mile farther on. Just as you cross the creek, look for a sign on the left marking the start of the canyon trail.

The canyon is very quiet and secluded, with plenty of nice spots to stop and rest, though no pools to dip in. Along the lower section the trail crosses and re-crosses the creek a number of times, and rarely will you find yourself very far from the creek. After the first crossings the trail stays mostly on the right side of the creek for a bit, following a small ridge steadily uphill through a series of oak forests. Then a very narrow section takes you back and forth across the creek several times, eventually leading to a crossing where there is a small but very pretty moss- and fern-lined waterfall and pool. This is a wonderful spot to stop for lunch.

From here it is about a half-mile to the end of the canyon section. The trail leads up along the right side of the creek through a sweet-smelling forest of California bay trees, then crosses to the left side of the creek and switches back and forth several times until it reaches Romero Road.

From here most people will turn right and return down the old road. It is a longer trip back if you take the road—3.5 miles versus 1.5 miles via the canyon route—but the views are great and it is easy walking.

The upper part of the Romero Canyon Trail is just across the road. It rises steeply up the mountainside through thick chaparral for a mile to the to the top of the Santa Ynez Mountains and the best views around. Though no longer maintained and somewhat scarred by motorcyclists, an old trail—the Island View Trail—leads along the crest. If you follow the ridgeline to the west it leads to Romero Saddle. From there you can take the road back down. It is 1.5 miles down to the intersection with the canyon trail on which you came up. You can either retrace your path back down the canyon or continue down on the old road.

27. Romero Road

TRAIL INFORMATION
Distance—2 miles to saddle where road narrows to become a trail; 3.5 miles to the upper canyon trail intersection
Elevation Gain—875' to the saddle; 1100' to the upper trail intersection
Difficulty—Easy to moderate
Topo—Santa Barbara and Carpinteria
URL—http://www.sb-outdoors.org Keyword Search: Romero Road

HIGHLIGHTS
Romero Road leads up and around a large peak and provides views of the entire coastline. The road is steep in parts, but well maintained and easy to walk on. At the halfway point, as you finish rounding the peak, there are very nice views of the upper canyon. It is also possible to continue along

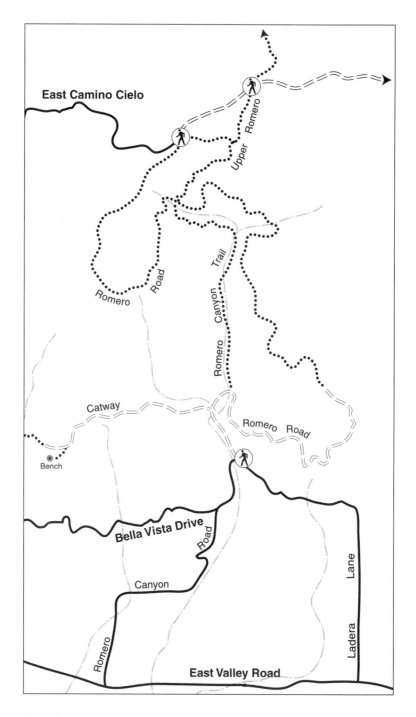

East Camino Cielo

Upper Romero

Romero Road

Romero Canyon Trail

Catway

Bench

Romero Road

Bella Vista Drive

Canyon Road

Romero

Canyon

Ladera Lane

East Valley Road

the road, which becomes more of a trail after the power lines, until you reach the intersection with the canyon trail and loop back down it.

DIRECTIONS
See directions for the Romero Canyon Trail (#26).

THE HIKE

For hikers who would like to experience the feeling of a walk up historic Romero Road, following it up as far as you feel like walking is a very nice alternative to the canyon hike. The road is wide, easy to walk on, and the views are spectacular.

From the locked gate the route-finding is easy—just follow the dirt road. Just beyond the concrete bridge a secondary road splits off to the left (Day Hike #28). Continue to curve to the right, cross the creek, and follow the main road along a very pretty oak-lined section to a second creek crossing. The canyon trail cuts off to the left just beyond this crossing. The road continues to curve to the right and begins to head more steeply uphill.

Romero Road is also very popular with mountain bikers, so be on the lookout for them as you wind your way up and around a large peak. Within a few minutes you will find yourself high enough above Buena Vista Road to enjoy spectacular views of the coastline.

Gradually the road curves back to the left, winding counter-clockwise around the peak. As you round each turn you'll spot another section of road leading upward to the next turn, and you will wonder when you will finally reach the high point. Eventually you do. At one particular turn in the road there is a small turnout that provides great views of the Carpinteria Valley, and if the day is clear you can see all the way to Point Mugu.

Beyond here the hiking is much mellower. A half-mile of easier hiking leads to a saddle and a series of powerlines. On the right side of the saddle a power line road drops down into Toro Canyon, and it is possible to follow this across the canyon and over another ridge to upper Toro Canyon Road.

If you continue through the saddle area you will find yourself looking back down on Romero Canyon. The road crosses under the power lines and winds around several steep hillsides, bringing you back into Romero Canyon. Then suddenly, just as you round one more turn, you can see all of the way up into the canyon. This marks the end of the maintained section of Romero Road.

Beyond this point, because the road hasn't been maintained, the chaparral has moved back in, so what is left of the roadway is a trail.

The next mile and a half of hiking takes you along the right side of the canyon, winding in and out of several small side canyons, and the hiking is very pleasant. There is almost no elevation gain, and the views are great. Before you know it you will reach the point where the canyon trail intersects with the road. It is 1.5 miles return trip via the shaded canyon, and a very pretty way to loop back down to your car.

If you want to continue on the road all the way to the crest, it is 1.5 miles up to Romero Saddle. If you are extremely adventurous, it is possible to head east straight up onto the top of Romero Ridge from the saddle and continue along it until you come to the top of the Romero Canyon Trail, then drop back down.

28. Romero Catway

TRAIL INFORMATION

Distance—.4 miles to power line intersection and start of Buena Vista Trail; 1.25 miles to top of power lines; 2 miles to Buena Vista overlook
Elevation Gain—700' to top of power line road; 100' loss to the Buena Vista overlook
Difficulty—Moderate
Topo—Santa Barbara and Carpinteria
URL—http://www.sb-outdoors.org Keyword Search: Romero Catway

HIGHLIGHTS

For hikers who would like to experience the feeling of a walk along the upper edges of Montecito, where they can look down on the coastline from a lofty perch nearly 1200' above the valley floor, the route up to the Buena Vista lookout provides just such an experience. The power line road is wide and easy to walk on, and the views are spectacular. It is possible to reach the Buena Vista Trail or hike all the way to San Ysidro Canyon on the power line road.

DIRECTIONS

See directions for the Romero Canyon Trail (Day Hike #26)

THE HIKE

From the locked gate the route-finding is easy—as you walk up the oak-lined road, the power line road splits off to the left a bit beyond the concrete bridge. This is where the hard part begins. The road leads up a side canyon and begins to gain elevation fairly rapidly. Fifteen minutes of strenuous climbing will get you to the sum-

Montecito Trails Foundation bench

mit, and from here the next mile along the power line road is easy. The road is almost, though not quite, level as it winds along the side of the Santa Ynez Mountains.

There are several promontories along the way that provide great places to stop, but the best is near the end of the road on a knoll that is marked on the Carpinteria topo with a small triangle and the elevation—1543 feet. Look for a trail in the chaparral leading out to the top of the knoll. On it you will find a beautiful hand-carved bench to sit on and enjoy the sunset views. You can thank the Montecito Trails Foundation for providing this magnificent bench.

The power line road ends just a few hundred yards beyond the knoll trail. If you look closely you will spot the Buena Vista Trail sign without too much difficulty. The trail drops down into a very pretty sycamore-filled canyon, which is the most colorful front country canyon in November and September, when the leaves are a golden yellow.

If you would like more information about hikes in this area, check out these San Ysidro Canyon hikes: Buena Vista Trail (Foothill Hike #23) and Buena Vista Catway (Foothill Hike #24).

The Narrows at the Playground

Mountain Crest Hikes

The drive is awesome. Breathtaking. Winding from the 2,250-foot summit of San Marcos Pass to the tiptop of 3,985-foot La Cumbre Peak, each turn along East Camino Cielo Road uncovers a new vista—Santa Cruz Island, the Santa Barbara coastline, Lake Cachuma, Figueroa Mountain, the Big Pine cliffs, Little Pine, Gibraltar Lake, a blend of images that suggests a wildness and an isolation rarely to be found so close to civilization.

In actuality, the road is not a single continuous route but is composed of two distinct sections: East and West Camino Cielo.

Historically, perhaps what symbolizes the essence of Camino Cielo is the work of George Owen Knapp, whose efforts lead to the development of the roads that snake their way across the top of the crest from Gaviota almost to the edge of Ojai.

EAST CAMINO CIELO—KNAPP'S ROAD

Camino Cielo was begun during World War I, one of the many routes made possible by George Owen Knapp, who came to Santa Barbara in 1912. Born in 1855, Knapp graduated as a civil engineer from Rensselaer Polytechnic Institute of New York in 1876. He went on to work for People's Gas, Light and Coke Company in Chicago, building gas plants. Eventually Knapp became president of the company before moving to Union Carbide, where he was chairman of the board for twenty-five years.

Retiring in Santa Barbara, Knapp quickly became involved with everything that seemed to be identified with the city's progress. Within a few years he had funded a nursing school at Cottage Hospital with a $200,000 contribution, donated substantial sums toward the construction of both All Saints-by-the-Sea Episcopal Church and Montecito Presbyterian Church, and provided money for a number of costly pipe organs in other churches.

Next to building organs and hospitals, Knapp's abiding passion was building roads. Although he was past sixty years of age at the time, he personally supervised the construction of mountain roads to and from a lodge he was constructing in the Santa Ynez Mountains "with all the interest and enthusiasm of a man half his years." More than anyone, it was George Owen Knapp who was responsible for the construction of Camino Cielo.

Knapp himself built four palaces in the mountains: the "Castle" above Painted Cave; one near Wind Cave (it is likely that the steps at the Chumash cave there were built by him); a third near Refugio Pass, now the site of Rancho la Sherpa; and the last next to a hot spring in the upper Santa Ynez drainage, now known as Pendola Hot Springs. The cement pool you will find there was added by Knapp.

KNAPP'S CASTLE

On April 9, 1916, George Owen Knapp purchased a 160-acre tract east of the Laurel Springs Ranch, wanting, in his words, "to make the tract a private mountain lodge that in natural beauty and grandeur will have few to equal it on the American continent." If the structure itself was anything like the view, it must have been awe-inspiring.

There were seven buildings in all, carved from thick sandstone blocks. The main house had five bedrooms, a large hallway, dining room, observatory, and a room especially designed for Knapp's pride and joy, a pipe organ. Over twenty men were employed during the construction of the lodge, which took more than four years. In addition to the main house, there was a studio next to it, a workman's cottage below, a dormitory that housed six servants, and a superintendent's house in the hollow where the lower road forks away from the path leading up to the lodge.

Soon after the lodge was constructed, Knapp discovered a series of cascades in the canyon east of the lodge, known now as Lewis Falls. Shortly thereafter an automobile road led down to them. If you look closely after you have hiked down this road about a mile, you will see the faint remnants of the rock steps Knapp had built to the base of the falls, now mainly a dirt path with sandstone rocks lining the way. There he also added a bath house and a pool fed by the falls, installed lighting to illuminate the falls at night, and even had the organ music piped all the way down from the house!

The music was provided by resident organist Dion Kennedy. Concerts were given at the rustic retreat from time to time, by Kennedy as well as by invited guest artists of local and national repute, including Bruno Walter and Otto Klemperer.

Today all that remains of the castle is the foundation and several chimneys rising like solitary spires into the sky. In 1940 Ms. Francis Holden purchased the lodge, but tragically five weeks later it was destroyed when a fire started in Paradise Canyon and raged out of control up the north slope of the Santa Ynez Mountains.

As the fire burned nearer, a friend of Ms. Holden painted the fiery mountain scene around her until she was forced to evacuate. Rather than worry about her fate, the woman seemed more concerned about her artwork, complaining of all the ashes falling in her paint and on her canvas. While everyone else panicked, including Ms. Holden, she calmly sat and painted.

The Forest Service finally made the women leave, with time enough only to throw a few belongings into a sheet, jump into a car, and go. When Ms. Holden tried to go back later to retrieve more, she was unable to get through a roadblock, though her chauffeur was able to climb a hill in time to see the flames reach the house and engulf it.

Five days later, only the observatory, built by Knapp in 1931 to house a large telescope, remained intact. Francis Holden never rebuilt, for the cost was simply too high. In 1964, the Coyote Fire claimed the observatory too, and the last of Knapp's dream.

Still, the beauty that Knapp saw as he first walked over the crest to his newly purchased property remains. Stepping onto the floor of the old observatory, its octagonal walls long since destroyed, one can gain a vision of what life in the Santa Ynez Mountains must have been like a half-century ago.

MUCH MORE

There is more—much more—to the crest though than just taking an afternoon's drive. There are a host of hidden places to explore, like the Playground or Lizard's Mouth on West Camino, and trails to enjoy, such as the Fremont, Snyder, and Arroyo Burro trails on the central section of East Camino Cielo and the Cold Springs, Forbush, San Ysidro, and Blue Canyon trails on the portion east of Gibraltar Road.

Most of all there is the castle—Knapp's dream and gift to us—a place where it is possible to gain an appreciation and perhaps a bit more of an understanding of a time in history that has passed us by.

WEST CAMINO CIELO DRIVE

1. Crest Drive

At least once a year I take the trip across the breadth of West Camino Cielo Road on my mountain bike to get a reminder of what it might have been like to travel the rough and dusty dirt road a century ago.

The route begins a half-mile below the crest of San Marcos Pass. Leading across the rugged and extremely remote western portion of the Santa Ynez Mountains, the road snakes its way across a series of bony spines and high prominences for 19 miles Refugio Pass. For four miles the road is paved, and the going seems easy, but just beyond Lizard's Mouth the road abruptly turns to dirt and begins a series of sharp downhill switchbacks that seem to lead backward in time to a frontier era.

Once I've left the pavement and coasted quickly down the switchbacks, the pedaling takes on a different sort of rhythm. The riding is slower in the dirt, and the potholes and ruts that are characteristic of the backcountry roads cannot be ignored. I stop often, savoring the views leading my eye from horizon to horizon on either side of the crest. Perhaps one day I will walk this route, though for now I am content to enjoy it by bike.

To the south the island profiles can be seen clearly: on a clear day, especially on those after a storm, Santa Cruz, Santa Rosa and San Miguel seem close enough to reach out and touch. To the north is the Santa Ynez Valley, Lake Cachuma, and in the distance the wilderness areas, the places you need a backpack and a few days of free time to explore in depth.

Though barely a mile inland from the Pacific, this is rugged country. Huge layers of sandstone have been thrust up to create the tallest peaks in the Santa Ynez range: Broadcast and Santa Ynez peaks—each more than 4,000 feet tall. The thick slabs of stone, deposited more than 50 million years ago, have weathered slowly, creating the beautiful formations to be found at Lizard's Mouth, the Playground, and other places along the crest.

To get the flavor of what travel might have been like three-quarters of a century ago, take an afternoon and drive from San Marcos Pass to Santa Ynez Peak along West Camino Cielo. It is rough and bumpy and has plenty of places for you to curse me for my advice, but it is well worth your time. Though I've done the drive in a passenger car you will definitely want to be in a high-clearance vehicle to make sure you don't bottom out.

Most likely you won't meet more than a car or two on the entire 19-mile drive and you won't see sprawls of tract homes dotting the valley below. Only rarely will you see either Highway 101 or the Southern Pacific Railroad tracks. What you will see is a land almost unchanged since the days in which Chumash Indians lived here, a place that must be taken slowly and with care, as your springs and shocks will tell you.

MILEAGE ALONG WEST CAMINO CIELO ROAD

0.0	West Camino Cielo
0.1	San Jose Creek crossing
0.2	Kinevan Road. Bear left and up the switchbacks
0.9	Old Indian Rock
2.4	The Playground trailhead
3.5	Lizard's Mouth
3.6	Winchester Gun Club
3.8	Winchester Skeet Area
4.0	End of the paved road
4.7	Bottom of switchbacks
5.3	Shooting Range
8.6	The Pines picnic area
11.0	Tequepis Trail
11.8	Santa Ynez Peak
13.0	Broadcast Peak
13.5	Start of pavement
19.0	Refugio Road

2. Lizard's Mouth

TRAIL INFORMATION
Length—300 yards
Elevation Gain—None
Difficulty—Easy
Topo— San Marcos Pass (not shown on map)
URL—http://www.sb-outdoors.org Keyword Search: Lizards Mouth

HIGHLIGHTS
Lizard's Mouth is located in a large amphitheater-shaped rock formation at the point where the Coldwater Sandstone formation crosses over the Santa Ynez Mountains. Its chaparral vegetation is interspersed with

massive sandstone outcroppings. The forces of wind and water have created an intricate network of caves and crevices that are wonderful to explore. Unfortunately, it has also been trashed by careless visitors, and it is not nearly so attractive as it once was. You can help out by coming up here and helping collect the trash every so often.

DIRECTIONS

From Highway 154, turn left on West Camino Cielo Road and drive approximately 4 miles to a point just before the Winchester Gun Club, which is on the left. If you reach the Gun Club, you've gone a hundred yards too far. The trail is only a few hundred yards in length and opens onto a massive rock formation. You'll know when you get there. The Lizard is off to the right.

SETTING THE SCENE

Lizard's Mouth is a sliver of bedrock nestled high in the Santa Ynez Mountains west of San Marcos Pass, a place filled with sandstone boulders, underground caves, and water-worn channels that separate huge slabs of rock as though they were pieces of a gigantic puzzle. This is land that has yielded only stubbornly to the forces of nature, a place where one can appreciate and begin to understand the slow pulse of the earth's evolution.

It is a land that has undergone radical changes over the past several hundred million years, including some very dramatic ones in the last three or four million years. The bedrock has shifted, the climate has changed many times, and every earthquake reminds me that the entire process is in constant flux even today. The land may remain rigid for the balance of this day perhaps, for the month, the year, or, for that matter, the rest of my life. Nonetheless, it is part of a fluid, ongoing process.

I made a very special trip to Lizard's Mouth several years ago. It was in autumn, during Santa Barbara's Indian summer, and the air was warm and moisture-laden. A tropical storm had invaded from the south. From the perch of a small cave, a friend and I sat huddled as we watched dark billowing clouds head our way. Below in the valley I could see cars streaming down the freeway, but it was with the sound of the city turned off, and it lent a sense of detachment to the air. Solitude filled me.

Suddenly the storm was upon us. The intensity of the heat broke as clouds pounded against the mountain, peppering the sandstone with popcorn-sized pellets of water. The smell of the first drops of rain washed over me. Steam rose off the rocks. Rumbling

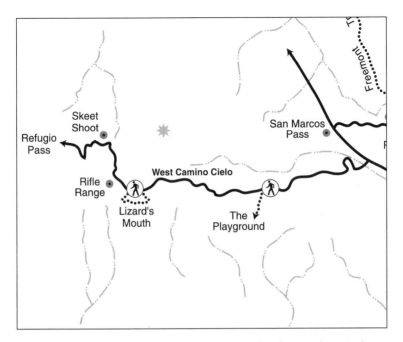

and grumbling in the background were peals of ear-splitting thunder. And the lightning.

For a moment I became frightened as I remembered that neither mountaintops nor caves were proper places to be when lightning struck, but as quickly as it had pounced on us, the storm dissipated and was gone, and the fear faded with it. Along the coast, the long curving arch of a rainbow split More Mesa in half. Rays of sunlight peeked through somber banks of clouds now in full retreat. As the storm faded to the west, the pattern repeated itself. Cloud, thunder, rain.

A half-hour later we left the shelter of the cave and made our way to the tawny back of the stone lizard. The sun neared the horizon and, as always, the breeze quieted, leaving an unearthly silence. Colors were trapped along the western horizon—reds, yellows, and oranges that shimmered in the haze. As the sun dipped into the water its shape broke, undulating against the skyline. Slowly it eased itself into the dusk, and I was left touched by its momentary grace.

To the east, the mountains gave birth to a second moment of beauty. Moonrise. The globe ascended like a hot-air balloon, its light streaming across the valley floor to replace that of the receding sun. City lights were being turned on, but other than that, to the east and to the west, and especially to the north, all I saw were the serrated silhouettes of ridge after ridge, like riders on a purple haze.

3. The Playground

TRAIL INFORMATION
Length—.75 miles
Elevation Gain—300'
Difficulty—Moderately easy
Topo— San Marcos Pass (not shown on map)
URL—http://www.sb-outdoors.org Keyword Search: Playground

HIGHLIGHTS
The Playground is a circular boulder field about three-fourths of a mile in diameter that you can see from the Goleta Valley. It features the best rock scrambling anywhere in Santa Barbara, with channels and water-worn crevices separating the sandstone into individual pieces, making it seem like a picture puzzle. You'll discover beautifully sculpted sandstone "art forms," a network of rough-hewn trails that don't really lead anywhere but allow you to romp through most of the boulder field, and of course, the Narrows.

DIRECTIONS
From Highway 154, turn left on West Camino Cielo Road and drive approximately 2.5 miles to a point where a power line crosses the road. Look for this well-hidden trail on the left side of the road.

SETTING THE SCENE

One of the wonderful things about the Santa Ynez Mountains is its hidden places, such as Teardrop or Cat Canyon, where there are steep water slides and deep pools, or Mist Falls, which, if you explore long enough, you will find somewhere out in the Gaviota area, or the sites of Chumash rock art—all to be found only by spending many moments of exploration.

A favorite of mine is the Narrows, a quarter-mile long crease carved by water in the Coldwater Sandstone, part of a land of mystery and enchantment known now as the "Playground." The Narrows is less than body-width wide, forcing you to turn sideways to climb up and over a small ledge and into the interior.

Actually, the Playground was discovered by a former student of mine—Jeff Finear. In the 1970s we looked everywhere for places to climb. No matter how hard it was to get to, we checked out every wall we could find—even those that meant a half-mile crawl through the chaparral. Jeff was the fortunate one to find this place.

The weekend after Jeff discovered the Playground I set out

through the chaparral, not knowing quite what to expect. The route down turned out not to be too hard. Eventually I ended up on the west side of the Playground, and from there I worked my way up onto the boulder field. I was amazed, unable to believe that such a place could exist.

I found myself staring across at a boulder that I needed to get to, only to find that it involved a six-foot jump, easy enough if the drop isn't too far, but here the channels were 15 to 20 feet deep. No way I was going to try that!

Instead, I found myself frustrated constantly, and I worked my way down and then back up over boulder after boulder. I started to wonder if this was worth it. Then I found the Narrows. I was at the bottom of the Playground, exhausted, wondering how I would find my way back up to the upper end, when I spotted the thin crease. The rest, some would say, is history.

Through the first part of the Narrows you walk with your shoulders touching the walls, a perfect place to practice "chimneys" if you are a rock climber. After several hundred yards the walls close in, but this time large boulders and tons of earth have been poured into the opening, making this appear to be a box canyon. At the base the rocks have formed a superstructure of sorts, and the earth covers it to create a small cave-like entrance leading into a dark interior.

Hunched over, you can make your way for fifty yards, then it is on all fours to scramble through a tunnel not more than two feet high, with only a starburst of light to lead you on. At one point the way ahead is in total darkness. Just when proceeding further seems hopeless the cave makes a dogleg to the left, and as you turn the corner there is more light.

Fifty more yards bring you to the end of the tunnel and into a chamber the size of a small bedroom. Water falls from directly overhead, a shower of trickles. From here the only way out is by climbing a series of boulders stacked one upon the other.

At this point, deep inside the bedrock, there is just enough light to distinguish the interior features, a soft and indirect glow that heightens the sense of adventure. The underside of the rock is cold to the touch and the air is crisp, in contrast to the warmth topside. Water seeps drop by drop into a tiny pool, not enough to sustain much life, but enough for a cluster of maidenhair fern that grows by the edge of a thimble-sized basin.

It is a miracle that in the space of a few feet such disparate plant communities as the chaparral and the ferns can exist, each with such seemingly different needs, plants from climatic periods that existed so many millions of years apart. But that juxtaposition is what makes the vegetation of the mountain wall, nondescript in appearance from the city, so surprising, and so delightful, when confronted up close.

Pockets of prehistoric beauty still remain, albeit hidden—a surprising beauty that is all the more special because it is rare. Perhaps not as surprising as this hidden beauty is the fact that I haven't included much of a trail description with this information. But why should I? Places like this should be found on your own, part of the process of discovery I've found so important to me.

EAST CAMINO CIELO ROAD

1. An Afternoon's Drive

I lived just a quarter-mile up East Camino Cielo Road from San Marcos Pass for more than ten years, so this area will always provide me with fond memories: of snowball fights at Knapp's Castle, evening rides up the road to visit friends in the Painted Cave area, and hundreds of hours exploring the nooks and crannies to be found in the ten-mile stretch from my house to Gibraltar Road.

The favorite place to visit for most everyone is Knapp's Castle, but there are lots of other places along the way too. The long, thin escarpment leading down Fremont Ridge is a favorite, as is the miniature pine forest that you will find not too far away.

For those of you who don't want to test your vehicle on the more primitive western section of Camino Cielo, a drive on East Camino Cielo across the central portion of the Santa Ynez Mountains will provide a worthwhile afternoon full of beautiful views: islands and the coastline on the south side of the road, and the Santa Ynez Valley, the San Rafael Mountains, and wilderness areas on the north.

The 30-mile loop takes about two hours (not counting all the times you will stop along the way) and can be made by taking Highway 154 to the crest of San Marcos Pass, turning east and following Camino Cielo for 10 miles, and then dropping back down to Santa Barbara on Gibraltar Road.

Following is a guide to the drive from San Marcos Pass to Gibraltar Road. Mileage is from San Marcos Pass. You might also start by heading up Gibraltar Road and enjoying a late afternoon of music at Cold Springs Tavern later.

MILEAGE ALONG EAST CAMINO CIELO ROAD

0.0   San Marcos Pass

0.2   Cielo Store. Unfortunately, due to hard times, the store will most likely not be open when you pass by. Perhaps this will change and we will have the old store back. It has always been the perfect place to stop on the way to or back from a hike in the mountains.

1.75   The Pines. Look for an open parking area on the left with a large pine tree in the center of it. A short hike up to the top of a small saddle and back to the west leads to a picturesque forest of pines and a series of wind-sculptured caves. This is an excellent short hike, a great place for kids to scramble on the rocks, and a nice picnic area.

2.0   Fremont Ridge Road. Follow the dirt road beyond the locked gate down and then across the long ridgeline. Great views everywhere.

2.5   Painted Cave Road. Painted Cave is approximately a mile down this narrow road, which winds past Laurel Springs Ranch and the Painted Cave community, eventually leading back down to Highway 154. An excellent small book, *Guide to Painted Cave* can be purchased at most bookstores or the Cielo Store.

3.75   Knapp's Castle turnoff. Park near the locked gate. The road leads gently downhill to the castle. Several hundred yards of walking will bring you around a corner and present you with great views of the ruins.

6.0   Arroyo Burro Road. A shooting area is just to the north side of the road where Arroyo Burro intersects with Camino Cielo, so be extremely careful should you decide to explore anywhere in this area. The historic Arroyo Burro Trail crosses here. You can hike down it in either direction.

8.0   La Cumbre Peak. At the 3,985-foot peak you'll not only have the best views in town, but there are picnic tables for a pleasant afternoon's feast and plenty of rocks for the kids, or you, to explore on the coast side of the crest. For those with a real sense of adventure, it is possible to work your way down the front side of the mountain, across a saddle, and up to the top of a lesser mountain called Cathedral Peak.

10.0   Gibraltar Road. On the way down, look for Gibraltar Rock, a large ice cube-shaped boulder made of extremely resistant Matilija Sandstone where you will usually be able to watch climbers testing their skills (and courage).

2. Fremont Ridge Trail

TRAIL INFORMATION:
Length—Variable, up to 1.5 miles
Elevation Gain—200'
Difficulty—Easy
Topo— San Marcos Pass
URL—http://www.sb-outdoors.org Keyword Search: Fremont

HIGHLIGHTS

Fremont Ridge Trail provides a short hike with great views of the Santa Ynez Valley and is easy enough that you can take small children on it. The ridge is sharp, and after an immediate downhill it meanders over a series of knolls to a point where you can sit and look out on the backcountry and all of the valley. It makes a nice evening hike, just before sunset.

DIRECTIONS

To reach the trailhead, follow East Camino Cielo Road approximately 1.75 miles from San Marcos Pass until you spot a locked metal Forest Service gate on the left side of the road. You'll find it several hundred yards after a small turnout by the Pines, which is described above in the section "An Afternoon's Drive."

CAUTION

Stop at the point where the trail drops steeply down into the valley. Not too far down from there it goes onto private property.

SETTING THE SCENE

Though not a long hike, the Fremont Ridge Trail is a very enjoyable one, especially in the spring, when the hills fill with green grass and colorful wildflowers. The feeling here is one of openness, for the ridge is rather sharp, offering views up and down the Santa Ynez Valley. To the east the silhouette of Knapp's Castle provides an interesting backdrop, while Lake Cachuma and Figueroa Mountain make for a breathtaking view to the west. This is a nice hike anytime, but especially at sunset or on a moonlit night.

Just to the side of the locked gate you'll notice a very picturesque pine tree, its presence remarkable in the midst of this sea of chaparral. It is a Coulter pine, best known for its huge cones, which can reach 30 pounds in weight.

Originally an Indian trail, the Fremont Ridge Trail is believed to be the route by which the Chumash Indians dragged giant

Ponderosa pine logs from the top of Mission Pine Mountain, across the wide expanse of the Santa Ynez Valley and up over the mountain wall to Santa Barbara, where the logs became the ceiling beams for the new mission.

It is also the route by which John C. Frémont led a battalion of American troops south from Monterey to capture Santa Barbara in 1846. It is a story chronicled by Jim Blakely, Santa Barbara's most famous local historian. "After camping in Foxen Canyon near what is now Los Olivos the troops, along with horses, mules, and cannons, began the ascent of the Santa Ynez Mountains on Christmas Eve," Blakely noted. "The weather was terrible. Lots of rain and mud made the trip almost impossible."

It was "the hardest day's work we have yet had," battalion trooper Louis McLane wrote in his journal. "The guide says we are over the worst of the road, if a path full of rock and timber can be called a road."

Frémont's battalion reached the crest via Laureles Canyon, crossed over to San Marcos Pass near the Cielo Store, then descended into Santa Barbara in the pouring rain on Christmas Day, capturing the city on December 27 without firing a single shot. No one had expected his troops would be able to make the trip over the mountains in this weather.

One hundred fifty years later the ridge still bears Frémont's name.

THE HIKE

The Fremont Ridge Trail is actually a bulldozed road that provides a lateral firebreak down the north side of the Santa Ynez Mountains. The road leads downhill for several hundred yards, making it appear as if this will be a strenuous hike, but shortly after this it levels off and meanders over soft, rolling hills. The scent of sage in the air and the colorful pastels of the spring wildflowers in the midst of the rocky outcrops and thick green grasses make the walk in and around and up over the gently rolling hills a treat.

Look carefully on the left once you've dropped down from the locked gate and started along the ridgeline. You may spot a few rocks stacked to create a "duck" that marks the old route taken by Frémont across the upper end of Laureles Canyon to San Marcos Pass.

The main ridge continues for a bit less than a mile before finally beginning to drop steeply downhill. My advice is to turn around at the point where the Fremont ridge begins its plunge down into the Santa Ynez Valley. After this point the trail is loose and steep.

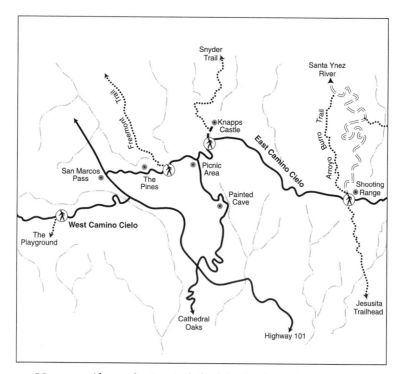

However, if you don't mind the hike back up the steep section, try hiking on down the road. Soon you will find yourself almost directly beneath the power lines and at an intersection. Go right.

Almost immediately you will find yourself in the shade of a steep wall and an almost entirely different type of vegetation. Oak forests and more open hillsides filled with grasses and softer chaparral begin to appear, and as you lose even more elevation the chaparral gives way, leading you into rolling hills of oak and grass and eventually an enchanting meadow, nearly flat and several hundred yards in width, perfect for a picnic.

Beware, though, it is a long way back up to the crest.

For the adventurous, those who like the little niches that the mountain wall has hidden within and who don't mind the effort involved in finding them, a wonderful day's exploration can be found in the canyon on the east side of the ridge. This is Paradise Canyon, a narrow, rocky creekbed filled with small waterfalls, pools, and the quiet solitude of a wilderness setting. A small, rough trail leads down into the canyon a short distance after the initial drop from the paved road. Look for it just after the dirt road levels off. Beware though, poison oak will be found along this section.

3. Knapp's Castle

TRAIL INFORMATION

Length—.75 miles to the ruins; 3.75 miles from Camino Cielo down the
   Snyder Trail to Paradise Road
Difficulty—Easy to moderately strenuous
Topo—San Marcos Pass (the trail shows only as a jeep road down to
   Lewis Falls)
URL—http://www.sb-outdoors.org Keyword Search: Knapps Castle

HIGHLIGHTS

Knapp's Castle is a short hike that is perfect for children, and it is very nice
at sunset. The trail is only three-quarters of a mile in length and almost
level. The silhouettes of the chimneys form one of the most dramatic sights
to be found anywhere in these mountains, and kids love playing around
them. From the castle you have 180-degree views of the entire backcountry.

DIRECTIONS

To reach the trailhead, follow East Camino Cielo approximately 3.5 miles
from San Marcos Pass until you spot a locked metal Forest Service gate on
the left side of the road, approximately 1 mile past Painted Cave Road.

CAUTION

The castle is actually on private property, though for the present access is
allowed. But this could change. Be extremely careful and considerate
while you are here.

SETTING THE SCENE

Even if you only have a few minutes to stop on your drive over
the crest, the short hike to visit the remains of Knapp's Castle is well
worth the time. The easy hike not only offers a glimpse back into a
period of time when this was wild, rugged country and the people
who inhabited it were truly pioneers, but the most spacious views of
the Santa Ynez Valley and the backcountry available anywhere.

THE HIKE

For a half-mile, the dirt road winds through the chaparral, with
enjoyable views out over the valley. Then suddenly you make a turn
to the right and the castle comes into view, a series of chimneys,
rock walls, and arches that takes your breath away.

At the ruins the walls provide abundant places to rest, to marvel

Knapp's Castle

at the 180-degree views offered of Santa Barbara County's mountainous interior, and to begin to imagine what the castle might have been like when the rich made their way here for one of Knapp's famous social engagements. If you listen carefully, you can almost hear the haunting melodies of Dion Kennedy's pipe organ floating on the breeze.

Just before the castle, the road splits. The left fork marks the start of the Snyder Trail, which winds its way for three miles down to Paradise Road. This is an excellent hike that I highly recommend.

The first half of the three-mile trail is a jeep road. The route is relatively open, not too steep, and fairly easy on the return trip. This is the original route taken by Knapp's guests on their way down to the bath house.

For a half-mile the road curves around the base of a large knoll then turns east and cuts across its flank through a forest of oak and bay trees. After a mile it opens onto a series of large grassy knolls and passes under a prominent set of power lines. This is a good spot to turn around. Beyond here the trail starts dropping steeply.

The second half of the Snyder Trail begins not too far beyond the power lines. You may or may not see a trail sign, but look for a trail on the left. You should be able to spot it without too much difficulty. The road continues east toward Lewis Canyon, degrading quickly as it nears the canyon's edge. Erosion and the encroachment of the chaparral have almost eliminated any sign of it once it begins descending down into the canyon.

Once you are in Lewis Canyon, the trail drops quickly and almost directly down a series of small, grassy hills, then switches back and forth through forests of oak, eventually leading to a dirt road that services a water tank supplying the nearby Forest Service homes.

4. Arroyo Burro Trail

TRAIL INFORMATION
Length—3.25 miles
Elevation loss—2035'
Difficulty—Strenuous
Topo—San Marcos Pass and Little Pine Mountain
URL—http://www.sb-outdoors.org Keyword Search: Arroyo Burro

HIGHLIGHTS
This is a delightful trail that leads down into a narrow canyon, and because it isn't traveled too often, it is a nice hike for those who want a bit of solitude. From the saddle you can also walk down Arroyo Burro Road. You can also explore a little of the front side of the mountains. The trail actually goes all the way down into San Roque Canyon, and has just recently been made accessible through agreements with property owners near the bottom.

DIRECTIONS
To reach the trailhead, follow East Camino Cielo Road approximately 5.5 miles from San Marcos Pass. From the pass, Camino Cielo rises steadily for 5 miles to a high point then drops abruptly to a saddle where Arroyo Burro Road intersects it. Turn left on the dirt road and continue past the shooting area. The Arroyo Burro Trail is on the left, .2 miles down this road.

CAUTION
A Forest Service-approved shooting area is located in the saddle at the intersection of Arroyo Burro Road and Camino Cielo Road. Use care when hiking near it.

THE HIKE
The north-side portion of the Arroyo Burro Trail winds through chamise chaparral at first, then begins to drop steeply down into a narrow, rocky canyon, which is shaded and filled with lush riparian vegetation and a cool creek that runs year round except in extremely dry years.

Depending on how far down the trail you go, the hike ranges from easy to strenuous. At the bottom the trail ends on the lower part of Arroyo Burro Road at the edge of Rancho Oso (now a motor home park), approximately .8 miles from the Santa Ynez River. A loop can be made by following the dirt road back uphill to your car, a distance of about 3 miles.

If you'd like to sample a little of what the Arroyo Burro Trail was once like on the coastal side, the trail is still in passable shape and it is possible to make it all of the way down to the Jesusita Trail (see trail description in Santa Barbara Foothill section). The trail-head is opposite Arroyo Burro Road on the ocean side of East Camino Cielo. Look for a small turnout.

Just a few yards after you leave your car, the trail turns to the left and winds down through shaly slopes into the east fork of San Antonio Creek. The trail drops fairly quickly into the canyon.

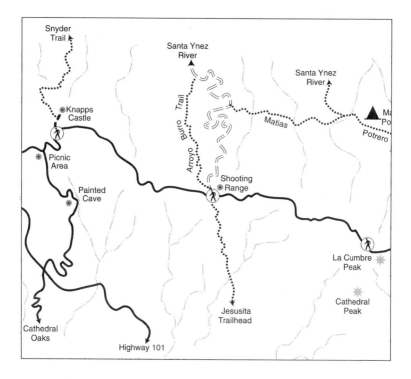

Atop La Cumbre Peak

5. La Cumbre Peak

TRAIL INFORMATION

Length—.75 miles to top of Cathedral Peak

Elevation Loss & Gain: 900' loss to Cathedral saddle; 250' elevation gain to Cathedral Peak

Difficulty—Strenuous

Topo—Santa Barbara

URL—http://www.sb-outdoors.org Keyword Search: La Cumbre Peak

HIGHLIGHTS

Most likely you will agree with me that the top of La Cumbre Peak—3,985 feet above sea level—provides the best views Santa Barbara has to offer. The panorama is full circle, great views of the islands, the long arms of the San Ynez Mountains stretching in either direction toward Ojai and Gaviota, and breathtaking vistas looking back at the San Rafael Mountains. A short loop can be made by following the remnants of the paved road leading up to the lookout tower. You will find benches and picnic tables at strategic locations, placed just right to enjoy the spacious views while you munch on your lunch treats.

DIRECTIONS

To reach La Cumbre Peak from Santa Barbara, follow Gibraltar Road 6.5 miles to East Camino Cielo Road, then turn left and drive another 1.8 miles to the peak. Park near the locked gate leading to the lookout station.

SETTING THE SCENE

The La Cumbre Lookout Station was first built in the 1920s and replaced in the 1940s. It is a reminder of the days when seasonal spotters would live on the tops of these gnarly peaks, looking for the first hint of smoke that might signal the start of a forest fire. Today the tower is abandoned, surrounded by barbed wire, and the windows have been broken out. The peak now serves a different function: it hosts a satellite communications systems.

Nevertheless, this is an enchanting place. Tumbles of huge tan and orangey-yellow boulders sit atop the peak, almost as if stacked there to create the pyramid-shaped crest. There are small trails that lead here and there. My favorite leads down from a bench you will see as you walk toward the tower. Inscribed there are these words:

CHRISTOPHER AND SHANNON

ETERNAL LOVE

REAL MAGIC

At the turn of the century the newly formed Santa Barbara Chamber of Commerce helped develop one of the first tourist routes up to the top of the mountains. It was known as the "Chamber of Commerce Trail" and followed what is now Gibraltar Road. Visitors at the town's plush hotels could rent horses for a day's outing to La Cumbre Peak. Today's hikers usually make this pilgrimage via Tunnel Trail.

Near a large flat rock by the lookout tower you may also spot a cross inscribed in the rock along with the words "Old Mission" and the date "1902." According to historian Jim Blakely, brothers in training at the mission had a day set aside for hiking and they would climb the Tunnel Trail to the peak. Most likely they are the ones responsible for the inscriptions.

THE HIKE

The hike to the tower is short and requires little in the way of directions—just follow the asphalt road. However, if you would like to try a bit of "off-trail" exploration there are numerous paths leading through the boulders and manzanita, mostly to spots where you can lean back, settle in against the warmth of the tawny sandstone, and enjoy the sound of the wind, the birds hidden in the brush, and the butterflies flittering from blossom to blossom—and, of course, the incredible views.

The premier hike, actually a combination of boulder-hopping, rock scrambling, and down-climbing, leads to the peak you can see a bit below you and just out of reach—Cathedral Peak. When I first saw the peak I named it "Monkey's Tooth," because that's what it looked like to me. From Santa Barbara you can't see it because of its location. From Goleta or the San Roque area, however, it is easily spotted.

Perhaps it was the rock climbers who created these thin openings in the chaparral, just wide enough to make your way along, but there are numerous off-trail routes hidden in the mountain walls of Mission Canyon, mostly all of them leading to very special places.

The route to Cathedral Peak leads from Christopher and Shannon's bench down through sandstone boulders and waist-high manzanita to a larger boulder. To the right of the boulder is a 30-foot tall Coulter pine that marks the start of a precipitous plunge down for 900 feet to a saddle where you are presented with the challenge of climbing up through relatively overgrown chaparral to the peak.

The down-climbing isn't too difficult but requires care. Pay close attention to the route-finding, and make sure you stay on the "trail"—or what there is of one. In the 1970s, when we first made the hike to Cathedral Peak, the brush was fairly open and the routes easy to find, but that isn't the case anymore. Bucking through the brush is tough if you get lost.

About halfway down to the saddle you leave the boulders behind and enter hard chaparral. The hiking is a bit easier and the route-finding straightforward. However, once you are at the saddle, the climb up to the peak is demanding—250 feet of steep mountainside and lots of overhanging brush. Once you reach the top of the ridge it is still a hundred-yard scramble over several spiny outcropping to the peak. Use extreme care. The drops are fairly long, and rescue from places like this is very difficult.

The view from the top of Cathedral Peak, however, and the feeling of being perched out in the middle of the mountain wall, almost on your own pedestal, are incredible.

From here it is possible to work your way to the left side of the peak and down to its base, where you will find an enormous cave, situated almost like a large cavity in a 300-foot high tooth. It is also possible to continue south along the ridgeline several hundred yards farther to a second peak. You will find a trail register there and plenty of boulders to sit back against while you enjoy a well-deserved lunch.

From this point it is a long way in time and effort back up to the top of La Cumbre Peak. Give yourself plenty of time to make the return trip. However, if you have made arrangements to be dropped off, you can continue down the eastern escarpment to the Seven Falls area and the Tunnel trailhead. This is a great way to finish this hike.

6. Angostura Pass

TRAIL INFORMATION
Length—3 miles
Elevation loss: 2000'
Difficulty—Easy to strenuous
Topo—Santa Barbara and Little Pine Mountain
URL—http://www.sb-outdoors.org Keyword Search: Angostura

HIGHLIGHTS
The dirt road leading from Angostura Pass down to Gibraltar Dam provides a nice hike with expansive views of the backcountry. For those who want a long day hike, the Matias Potrero and Devil's Canyon trails will take you to the river and the road will take you back up. Or, with a shuttle, you can follow the Matias Potrero Trail all the way to Live Oak picnic area.

DIRECTIONS
From Santa Barbara, follow Gibraltar Road 6.5 miles to East Camino Cielo Road, then turn left and drive another .7 miles to Angostura Pass. The dirt road is on the right, leading 6 miles down to Gibraltar Reservoir.

SETTING THE SCENE

With the exception of a few mountain bikers, not too many people venture down the road. You should. Because of the locked gate there is almost no vehicle traffic on the dirt road, thus providing an open and easily traveled path for those who would like to enjoy the beauty of the backcountry without the rigors that often accompany it.

As the canyon opens, so do the views. As you look almost directly down on Gibraltar Reservoir, the Santa Ynez river canyon is exposed before you. In the fall (late November and December) the leaves of the sycamore turn a vivid yellow, filling the canyon with color.

THE HIKE

Once you are beyond the locked gate, the road is smooth and well graded. It winds gently downhill through the pass then begins to cut across the back side of the Santa Ynez Mountains. In the process it provides expansive views of Little Pine and Big Pine mountains as well as Gibraltar Reservoir.

The hike is leisurely, and you can make it as long as you want. Hike as far down as you feel comfortable walking back up.

Two miles down from Angostura Pass, the Matias Potrero Trail

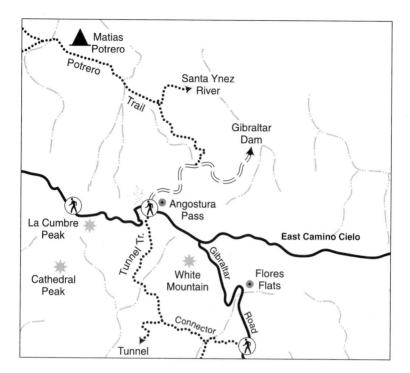

leads steeply down and to the left. It isn't marked, so you need to look for it carefully. This trail cuts across the north side of the Santa Ynez Mountains for 6 miles, eventually intersecting with Arroyo Burro Road. Along the way two connector trails lead down to the Santa Ynez River, one in Devil's Canyon and the other near Live Oak Picnic Area.

The Matias Potrero Trail switches back and forth down the back side of the Santa Ynez Mountains, losing elevation rapidly, until you are about halfway down to the river. It then turns to the west and across the mountains, dropping more gently to the Devil's Canyon Trail intersection, which is 1.5 miles down from the road. Check out the old trail signs, which you will find lying off to one side of the intersection.

Devil's Canyon leads directly down into the Santa Ynez Fault and then through a narrow and very picturesque canyon to the Santa Ynez River near the base of Gibraltar Dam. The route follows the left side of the canyon through very pretty oak-and-grass-covered hillsides before descending into a narrow, alder-lined canyon.

To make this a loop trip, turn right at bottom of Devil's Canyon, hike up to the top of the dam, then follow the dirt road back up to Angostura Pass. This is an 11-mile hike in total, so plan on a full day. The unfortunate part of this hike is that you have to do the hard work at the day's end, but this is a great trip and well worth it. Along the way up the road you will pass through a series of rocky ridges that provide nice resting spots, one of them composed of limestone, a reminder of the time when Santa Barbara was entirely underwater.

7. Forbush Flats

TRAIL INFORMATION
Length—Gibraltar Trail 3 miles; Santa Ynez River 3.5 miles; Cottam Camp 3.8 miles
Elevation loss: 1075' to Forbush Flats; 2000' to the Santa Ynez River
Difficulty—Moderate to strenuous, depending on route chosen
Topo—Santa Barbara, Little Pine Mountain, Carpinteria, Hildreth Peak
URL—http://www.sb-outdoors.org Keyword Search: Forbush Flats

HIGHLIGHTS
Forbush Flats is a delightful camp situated right in the middle of the Santa Ynez Fault. Because of this, shell fossils are exposed in the rock in this area, making it a geologist's paradise. You'll find an apple orchard here, the only remnants of Fred Forbush's pioneer homestead. Gidney Creek leads off to the left, which is interesting to explore. Or you can follow the main trail to the river. Overnight camping is possible here.

DIRECTIONS
From Santa Barbara, follow Gibraltar Road 6.5 miles to East Camino Cielo Road, then turn right and drive another 3.75 miles to the trailhead, which is opposite the end of Cold Springs Trail, at a saddle just after a downhill section of road. A trail sign on the left and a cement water tank on the right side of the road should make it easy to spot.

SETTING THE SCENE

The Forbush Flats Trail (actually a continuation of the Cold Springs Trail) offers access to a number of parts of the upper Santa Ynez Valley and day loops, shuttle trips, or overnighters, depending on the type of arrangements you make. Originally it was one of the main thoroughfares into the backcountry, leading from Montecito through the upper part of the Santa Ynez drainage, along Mono Creek, and over a window in the San Rafael range known as the

Puerto Suelo to Santa Barbara Canyon and the Cuyama Valley. When the Chumash revolted briefly in the 1820s, fleeing to the tule marshes in the lower San Joaquin Valley, this was the route taken by soldiers whose task was to round them up and bring them back.

THE HIKE

The first 1.5 miles of the trail leads through chaparral to Forbush Flat, dropping a thousand feet in elevation. The camp is pleasant, well shaded and at the foot of Gidney Creek which often flows year round, though not always. Nearby is a small meadow, complete with an aging apple orchard, courtesy of Fred Forbush, who built a cabin there about 1910.

The camp is situated on top of the Santa Ynez Fault, which cuts directly through it, forming the crease along which Gidney Creek flows. Due to the uplifting that has occurred here, numerous layers of bedrock rich in fossils are exposed here, making this an amateur geologist's paradise. A wonderful afternoon can be spent here, either meandering down the creek checking out the exposed layers of bedrock, or continuing down the trail toward the Santa Ynez River.

To continue on, look for a trail intersection just north of the meadow. The main trail continues north over a 50-foot-high ridge and then down another 1,000 feet in elevation for 1.5 miles to the Santa Ynez River. Along the way are more fossils and a pool or two for refreshment.

The trail on the right leads 2 miles east down through the Santa Ynez Fault and rugged chaparral to Cottam Camp, located at the bottom of Blue Canyon. The Santa Ynez River is a half-mile downstream from Cottam Camp.

For hardcore hikers, a long but extremely rewarding day hike can be made by staying on the left side of the river and continuing downstream for a mile to the Cold Springs Trail, then heading back up it to Forbush Flats and eventually to your car on East Camino Cielo.

Should you spend the night at Forbush Flats, the route down into the Cottam area and then back up the Cold Springs Trail makes an excellent and much more reasonable loop. We often hike in on Friday night, enjoy the loop hike on Saturday, then a very pleasant Saturday night's campfire, before heading back up to the car on Sunday.

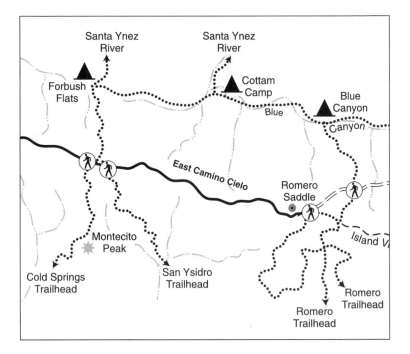

8. Montecito Peak

TRAIL INFORMATION

Length—1 mile

Total Elevation Loss and Gain: 600' loss to the saddle; 250' gain to the top of the peak

Difficulty—Moderate to strenuous

Topo—Santa Barbara

URL—http://www.sb-outdoors.org Keyword Search: Montecito Peak

DIRECTIONS

From Santa Barbara, follow Gibraltar Road 6.5 miles to East Camino Cielo Road, then turn right and drive another 3.75 miles. The trail is at a saddle just after a downhill section of road. A trail sign on the left and a cement water tank on the right side of the road should make it easy to spot. San Ysidro Trail is .2 miles farther.

HIGHLIGHTS

The upper part of the Cold Springs Trail leads a mile to Montecito Peak, a great place to spend the afternoon or enjoy a sunset. You can be dropped off at the top of either the Cold Springs or San Ysidro trail and picked up by a friend back down in town. If you've just hiked down to Forbush Flats, why not walk back to town rather than drive?

THE HIKE

From town, Montecito Peak looms like a giant knob above the foothills. If you look closely you can see the long thin line of upper Cold Springs Trail etched across its face and, if you look really closely, the lonely eucalyptus trees jutting up out of the chaparral. The hike to this point from the bottom requires much effort, and many prefer to make the trip to the top of the Montecito Peak from East Camino Cielo.

The peak is at 3,214 feet, nearly 300 feet higher than the surrounding countryside, providing the feeling of an angel's rest. The top is about 50 feet in diameter, nearly flat, and the perfect spot for a beach chair, a book, and an afternoon of relaxing reading. Getting there, however, is not so easy.

From the parking area the trail leads slightly downhill along the side of a large water tank, then begins dropping down into the chaparral as it curves around the upper end of Cold Springs Canyon. A mile of hiking brings you to a gently sloping ridgeline on the left, where you have the first views out toward the Carpinteria coastline. Montecito Peak looms steeply in front of you.

At first glance, the easiest route to the top seems to be the one following the ridgeline; however it is much easier to continue a bit farther down the trail. Look for an unmarked trail leading up to the left when you are almost right at the peak's edge. From here there really isn't a trail—rather, it is a scramble up a steep slope with little traction underfoot. But once you are on top you will find the views well worth the few minutes of hard work it cost to get there.

If you are like me, after you have been to places such as these, the next time you look up at the peak from the city it will no longer seem quite the same. Memories of the hike up to the top and the feeling of being up there will leave you with a different impression from what you had before. As you visit more and more places such as this, bit by bit the experiences will build up, until at some point you will discover that the mountains have become a part of you.

9. Upper Romero Loop

TRAIL INFORMATION
Length—5 miles
Elevation Loss and Gain: Elevation loss of 500' and gain of 600'
Difficulty—Moderate
Topo—Carpinteria
URL—http://www.sb-outdoors.org Keyword Search: Upper Romero

HIGHLIGHTS
If you like great views, you'll love this trail. The route follows Romero Road for 1.5 miles down until it intersects the Romero Trail, then follows this up to the top of the mountains. Though you will have a steep hike to the crest, once there you'll feel like you are on top of the world.

DIRECTIONS
From Santa Barbara, follow Gibraltar Road 6.5 miles to East Camino Cielo Road, then turn right and drive another 6.5 miles to Romero Saddle, where the road begins. The saddle is just after a downhill section and marks the end of the paved section of road and the beginning of Pendola Road, which leads into the upper Santa Ynez Recreation Area. A cement water tank on the right side of the road marks the beginning of Romero Road and is easy to spot.

SETTING THE SCENE
Prior to 1978, Romero Road was the last remaining vestige of the primitive system of roads built in the early part of the century, the only route to the mountain crest that hadn't been paved. A reminder of what travel over the mountain wall was like fifty years ago, this rugged and extremely narrow dirt road was still open to the public. But 42 inches of rain that year caused massive mud- and rockslides. Too expensive to repair, the road was closed for public use. Today it is overgrown enough that it is almost impossible to image that it could ever have been used for automobile travel, but it is still in service, though now used by hikers and mountain bikers.

THE HIKE
From the saddle, follow Romero Road down toward the coast for 1.5 miles to its intersection with the Romero Trail. At this point turn left and take the upper section of the trail, which rises steeply through the chaparral for a mile to the mountaintop. At the crest are remnants of an old trail—the Island View Trail—which once yo-

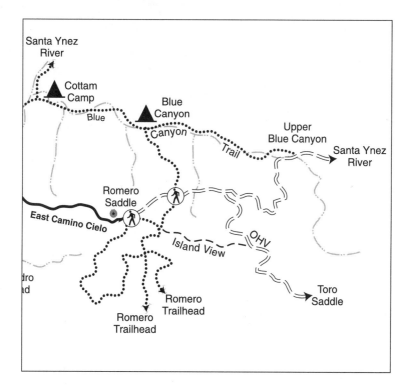

yo'ed across the eastern part of the crest toward Carpinteria. Some of it has been lost due to the construction of a fuelbreak along the top of the Santa Ynez Mountains and partly because of the encroachment of motorcycles.

Yet the view is still magnificent, the trail name still appropriate, and the feeling is one of almost being able to float over the land like a hang glider soaring on the currents.

From the crest you have several choices. The most direct is to head west following the ridgeline as it bobs up and down until you arrive back at Romero Saddle. A second choice is to continue north on Romero Trail, dropping down to Pendola Road. There you will turn left and follow the road uphill for a half-mile to the saddle. A third choice would be to head east on the old Island View Trail until you intersect the Divide Peak Jeepway. Turn left and walk down the jeepway to Pendola Road, then left again for 1.2 miles back up to the saddle.